NEW DEVELOPMENT PARADIGMS AND CHALLENGES FOR WESTERN AND CENTRAL INDIA

About the Editors

R. Parthasarathy is HUDCO Chair Professor at School of Planning, CEPT University, Ahmedabad. Till recently, Parthasarathy was a Professor at the Gujarat Institute of Development Research, Ahmedabad. Email: rpsarathy@spcept.org.

Sudarshan Iyengar is Vice Chancellor, Gujarat Vidyapeeth, Ahmedabad. Iyengar was earlier the Director of Gujarat Institute of Development Research, Ahmedabad. Email: iyengars@icenet.net.

New Development Paradigms and Challenges for Western and Central India

VOLUME TWO

Editors

R. Parthasarathy
Sudarshan Iyengar

Published for
Gujarat Institute of Development Research, Ahmedabad
by
CONCEPT PUBLISHING COMPANY, NEW DELHI-110059

Cataloging in Publication Data—DK
Courtesy: D.K. Agencies (P) Ltd. <docinfo@dkagencies.com>

New development paradigms and challenges for western and central India
/ editors, R. Parthasarathy, Sudarshan Iyengar.
p. cm.
Papers presented at the National Seminar on New Developmental Paradigms and Challenges in Western and Central India, held at Ahmedabad.
Includes bibliographical references.
Includes index.
ISBN 8180692809

1. India—Economic conditions—Congresses. 2. India—Economic policy—Congresses. 3. Sustainable development—India—Congresses. 4. India—Social policy—Congresses. 5. Natural resources—Co-management—India—Congresses.
I. Parthasarathy, R. II. Iyengar, Sudarshan, 1954-

DDC 330.954 22

The views and opinions in this book are those of the authors and not necessarily reflect the views of the organizations to which they belong.

ISBN 81-8069-280-9 (Set)
ISBN 81-8069-312-0 (Vol. I)
ISBN 81-8069-313-9 (Vol. II)

First Published 2006

Published and Printed by
Ashok Kumar Mittal
Concept Publishing Company
A/15-16, Commercial Block, Mohan Garden
New Delhi-110059 (India)

Phones : 25351460, 25351794
Fax : 091-11-25357103
Email : publishing@conceptpub.com

Dedicated to

Professor Pravin Visaria

Foreword

Western parts of India, especially Gujarat and Maharashtra have, during the past 15 years, led the charge in India's economic growth. Gujarat, in fact, has been matching growth rates of China whose example many of us would like India to emulate. These regions are in the throes of a rapid socio-ecological transition. Aside from creating wealth for entrepreneurial agents and the educated-employed, however, what this transition has in store for the majority of the region's people is a growing hiatus between rising expectations and stagnant pool of opportunities. What the transition also holds in store is a growing conflict between economic growth and environment. In many ways then, the region is wading through a turbulent phase, presenting numerous challenges of transforming economic growth into wholesome, all-round and equitable development. Meeting these challenges requires deft handling of the economy and the political processes of public choice.

This collection, to which, I have the honour to write this foreword, brings together a collection of 25 writings and reflections which deal with variations on this overall theme of the development of Western and Central India during recent times. These writings were first presented in a 2003 workshop organized to commemorate half a century of development partnership between the Ford Foundation and India. These volumes, in many ways, is a tribute to the sterling catalytic role played by the Foundation during the early decades after independence and reflects a broad spectrum of the developmental issues with which the Foundation has engaged.

The collection is interesting because of the variety of concerns, perspectives as well as styles it seeks to accommodate. It includes essays as well as empirical research papers. It has erudite thought pieces on one hand and practical notes written by practitioners. Several authors write on alternative strategies of economic growth and their fall out. But others also share their views on the social sector and environmental issues. These volumes will disappoint a reader looking for a comprehensive treatise on economic growth and social transformation in Western and Central India. But with the variegated perspectives it presents, it will delight someone in search of a mosaic that attempts to address a huge diversity of issues and concerns that the society in this region is experiencing.

November 2005 **Tushaar Shah**

Preface

In the second half of 2001 in a meeting in Jodhpur between the Ford Foundation grantees and the representatives of the Ford Foundation, Delhi, there was a discussion on how to suitably commemorate the 50 years of partnership of the Foundation with India in the year 2002. The freewheeling discussions hovered on themes of varied hues from culture to economy and democratic governance to fortifying the mechanisms for social justice. For an academic who had the support of the Foundation for a number of research projects, the whole discussion initially looked a little gentle, however, when it picked up the significance of the dimensions of the Foundation's support to the institutions and processes in India and South Asia became clear. During the half-a-century ending 2002, the Foundation's first and oldest overseas office in New Delhi has played a key role in the establishment of institutions which have contributed to the development and often introduced some challenging processes of developmental discourse. The Foundation has been widely credited for the "Green Revolution" in India and more recently for introducing the concept of micro-finance. Further, it has supported many prestigious institutions in India including institutions of academic excellence, fundamental research, policy design, advocacy and action, besides, India's Planning Commission among others. The discussion lingered in the mind and led to the thought that these interventions would have introduced a new spin not only in the developmental processes but also in the multi-dimensional outcomes. It also led to a desire to assess how much of this support had been absorbed and how could the next phase of the Foundation's work in India could contribute in identifying a new agenda. The developmental stage of the States is to be looked at first, and the challenges of the future identified. Invariably, a mutually beneficial partnership evolves when the stakes are shared between the interested and the gains are also shared. Thus, the Ford Foundation-50—Gujarat Institute of Development Research (FF50-GIDR) partnership platform to undertake a commemorative journey in 2002-03 took shape. In this, the Surabhi Foundation and Mandala are partners besides the GIDR which hosted the *National Seminar on New Developmental Paradigms and Challenges in Western and Central India.* Surabhi organised a Film Festival on *Images of India: Traditions and Transitions,* and Mandala planned Theatre Productions and installations: *The Rivers of India, Voices and Dreams and Haasyaras.*

The Seminar's goal was to bring together academics, scholars, government officials and NGOs to share the progress and the processes, and to take stock of where we are in the changing developmental paradigms and to identify the challenges ahead. The participants and contributors of research papers to the Seminar focussed on a wider context of Indian Economic and Social Development.

The focus therefore was not on providing a treatise on economics or sociology but to identify the variety of issues and challenges in a developmental challenge perspective. Thus, an important contribution of this exercise is the conceptualisation of developmental paradigms in an identifiable ground of social and economic progress initiated by the government and civil society efforts. This, in the Editors' point of view, could henceforth be taught in the undergraduate to graduate courses as Indian Economic and Social Development in place of what the authors (and even the current students of economics) study as Indian Economic Development (popularly known as IED). This is not an imagined vision—the papers in these two volumes would bear testimony.

An ambitious task of this kind cannot obviously be achieved without kind support from many. First, we would like to thank the Chief Guest for the Seminar, Prof. Kirit Parikh, Chairman, GIDR and currently Member, Planning Commission, Government of India, who also helped the Editors immensely in the subsequent stages of the work. Prof. Yoginder K. Alagh, former Member, Planning Commission, and a Central Government Minister, inaugurated the Seminar and Mr. Jay Narayan Vyas, former Minister for Narmada Development, Government of Gujarat, chaired the panel discussion and delivered the Valedictory Address. Prof. Tushaar Shah willingly agreed to our request to write the Foreword for these volumes. Words of thanks cannot adequately express our gratitude to these eminent persons yet we would like to convey our deep sense of gratitude to each one of them.

Institutions and individuals are inextricably linked in the politico-economic fabric of the Indian society. One of the institutions that have been supported by the Foundation to come up is the Gujarat Institute of Area Planning (GIAP). The GIAP transformed itself into the Gujarat Institute of Development Research (GIDR) under the leadership of Prof. Pravin Visaria whose erudition and commitment to developmental paradigms is known. The Foundation supports to the Seminar came at a time when the GIDR—the host institution—had been, for a couple of years without Prof. Visaria. He died in 2001. The editors of these volumes who grew under the tutelage of Prof. Visaria dedicate these volumes to his memory.

In fact both the GIDR and the Editors of these volumes were only keen that a suitable commemorative academic event coincides with the Seminar. A *Professor Pravin Visaria Memorial Public Lecture* was organised and Prof. Tim Dyson of London School of Economics, delivered the lecture. The topic of the lecture, "India's Population: Past, Present and Future," held as part of FF50-GIDR seminar was also an occasion for the people, policy makers, politicians and social activists to take stock of the developments on the social front today. The lecture also helped in taking to the people the developmental contours of the region.

A Seminar of this scale and volumes would not have been possible but for the able support of the Director, the administration and the support staff at the GIDR: Mr G. G. Nair, Mr Upendra Upadhyay, Mr K.P. Solanki, Ms Kalpana Mehta, Mr Jignashu Yagnik, Mr Bharat Adhyaru, Mr Dixit Parmar, Mr Dinesh Parmar, Mr Niranjan Bhatt, Mr Shivsingh Rathod, Mr Joravar Singh and Mr Raju Vaghela. Ms Girija Balakrishnan, Ms V.A. Vasanthi and Ms Sheela Devadas word-processed the papers for the Seminar and subsequently for these volumes. The Director and members of the GIDR Faculty deserve a special mention and thanks for their encouragement and crucial support at all stages.

During the organising of the Seminar, in the follow-up with the authors and in brining out these two volumes, Ms Jharna Pathak, Mr Harish Joshi and Mr Jayanti Solanki played a significant supportive role. But for their enthusiastic and ungrudging support the task would have been unmanageable for the Editors. We express our gratefulness to all of them.

These volumes are envisaged with a plan, although the delay in giving it a final shape is inexplicable. Other commitments and some reticence in writing down the thought processes that finally appear as the overview were partly responsible for the time lapse. In fact Prof Leela Visaria, present Director, GIDR, persuaded the Editors to accomplish the task in the shortest possible time and we gratefully acknowledge her efforts. However, the timeliness of the publication is not optimistically lost, as the development processes that have unfolded in the past two years lend further credence to some of the diagnosis, prognosis and policy imperatives. The papers received for these volumes were reviewed and revised and in some cases re-reviewed before acceptance as a publishable material. A professional editor, Dr. Rohini Patel, subsequently edited these revised papers. We would like to credit immense gratitude to the paper writers, reviewers, and the Editor for their committed work and encouraging response.

It would indeed be knotty to suitably thank the Foundation for its support and the distinguished participants of the Seminar and the contributors to these volumes. A Seminar of this importance would not have been possible but for the strong, committed and responsive acknowledgement of all of them. It is with delight the editors express their gratitude to the Foundation, participants of the seminar and the authors contributing to these volumes. The Ford Foundation, New Delhi, was indeed generous to a fault as perhaps they were in the Indian context, to support what was originally an intellectual knowledge generating activity that turned out to be a fruitful discourse between the various stakeholders of the developmental debate.

We owe a great measure of deep gratitude to the Ford Foundation officials and staff: Dr Gowher Rizwi, the then Representative, Dr Steven Lawry, Dr Dorris Capistrano, Ms Roshmi Goswami, Ms Renuka Agarwala, Ms Mona Challu, Ms Soha Khan, Mr Tuhina Sunder, Mr Nagasubramaniam and Mr Deep Chand. Our special thanks to Mr Ganesan Balachandaran, the present Representative, and Dr Vasant Saberwal for showing concern, and giving support and encouragement to complete the remaining portion of the process culminating in this publication. In the collaborative exercise with Surabhi and Mandala we appreciate the help of Mr Siddharth Kak and Ms Mita Vasisht.

While we were in the process of bringing out these volumes, both of us moved out from GIDR: R. Parthasarathy to the School of Planning (CEPT), Ahmedabad, and Sudarshan Iyengar to Gujarat Vidyapeeth. Both these institutions provided excellent academic and accommodative atmosphere for our pursuit. We would like to place on record our gratitude to these institutions.

While organising the Seminar and subsequently bringing out these volumes, the aim and purpose was to learn from the past approaches, the emerging scenarios and the paradigm shifts informed by the New Institutional Economists. If, as we had hoped, the FF 50-GIDR Seminar and the collection of papers in these volumes bring about an intercourse of the developmental paradigms and challenges and the academics, policy-makers and practitioners, the efforts and the purpose would be well served. Lastly, we are grateful to Mr Ashok Mittal of Concept Publishing Company who readily agreed to our request to contribute towards the dissemination part of the process by publishing the collection of papers.

R. Parthasarathy
Sudarshan Iyengar

Contents

PART II

Urbanisation and Industrialisation

PART III

Social Sectors

VOLUME TWO

PART IV

Management of Common Property Resources: Institutionalisation and Innovations

PART V

Watershed Development: As If People Mattered?

List of Tables

List of Charts, Figures, Map, Graphs and Appendix Figures

Charts

Figures

Map

Graphs

Annex Tables and Appendix Figure

Tables

Figures

The Contributors

Bakshi, Nishita, Indian Institute of Forest Management, Bhopal.

Ballabh, Vishwa, Institute of Rural Management, Anand.
Email: vb@fac.irma.ernet.in

Bhende, M.J., Institute of Social and Economic Change, Bangalore.
Email: bhende@isec.ac.in

Biswas, P.K., Indian Institute of Forest Management, Bhopal.
Email: pkbiswas@iifm.org

Chatterjee, Mirai, SEWA, Ahmedabad.
Email: sewass@icenet.net

Deshpande, R.S., Institute of Social and Economic Change, Bangalore.
Email: deshpande@isec.ac.in

Dholakia, Archana, Gujarat University, Ahmedabad.
Email: archana_dholakia@hotmail.com

Dholakia, Ravindra H., Indian Institute of Management, Ahmedabad.
Email: rdholakia@iimahd.ernet.in

Duggal, Ravi, CEHAT, Mumbai.
E-mail: raviduggal@vsnl.com

Ghate, Rucha, The Institute for Research and Development, Nagpur.
Email: shodh@nagpur.dot.net.in

Hirway, Indira, Centre for Development Alternatives, Ahmedabad.
Email: hirwayad1@sancharnet.in

Iyengar, Sudarshan, Gujarat Vidyapeeth, Ahmedabad.
Email: iyengars@icenet.net

Khaitan, Neelima, SEWA Mandir, Udaipur.
Email: smandir@vsnl.com

Kundu, Amitabh, Jawaharlal Nehru University, New Delhi Email: Amitabh@jnuniv.ernet.in

Mahadevia, Darshini, School of Planning, Centre for Environment Planning and Technology, Ahmedabad.
Email: spceptad1@sancharnet.in

Marothia, Dinesh K., Dept. of Agril. and Natural Resource Economics University, Raipur Chhattisgarh.
Email: dkmarothia@yahoo.com

Mukhopadhyay, Pranab, Goa University, Goa.
Email: pm@thegym.net

Mukundan, K., World Bank, New Delhi.
Email: kmukundan@worldbank.org

Nair, Ramesh P.K., Indian Institute of Forest Management, Bhopal.

Parthasarathy, R., School of Planning, Centre for Environmental Planning & Technology, Ahmedabad.
Email: rpsarathy@spcept.org,

Ray, Sunil, Institute of Development Studies, Jaipur.
Email: sunil@idsj.org

Sarangi, Niranjan, Jawaharlal Nehru University, New Delhi

Shah, Amita, Gujarat Institute of Development Research, Ahmedabad
Email: amita@gidr.ac.in

Shah, Anil, Development Support Centre, Ahmedabad.
Email: dsc@satyam.net.in

Shah, Mihir, Samaj Pragati Sahayoj, Dewas, M.P.
Email: samprag@sifi.com

Singh, Katar, Chairman, India Natural Resource Economics and Management Foundation, Anand.
Email: inrem@earth.planet.net.in

Singh, Surjit, Institute of Development Studies, Jaipur.
Email: idsjaipur@sancharnet.in

Swamy, Shivananda, Centre for Environmental Planning & Technology, Ahmedabad.
Email: shivanand@spcept.org

Roy, Tirthankar, Gokhale Institute of Politics and Economics, Pune.
Email: tirthankar_roy@yahoo.co.in

Vijay, Shankar, P.S., Samaj Pragati Sahayoj, Dewas, M.P.
Email: samprag@sifi.com

Verma, Madhu, Indian Institute of Forest Management, Bhopal.
Email: mverma@iifm.org

PART IV

MANAGEMENT OF COMMON PROPERTY RESOURCES: Institutionalisation and Innovations

14

Alternative Institutional Structures for Sustainable Development of Common Pool Resources

Lessons from Chhattisgarh

DINESH K. MAROTHIA

Renewable Common Pool Resources (CPRs) have been managed and controlled under different property regimes in India. These resources can be managed sustainably under state common or private property regimes, and often, these are managed at the interface of state (public), community and private property regimes. Enough evidence is available in India when resources managed under a common property regime degraded into an open access due to weak property rights regimes, inadequate institutional arrangements and breakdown of authority systems. Examples are also available when renewable resources degraded under the open access system brought under a state, or private or community management regime through appropriate changes in the institutional arrangements (Arnold and Stewart 1991, Marothia 1993, 2002). Dissatisfaction with the traditional failure of 'pure' traditional community natural resource management and "pure" government control has led to great interest in distributed or shared governance. State or government control with active local communities involvement has recently been identified as a feasible option in managing the CPRs (Marothia 2002). A large number of the resource development programmes in India failed or could not yield anticipated outcomes due to lack of understanding on the part of the researchers, administrators, planners about the issues related to property rights regimes and institutional arrangements and their application in the socio-economic network of village life (Marothia 1993, 2002). In recent years, particularly in the 1980s, several developmental programmes for water, forestry, fisheries and rehabilitation of waste and wetlands resources have been introduced and a few of them were managed under alternative property rights regimes including distributed governance or shared management system. In a few projects local communities/ (or, resources user groups) and the state or local government shared the responsibility of managing the CPRs by combining the appropriate institutional skills of the local resource users, local committees and technical, administration and financial resources available with the states. In this paper an attempt has been made to discuss the outcomes of the CPRs-based development programmes implemented under different property regimes toward uplifting for the upliftment of rural poor in the state of Chhattisgarh.

CONCEPTUAL FRAMEWORK FOR FRAMEWORK FOR INSTITUTIONAL ANALYSIS

To analyse the strength and weakness of the alternative governance structure used to achieve sustainability of the CPRs, we have basically used the institutional framework developed in a number of analytical models (Oakerson 1992; Ostrom 1992; Tang 1992; Townsend and Pooley 1995). The attributes of the conceptual framework for an institutional analysis developed in these models have also have also been used in Indian conditions to understand the efficiency of alternative governance in managing the CPRs (Marothia 1993, 2002; Singh 1994; Arnold and Stewart 1991). Various physical and technical attributes of a resource, characteristics of resource users community, external and internal institutional arrangements affect management of the system. It is, therefore, important to recognize that the governance can be shared among states, communities and private interests groups in various ways. In other words, distributed governance is the extended version of the standard regimes of property rights (state, common and private property, open access). Distributed management system involves the share of authority among different groups/agencies at different decision-making levels. (Townsend and Pooley 1995).

Distributed governance involves the external institutional arrangements (rights-based management, co-management and contracted management) among government and local communities or resource users as well as internal institutional arrangements (self-organizing institutions, communal management and cooperative management) within the local community institutions or resource users (see Fig.14.1). These attributes usually configure in combination, i.e. to examine the effect of one an attribute, one must know what other attributes are also in effect. A change in one attribute may alter the way the entire configuration operates, thus creating quite different action situations. This principle implies that when one tries to explain the performance for various levels of resource management, one must be aware of the interrelationship among the internal and external arrangements involved in relation to resource and resource users. Fig. 14.1 shows how these assumptions, attributes and outcomes are related to one another within the conceptual framework for analysing management of the CPRs. Each component of the conceptual framework has sub-sets of attributes. Each set of attributes is related to the others. For example, characteristics of resource and resource users, alternative property regimes and distribution of authority system collectively affect external and internal institutional interaction patterns. Characteristics of a resource and the users can affect the performance directly or through patterns of interactions between external and internal institutional arrangements. The first two attributes of the framework can be treated as exogenous variables and the institutional arrangements as endogenous in the short run. Strategies chosen in the pattern of interactions between the state and Local Resource Management Committee (LRMC) reflect the combined set of constraints and opportunities found in the technical and/or physical attributes of a resource and the characteristics of the users and the institutional arrangement associated with its management. These collective choices form some pattern of interactions. The interaction results in outcomes and these outcomes are subject to evaluation. In the case of a negative outcome, backward linkages have to be traced to determine the relationships between resource and external and internal institutional arrangements and to modify the institutional arrangements for achieving a shared management system. The conceptual framework suggested herein also has a dynamic application. In the long-term analysis, institutional arrangements are exogenous and their effects could be iteratively assessed on the

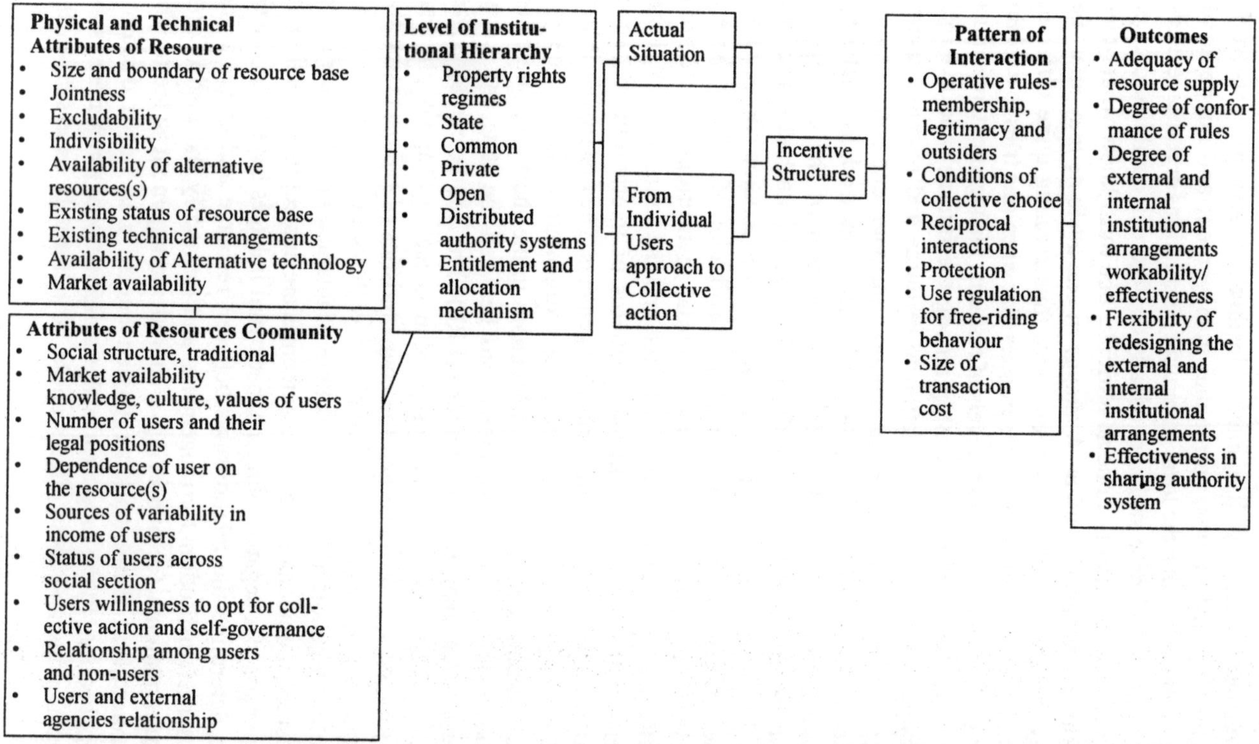

Fig. 14.1: Conceptual Framework for Institutional Analysis of Alternative Management System

interactions between external and internal arrangements and outcomes. (see Oakerson 1992). For example, in the case of Non-Timber Forest Products (NTFPs) many changes may occur in the physical and technical nature of these resources, and the outcome can affect the patterns of interactions among the different state agencies and the LRMC and between the LRMC and resource users. In such cases, institutional arrangements should be modified by the NTFPs' managements body and users should modify institutional arrangements. It is a continuous adjustment process of shaping institutional arrangements for shared management. To this end, we discuss CPRs-based development programmes operated under alternative property rights regimes.

ALTERNATIVE GOVERNANCE IN CPRS

In this section, capsule descriptions of instructive experiences about the role of institutional arrangements, type of property rights regimes and authority systems in managing the CPRs are discussed based on the studies conducted by this author during the last five years in the Chhattisgarh region. These case studies highlight the assessment of alternative management systems or alternative governance structures in managing the CPRs. Some CPRs-based programmes have been managed under a particular property regime while others under distributed governance structures.

Government, local communities and private parties utilizing common pool resources, each bring different interests, capabilities and understanding to the resource management process (see for details see Townsend and Pooley 1995). These alternative institutional perspectives shape the decision-making process among the government and local resource user communities and within the members of a local community for managing a resource by converting the unorganized structures into the organized ones (Marothia and Phillips 1985). To this end, we discuss cases of alternative governance systems in managing (i) Micro-Minor Irrigation Tanks (MMITs), (ii) Village Woodlots (VWLs), (iii) Community Fish Ponds (CFPs), (iv) Non-Timber Forest Products (NTFPs) and (v) Participatory Irrigation Management (PIM).

Case I. Micro-Minor Irrigation Tanks

The State Department of Agriculture (SDA) introduced an MMITs programme through its soil conservation wing in 1977-78 to provide irrigation facilities to increase foodgrain production, employment generation and minimize migration due to soil moisture stress. The MMITs were constructed on government-owned wastelands across the natural water courses to store rainfed run-off for irrigation. The command area of the MMITs is generally below 50 hectares. After construction, the panchayats were given the ownership rights of the MMITs and these were expected to be managed under the common property resource regime by group(s) of the farmers within the command area of a particular tank. (for details see Marothia 1992, 2002 and Table 14.1).

The MMITs programme was introduced in all the districts of the Chhattisgarh region with the conventional assumption that contributions of farmers in different types of resources-labour, materials and capital will be forthcoming, once it is determined that the benefits of the MMITs are significant to farmers and panchayats. The users have largely proved this assumption false in case of MMITs. Due to lack of legislative and administrative powers, panchayats could not manage the MMITs under the common property regime. One reason for the poor management was that the MMITs have extremely poor excludability. It is difficult to exclude non-contributors (in labour or capital resources) from taking advantage of the water use in the absence of a well-defined structure of rights and duties for the users and a breakdown of the local authority system to ensure that expectations of the water-users can be met through panchayats. All the MMITs were provided with iron sluice-gates. Water runs continuously in most of the cases. Its distribution is based on the crude negotiable rules. Despite the fact that a field-to-field irrigation water distribution method is operating within the command area, it has minimum external effects in terms of time and location due to the small size of the command area of the MMITs. Poor maintenance of the MMITs, lack of field channels and poor water control are the most pressing problems. Inadequate labour and capital share, non-payment of irrigation fees by the water users indicate their non-committal attitude towards the sustainable development of the MMITs and also

Table 14.1: Salient Features of Alternative Governance in MMITS, VWLS, CFPS, NTFPS, Canal Irrigation

S. No.	*Characteristics*	*MMITs*	*VWLs*	*CFPs*	*NTFPs*	*Canal Irrigation*
1.	Resource Management Programme (RMPs)	Dabri Yojna	VWLs Scheme	FFDA	NTFPs Coop	PIM
2.	Objectives of RMPs	Life saving irrigation to kharif crops and minimizing migration	Increase fuel, fodder and timber supply	Reliable and equal access to water to increase fisheries productivity	Provide market for nationalized and non-nationalised NTFPs, minimize exploitation of members	To transfer management of canal irrigation system to WUAs with financial and technical support
3.	Sponsoring Authority	SDA	SDF	SFD/FFDA	SDF	WRD
4.	Year of Initiation	1977-78	1986	1981-82	1988-89	1999-2000
5.	No. of Case Studies	18 (Tanks)	3 (Sites)	10(CFPs)	8(PMFPCs)	22 WUAs
6.	Social structure of users and organization	Multi_caste	Multi_caste	Fisheries Communities, SC/ST	Tribal dominant	Multi-caste users
7.	Size and boundary	Well-defined boundaries of tanks and command areas	Well defined area of common wastelands	Well defined boundaries of CFPs	Well-defined boundries of collection centres	Command area of WUAs is well demarcated.
8.	Original Ecological Status	Natural depressions, degraded Panchayat lands	Degraded/grazed village lands	Natural catchment, degraded Private lands	Protected and reserved forest	Natural drainage network beyond outlets of WUAs command area
9.	Original PRR	Panchayat	Village panchayat	*Private (Zamindars, Malgujlars)*	State	State

(contd.)

Table 14.1 (contd.)

S. No.	*Characteristics*	*MMITs*	*VWLs*	*CFPs*	*NTFPs*	*Canal Irrigation*
10.	Current PRR	Owned by VPs but open access status	Usufruct right to SFD (5-6 years)	CPR under cooperative governance/formal groups of fishermen	Usufruct rights to collect NTFPs	Distributed governance system
11.	Authority Sharing Arrangement	Absent	SFD control over project period	Internally dominated	Distributed governance (three tier organizations set-up)	Four tier organizational structure
12.	External Institutional Arrangements	Initially managed by SDA, handed over to panchayat	Implementation of project for (5-6) years by SFD.	External support –FFDA-	Financial, Technical and Infrastructure Support at different levels	Financial, Technical and Infrastructure Support at WUA, distributory, project and state levels.
13.	Internal Institutional Arrangements	Unorganized-weak authority system	Absent – No involvement of local community	Self-Cooperative formation/group formation	Cooperative structure with well defined rules.	Self governance system
14.	Outcomes	• High returns to individual users, without sharing labour, material and capital inputs • Inequitable distribution of water and income	• In some cases fodder is available • Babul sticks as tooth brush • Unsustainable use of wasteland • Conflict between SDF and village panchayat	• Fish sale • Wages paid to members • Common Pool fund for fish rearing assests • Social conflict between users and non-	• Proper and timely wages • Commission on total collection • Equal access to the NTFPs • FDT investment for Regeneration	• Nearly equitable distribution of water resources • Effective functioning of collective choice rules • Well specified work plan for main-

(contd.)

Table 14.1 (contd.)

S. No.	Characteristics	MMITs	VWLs	CFPs	NTFPs	Canal Irrigation
		• Unsustainable use of tank water		users over use of common village ponds	of NTFPs Biomass	tenance and repairs • Well structured mechanism for sharing • Well structured irrigation revenue at different management levels • Users and government officers learning and adopting PIMs norms.

Source: Table based on the synthesis of inferences drawn from NTFPs Cooperative (Marothia 1996), CFPs (Marothia 1997), MMITs (Marothia 1992), VWLs (Marothia 1993), PIM (Marothia, 2001).

Note: SDF: State Department of Forest, PMFPCs: Primary Minor Forest Product Primary Cooperatives, SFD: State Fisheries Department, FFDA: Fish Farmers Development Agency, SDA: State Department of Agriculture, VPs: Village Panchayats, CFPs: Community Fish Ponds, PRR: Property Rights Regimes, FDT: Forest Development Tax, WRD: Water Resources Department. PIM: Participatory Irrigation Management.

that they have yet have to develop a sense of belonging to the common pool MMITs (see Marothia 1992, 2002 for details). Simple working rules of keeping the sluice-gate closed on rainy days, controlled operation of the sluice according to the water requirement of the crop, introduction of water-measuring devices and appointment of water operators can increase the water-use efficiency. In the absence of appropriate administrative and legislative powers with the MMITs, the goal of sustainable management of the MMITs may not be achieved. The MMITs are common property resources and their operation and management should be based on community action on the basis of rules and regulations which that influence water control and resource base. The panchayat system broke down due to lack of a well-defined structure of water rules, regulations and acts; and the common property (*res communes*) MMITs ultimately degenerated into open access (*res nullius*).

To bring back the MMITs under a common property regime it is, therefore, necessary to develop incentives and sanctions that promote long-term participation and involvement of the water-users and panchayats in the management of the MMITs. These incentives, which may be economic or social in nature, should either reward those farmers or panchayats who are diligent in fulfilling their obligations, or penalize those who are delinquent. Such incentives and sanctions should constitute the major focus for the management of the MMITs. Currently these are poorly managed in absence of well-structured rights and duties, or incentives and sanctions and an MMIT management authority. Research on irrigation tanks in India has shown that tank irrigation efficiency may can be improved with effective institutional arrangements under a shared resource management regime. A series of studies conducted in Chhattisgarh has suggested the formation of a Tank Management Authority with distributed responsibility and rights structures to be shared by the government (State Department of Agriculture) and Panchayats; Tank Users Association and farmers and villagers (users of the tank water for domestic uses). The cooperative management system of governance may be adopted to restore the MMITs that are currently operating under an open access regime, where the government (panchayats) and village communities (water users) share the ongoing responsibilities for decision-making over the MMITs management decisions.

Case II. Village Woodlots

The State Department of Forest (SDF) undertook Village Woodlots (VWLs) plantation as part of its social forestry programme on village common grazing lands for a period of five years in various areas of Chhattisgarh. Based on the studies conducted in Kura, Kathadih and Saragaon villages in Raipur district of Chhattisgarh (Marothia 1993, 2002) it was concluded that the programme failed miserably due to the absence of a clear understanding of the sociological context, institutional arrangements (including property rights), insufficient consultation and involvement of the local people who dependent upon the grazing land on which woodlots were developed. For the entire project period of five years, village communities, particularly shepherds, were excluded through fencing of the woodlots and appointment of watchmen to guard the area. After the second year naturally grown regenerated grass was available in large quantities in the project area. However, grass-cutting was not allowed even for stall-feeding. In the opinion of the village community (including sarpanch and panches), the transfer of common grazing lands for woodlots was a losing proposition in terms of both shrinking grazing area for five-six years and conflicts generated between the SDF and village communities over the use of the resource. Village woodlots have resulted in poor patterns of interactions and inefficient, inequitable and unsustainable use of the village common grazing lands. Besides, dissatisfaction among the villagers is an important fallout (see Table 14.1). In 1993 the village panchayat was in the process in 1993 of getting back the grazing land under its control to develop collective fodder grounds.

Case III. Community Fish Ponds

Freshwater aquaculture, or fish farming is an important component of India's rural ecosystem and economy. The Government of India introduced the Fish Farmers Development Agency (FFDA) in 1973 to improve the productivity and income from aquaculture in village ponds and tanks. The network of the FFDA was also expanded in Chhattisgarh villages in 1979, alongwith other states of the country with the financial assistance from the World Bank. The FFDA has been specifically responsible for ensuring that all publicly owned ponds were leased out for fish culture and that all lease payments were made besides along with creating supportive infrastructure for promoting aquaculture in the community ponds.

Prior to the FFDA programme, panchayats did lease out a few specific community ponds for fish culture to the highest bidder from the village's fishing community, with the understanding that the water quality in the other community ponds would be maintained for the domestic use of the villagers. If conflicts arose between the fishermen and villagers, the panchayat resolved the issues. Community ponds have multiple uses for the human and animal population of the village. Traditionally these have been controlled and managed as common property resources by village panchayats. Under this system, they are governed not only by a well-defined set of institutional arrangements concerning who may or may not use the resource but also by the rules concerning the conduct of accepted users. The relationship of villagers with each other with respect to domestic and livestock uses on the one hand and to fish production on the other were bounded by formal and informal codes of conduct (Marothia, 1993,1997, 2002). The FFDA now has assumed many of these duties. It arranges the fishing leases between village panchayats and individuals, small groups and registered cooperatives. Pond size, lease sources, duration of the leases and the financial capacity of the lessees are the major factors in deciding to whom the ponds are leased. Fishing cooperatives are generally given preference when leasing large ponds; two or more fishermen often pool their resources to lease community ponds under two hectares and individual fishermen normally lease those under one hectare (Srivastava *et al.* 1993).

Based on a study conducted in three villages of Chhattisgarh (Marothia 1997) a few lessons are distilled here. Since the implementation of the FFDA leasing policies, the method of selecting the beneficiaries and the privatization of fishing rights in the community ponds have generated a social conflict between the leaseholders and other villagers. This has affected the productivity of fish-farming and created inequalities in the management of community ponds. Under the FFDA programmes, these ponds are normally leased to either members of the Scheduled Castes and Tribes or the fishing communities, individuals, or groups. To enhance their income, the rents fixed are fixed so low that they have no relation to with the profits received from fish-farming (Srivastava *et al.,* 1991; Marothia 1997). This creates conflicts with other villagers, especially other fishermen, who would have been willing to pay more for the right to fish but were excluded on the basis of community (Marothia 1997). Privatizing fishing rights of the community ponds often generates conflicts between their owners (panchayats) and fishermen. Community members at large are losers in terms of poorer water quality and increased water scarcity in water-stress years, a loss for which they receive little compensation. Thus, the process of privatizing the water resources of the community ponds creates social and economic inequalities (Marothia 1997). Poaching, restrictions on using medicines, feeds and manure, and class conflicts were the greatest problems, the fishing community was confronted with. On the villagers' side, skin irritations were reported due to the application of substantial quantities of manure and feed in the water-bodies for fish culture. Constraints were imposed in the case of individual fishermen, followed by fishing cooperative societies and fishermen's groups. These constraints created inequalities of income, yield and employment distribution in the management of the community ponds.

Before the involvement of the FFDA, aquaculture in the study villages had been managed as a common property resource. Under the FFDA, aquaculture now represents private property for the leaseholders. Like many development projects, the FFDA programme was implemented with no clear understanding of how restructuring of the property rights regime and its institutional arrangements would affect the social stability and economic productivity. On the one hand, it has reduced the productivity of freshwater aquaculture and, on the other, socio-economic disorder has been created. In some cases the ponds' many uses are reduced or obstructed and the mechanisms for leasing out ponds and selecting leaseholders are unsatisfactory. The magnitude of the disorder is more serious when the ponds are managed by groups of fishermen or individuals than when they are managed by cooperatives. The FFDA, in reality, has replaced the authority of the village panchayat, but it has not been able to ensure the stream of benefits to leaseholders. The study suggested to redesign the existing institutional arrangements for the CFPs that influence the ways in which these are used and maintained by the leaseholders and villagers alike. New institutional arrangements or modifications of the existing arrangements—such as reserving close-in ponds for common village use and more distant ponds for aquaculture—may resolve spatial and temporal conflicts. However, only organized institutions can reliably regulate the behaviour, since these institutions can impose working rules that define resource users/interactions with respect to the common property regimes. They do so by imposing a minimum cost on those whose behaviour or actions require modifications or by providing financial incentives to induce behaviour consistent with socially desired results. Cooperatives management with proper distribution of rights and responsibilities at different decision levels seems to be the better option for implementing new institutional arrangements (Marothia 1997).

Case IV. Non-Timber Forest Products

Non-timber Forest Produts (NTFPs) play a vital role in the socio-economic, ecological, cultural and political environments of the state of Chhattisgarh. For managing NTFPs, the State Department of Forests (SDF) has used several alternatives of distributed governance system in the post-colonial period. These varied from *contract management system* to monopoly arrangement with *purchaser-agent system* (see Marothia 1996 for a detailed discussion of the alternative property regimes in managing the NTFPs). However, a few nationalised NTFPs, namely, tendu leaves, sal seeds and gums are being managed under distributed governance using the Cooperative Management System. Other Non-Nationalized NTFPs are collected under usufruct rights systems and sold in the weekly local markets at prices generally dictated by the middlemen (Marothia 1994, 2002).

Cooperative governance is the most frequently suggested internal governance structure for managing the NTFPs at community levels. The cooperative governance operating in Madhya Pradesh has both external and internal institutional arrangements reflecting the core concept of distributed management. Recognising the problems associated with nationalisation or creation of private monopolies by assigning exclusive rights of collection and marketing to the private traders, and to eliminate the middlemen, cooperative management of the NTFPs was initiated in 1988 with the formation of Madhya Pradesh Minor Forest Produce Trade and Development Co-operative

Federation (MFPED) at the apex (state) level, District Minor Forest Produce Unions (MFPDUs) at the secondary (district) level and Primary Minor Forest Produce Cooperative Societies (PMFPCs) at the primary level. The organizational structure and external and internal institutional arrangements at different management levels are discussed in Marothia (1996).

For an effective implementation of the cooperative management of the NTFPs at MFPFED, MFPDU and PMFPCs byelaws have been framed for each level. The byelaws clearly spell out the working zones, objectives, functions, responsibilities, organisational, administrative and financial set-up, duties and rights of members of the governing bodies operating at the apex, secondary and primary levels. These byelaws reflect the relationships between the external and internal institutional arrangements for distributed management.

An analysis of the eight PMFPCs conducted by Marothia (1996) indicates that given the resource and resource users' characteristics on the one hand, and the internal decision-making environment, on the other, some pattern of interaction had emerged. This can effectively restrict the free riders or non-members and have framed internal institutional arrangements for regularizing different operations and payments to members. However, financial, technical and administrative control is still unevenly distributed at different levels of management. For example, PMFPCs has not been assigned my significant role for procuring and marketing of nationalized and non-nationalised NTFPs. In the past few years, owing to the collective pressure from PMFPCs, MFPFED made certain adjustments in the external institutional arrangements to allow some non-nationalized NTFPs collection and marketing by PMFPCs. However, owing to financial constraints, at PMFPCs, significant achievements have not been recorded in this effort. The external institutional relationship for distributed management is well defined (Table 14.1). However, for the self-governance of PMFPCs, the internal institutional arrangements have to be redefined for the greater involvement of the local resource users in managing NTFPs.

Case V. Participatory Irrigation Management

A few state governments, practitioners and scholars, involved in irrigation management in India have recently begun to realize the limitation of relying primarily on government bureaucracies to solve development related problems and to design complex institutional arrangements linking state agencies with local water users. The failure of many large, medium and small irrigation projects to deliver the projected benefits to farmers beyond pipe outlets clearly indicates the limitation of state control over canal irrigation water. Recently, Chhattisgarh has taken an initiative to reform irrigation by introducing Participatory Irrigation Management (PIM). For an effective implementation of the PIM a four-tier organizational structure at the WUAs, distributory, project and apex levels is in functional. By-laws for institutional arrangements have been framed for each level and made effective since June, 2000. The by-laws clearly spell out the working zones, objectives, functions, responsibilities, organizational administration and financial set-up, and the duties and rights of the members of the governing bodies operating at the WUA, distributory, project and apex levels.

An in-depth case analysis of 22 Water Users Associations (WUAs) indicates that PIM is in the process of transformation from state control to a self-governing irrigation system. It is important to realise that the PIM model was introduced only two years ago in the state of Chhattisgarh. Successful adoption of PIMs requires a complete change in the mindset of the bureaucracy. The office-bearers involved in water resource development, members of the managing committees of WUAs and farmers are still in the learning process. The preliminary results of the present study indicate that despite the maintenance and repair works that were carried out by all WUAs of the main canal, distributaries and field channels, a large number of WUAs and farmers located in different zones along the watercourses suffered water scarcity at the critical crop growth stages. In fact, the canal network was in a very bad shape even before transferring the irrigation management to the WUAs. Although, the external and internal institutional arrangements are well defined at each level of the PIMs and have the capability of structuring collective choices with respect to the irrigation system and farmers within a command area, the enforcement of these arrangements and outcomes thereof are at the best satisfactory, in terms of awareness and performance. In order to ensure an adequate and equitable water supply and minimal cleavages (social and economic differences among the farmers and the WUAs) an effective implementation of the institutional arrangements with dynamic WUAs is needed. This is important because many WUAs are socially, economically and politically very powerful and often influence repair, maintenance and water distribution. In the process, the WUAs without political leverage get a lower preference in seeking funds and approval of their proposals for repair and maintenance. In the WUAs with adequate water availability, there is cut-throat competition among the members to contest elections for the management committee and sub-committees. However, it is difficult to find candidates for the posts of president and members for the managing committee in the water scarcity zone. The nominated members are overburdened with departmental work and it is difficult for them to participate actively in WUAs. Also, to strengthen the WUAs, formation of Distributory Committees and Project Committees is urgently required. As per the provision in the Act, the share of the WUAs in the irrigation revenue may be transferred to enhance the financial capability of the WUAs. The responsibility for collecting irrigation fees may also be entrusted to WUAs for greater involvement in water management. In many cases, managing committees of WUAs face serious problems in maintaining records. In such a situation the managing committees are largely depending on the sub-engineer (co-ordinator of the managing committee) for maintaining the records and getting approval of the maintenance and repair works from the executive engineers of the WRD. Periodic training for the official members (superintendent and executive engineers), nominated and the elected members of the committee is required to educate them about the importance of institutional arrangements to achieve self-governance in the canal irrigation system. The sustainability of PIMs largely depends on the political and bureaucratic will to share power with farmers and creating a political environment for the smooth functioning of the WUAs.

CONCLUSIONS AND POLICY IMPLICATIONS

The foregoing analysis has obvious policy implications for the governance of CPRs and the welfare of the rural poor. It also suggests a general approach to policy designing in the CPRs management. Institutional arrangements (both external and internal) are important factors in CPRs management under different property rights regimes. Institutional movements have redefined the property rights structure in a number of the CPRs development programmes aimed at reducing rural poverty. This transition of institutional arrangements became a major source of eco-system degradation in many cases due to a lack of understanding of the policy makers about the social, economic and ecological linkages, users' participation in the programmes, and patterns of interactions. For example, institutional transition in the case of village woodlots has redefined the property right regime by converting common property to under into state property for undertaking social forestry programmes. This created social tensions as well as replaced the customary institutional arrangements to conserve the resource and eco-system. As a result the grazing area of the village was reduced and the villagers developed negative attitudes towards the plantation programmes due to the 'policing culture' in the implementation of social programmes. Similarly, the MMITs have been created on village wastelands but due to weak local governance and absence of well-defined institutional arrangements for common property regimes they have ended up in an open access resource regime. Experience from the management for fisheries has shown that multiple use of CFPs could create social tensions even if effective institutional arrangements are designed, keeping in view the number of the users. Unless an effective authority system is in place the social disequilibrium cannot be corrected. The findings of the NTFPs cooperatives clearly indicate that the cooperative management system still has an unevenly distributed governance, and excess state control is visible even at the PMFPCs level. The members still of the cooperatives remain mere wage-earners and their participation is almost negligible in the decision-making process. An important corrective could be that the state may use the local capacity of institutional building to support and gain strength for making the PMFPCs self-governing organizations at the local levels. An analysis of the participatory irrigation management clearly indicates that better understanding and management of the institutional arrangements, and political and bureaucratic will to share power with the farmers, can not only help improve the performance of the PIMs but also promote the goals of sustainable management of the scarce irrigation water resource.

The outcomes of these case studies suggest that the policy designers of the institutional arrangements for the CPRs development programmes in the rural areas should have an in-depth understanding of the strengths and weaknesses of alternative property rights regimes. Solely state, solely community-based and solely private property regimes have more negative effects in a large number of the cases. On the other side, distributed governance seems to be most appropriate for designing the CPRs management programmes. Promoting exploration of distributed governance as an acceptable model for institutional innovation to the local situation, should reflect in the policy and administration for a greater involvement of the resource users. However, this involves a major shift in the role of the policy-makers and administrators to share power for promoting greater involvement of the local people in decision-making and administration. Serious theoretical and empirical research efforts are, therefore, needed for testing the efficacy of alternative models of distributed governance in managing the CPRs.

REFERENCES

Arnold, J.E.M. and W.C.Stewart (1991): *Common Property Resource Management in India,* Tropical Forestry Paper No.24, Department of Plant Sciences, Oxford Forestry Institute, University of Oxford, U.K.

Bromley, Daniel W. (Ed.) (1992): *Making the Commons Work*, ICS Press, San Francisco, U.S.A.

Ciriacy-Wantrup, S.V. and R.C. Bishop (1975): Common Property as Concept in Natural Resources policy, *Natural Resources Journal,* 15:713-728.

Marothia, D.K. (1992): Village Irrigation Tanks: Institutional Design for Sustainable Resource Use, *Agricultural Situation in India* 47:479-487.

Marothia, D.K. (1993): Property Regimes and Institutional Arrangements: Concepts and their Relevance in Managing the Village commons, *Indian Journal of Agricultural Economics,* 48, 557-65

Marothia, D.K. (1994): *Decentralized Planning for Bastar District: An ACRP Approach*, Planning Commission Project (GOI) Indira Gandhi Agricultural University Publication Raipur (M.P.).

Marothia, D.K. (1996): Co-operative Management of Non-timber Forest Products: Issues of Property Rights and Institutional Structures, In R.Rajgopalan (ed.) *Rediscovering co-operation: Strategies for the Models of Tomorrow* (Vol.2), Institute of Rural Management, Anand, November.

Marothia, D.K. (1997): Institutional Arrangements in Common Fish Ponds. In J.M.Kerr, D.K. Marothia, K. Singh, C. Ramasamy and W.R. Bentley (eds.) *Natural Resource Economics: Theory and Application in India,* Oxford & IBH Pub. Co. New Delhi.

Marothia, D.K. (2001): Institutional Arrangements for Participatory Management: Initial Feedback from Central India. In Donna Brennan (Ed.). *Water Policy Reform: Lessons from Asia and Australia,* Australian Centre for International Agricultural Research (ACIAR) Proceedings No.106.

Marothia, D.K. (Ed.) (2002): *Institutionalizing Common Pool Resources*, Concept Publishing Company, New Delhi.

Marothia, D.K. and W.E. Phillips (1985): Analysis of Natural Resource Problems Using a Synthesis of Neoclassical and Institutional Economics, *Asian Journal of Economics and Social Studies,* 4, 263-81.

Oakerson, R.J. (1992): Analyzing the Commons: A Framework in D.W.Bromley (ed.) *Making the Commons Work*, ICS Press, San Francisco, U.S.A.

Ostrom, E. (1992): *Crafting Institutions for Self Governing Irrigation Systems*, ICS Press, San Francisco.

Singh, Katar (1994): *Managing Common Pool Resources: Principles and Case Studies,* Oxford University, Press New Delhi.

Srivastava, U.K., B.H.Dholakia, S.Srinivas Rao and S.Vathsala (1993): *Freshwater Aquaculture in India.* New Delhi: Oxford & IBH Publishing Company.

Tang, Shui Yan (1992): *Institutions and Collective Action: Self-Governance in Irrigation,* San Francisso: ICS Press.

Townsend, R.E. and S.G.Polley (1995): Distributed Governance in Fisheries in Susan Hanna and Mohan Munasinghe (eds.) *Property Rights and the Environment – Social and Ecological Issues.* The Beijer International Institute of Ecological Economics and the World Bank, Washington, D.C.

15

Management of Forest as a Common Property Resource for Sustainable Rural Development

P.K. BISWAS

Since independence we have devoted our resources and energies to economic development. A vast amount of money has also been spent by the government and the various international agencies for the upliftment of the poor. And yet the level of development remains alarmingly low. Poverty, malnutrition, unemployment and underemployment have not diminished appreciably. On the whole, the condition of the poor, in both urban and rural areas, has worsened, as the economic growth has taken place in an inequitable manner. In fact, the gap between the poor and the rich has widened considerably.

The lot of the rural poor as compared to that of the urban dwellers is perhaps worse. The rapid population growth and rising expectations make it almost impossible to maintain the desired level of production from the available land area. Therefore, to augment agricultural production and to set up industries, forestland is often cleared. This is more so in the thickly populated regions where the rural poor live.

The tribal communities in India largely occupy forested regions. They live away from the mainstream life but are in harmony with nature. The large-scale indiscriminate felling of trees and the resultant deforestation, soil erosion and environmental degradation have hit badly the rural poor in general and the tribals in particular. Further, the loss of forest cover creates ecological insecurity and increases poverty and misery among the rural poor.

Contribution of Forests to Development

In the above context, it is imperative to examine the contribution of forest in the development of the rural poor. Forests come second after agriculture in terms of land-use and play a vital role in the rural economy. In many rural areas, particularly where a majority of the population is landless, forests and trees are among the few resources available. They provide three different kinds of benefits: *jobs and incomes* often needed to supplement inadequate returns from agriculture; *produce* such as fuel wood, food, fodder and building poles for homes; and—less directly but just as importantly—a range of *environmental benefits*, without which other activities, such as agriculture might be impossible.

About 300 million people live in remote villages on the fringes of forests and depend on forests for their subsistence and livelihood. For about 100 million of them, forests are the main source of their livelihood; they obtain cash income from fuel wood, Non-Timber Forest Products (NTFP) and construction materials. More than half of India's 70 million tribal population, the most disadvantaged section of society, subsist on forests. Forests protect important catchments for water, conserve soil, protect watersheds, prevent water run-off and recharge groundwater. In addition, they ameliorate climate, combat global warming, and retard desertification. They also provide refuge for wildlife. Both wood and non-wood products are important for the economy as are flora and fauna for the environment.

India is rich in its biodiversity; it is one of the 12 countries in the world which collectively account for 60—70 per cent of the world's biodiversity. Its 10 bio-geographic regions represent a broad range of ecosystems. It has world's 6 per cent flowering plant species and 14 per cent avian fauna (World Bank 1996). There are nearly 45,000 species of flora and 81,250 recorded species of fauna in the country (Ministry of Environment and Forests 1999). It has 80 national parks and 441 sanctuaries (protected areas); they make up about 14.8 million ha. which constitute 4.5 per cent of the country's land area and 14 per cent of its forest area.

Forests contribute 1.7 per cent of the Gross Domestic Product (GDP) of the country. However, this figure does not take into account its numerous non-market and external benefits, nor does it include the vast amount of fuel wood, fodder, and other forest products—collected legally or illegally. One estimate shows that the total annual removals from the forest is worth about US$ 7.1 billion or Rs.30,000 crore which includes about 270 million tonnes of fuelwood, 280 million tonnes of fodder, over 12 million cubic metres of timber and countless NTFPs. This does not include the value of the environmental services provided by the forest which, according to one estimate, is worth US$ 19 billion per year.

For several tribal groups living in or near forests, about 30 per cent of their diet is derived from forest resources which include wild vegetables, tubers, fruits, nuts, bamboo shoots and small animals. The indigenous people have developed an interesting, even sophisticated, knowledge system of ethno-medicine and use of a vast variety of plants for medicinal purposes (Ministry of Environment and Forests 1999). Medicinal plants are important in the primary healthcare system.

The agricultural sector, essential for the survival of rural communities, depends almost entirely on the livestock for the energy needed for various farm operations. The main source of fodder, leaf or fruit, for the livestock is the forest. Wood (timber), bamboo, grass, creepers, and bark are used in the construction of houses, and wood and timber are used for making various types of ploughs and agricultural implements. Animal husbandry and dairy development programmes depend upon grass, fodder, leaves and so on. About 70 per cent of India's rural population depends on fuel wood to meet its domestic energy needs. The bullock-cart, the main means of transport in the rural areas, uses more than one produce from the forest to function. (According to one estimate, there are about 13 million bullock-carts in the country which accounts for an investment of about 3,000 crore. About two crore people find direct or indirect employment in the bullock cart transportation system.) The forest offers scope for the development of cottage industries for the tribal population. Many trees are a source of raw materials such as *tassar* for silk production, *pattal for* plate-making, and cane for basket-weaving.

The NTFPs play an important role in poverty alleviation. The rural poor and tribal communities collect various kinds of products throughout the year to sustain themselves. Activities related to NTFPs provide employment during the slack periods in the agricultural cycle and act as a buffer against risks and household emergencies. The NTFP-related activities are a part and parcel of the household activities, and in several cases they are the main source of income. Thus the forest is a part of the livelihood strategies of rural people in general and tribal communities in particular. It meets their basic needs, provides food security, alleviates poverty, meets health-related needs, and supplies materials for shelter in a sustained manner.

But that is not all—life of the tribal people is connected with forests in one way or the other right from birth to death. Their folklore, rites and rituals revolve around the forest. In times of distress forest is the last resort for them. Even in areas where forests do not exist, tribals continue to visit periodically the distant forests to procure their traditional requirements. Thus forests occupy a central position in the tribal economic and social life. Hence, tribal life is profoundly affected by whatever happens to the forest.

Status of the Forests

The land area of India totals 328.7 million ha. of which 142.5 million ha. (43.3 per cent) is under agriculture, and forests cover 76.5 million ha. (23.27 per cent). According to the State of Forest Report, published by the Forest Survey of India (FSI) in 1997, the actual forest cover is 63.34 million ha. (19.27 per cent), of which 26.13 million ha. are degraded forests (Ministry of Environment and Forests 1999). State-wise figures of recorded forest area and actual forest cover are shown in Table 15.1.

In terms of per capita forest area, India ranks amongst the lowest in the world, and the area has gone down from 0.16 ha in 1960-61 to 0.08 ha. in 1990 as depicted in Table 15.2.

The forest area is being rapidly depleted, and its quality has been deteriorating due to the heavy pressure of population on land. Having about 2.5 per cent of the world's geographic area, India at present supports 16 per cent of the world's human population and 18 per cent of its cattle population. Between 1950 and 1980 India lost about 4.3 million ha. of forest land to non-forest uses such as

Table 15.1: Recorded Forest Area and Actual Forest Cover in States and Union Territories as Assessed in 1997

State/Union Territory	*Geographical Area (in ha.)*	*Recorded Forest Area (in ha.)*	*Actual Forest Cover (1997) (in ha.)*	*Actual Forest Area as Per cent of Total Area*
Andhra Pradesh	275,068	63,814	43,290	15.7
Arunachal Pradesh	83,743	51,540	68,602	81.9
Assam	78,438	30,708	23,824	30.4
Bihar	173,877	29,226	26,524	15.3
Delhi	1,483	42	26	1.7
Goa	3,702	1,424	1,252	33.8
Gujarat	196,024	19,393	12,578	6.4
Haryana	44,212	1,673	604	1.4
Himachal Pradesh	55,673	35,407	12,521	22.5
Jammu & Kashmir	222,235	20,182	20,440	9.2
Karnataka	191,791	38,724	32,403	16.9
Kerala	38,863	11,221	10,334	26.6
Madhya Pradesh	443,446	154,497	131,195	29.6
Maharashtra	307,690	63,842	46,143	15.0
Manipur	22,327	15,154	17,418	78.0
Meghalaya	22,429	9,496	15,657	69.8
Mizoram	21,081	15,935	18,775	89.1
Nagaland	16,579	8,629	14,221	85.8
Orissa	155,707	57,184	46,941	30.1
Punjab	50,362	2,901	1,387	2.8
Rajasthan	342,239	31,700	13,353	3.9
Sikkim	7,096	2,650	3,128	44.1
Tamil Nadu	130,058	22,628	17,064	13.1
Tripura	10,486	6,292	5,546	52.9
Uttar Pradesh	294,411	51,663	33,994	11.5
West Bengal	88,752	11,879	8,349	9.4
Andaman and Nicobar Islands	8,249	7,171	7,613	92.3
Chandigarh	114	31	7	6.1
Dadra and Nagar Haveli	491	203	204	41.5
Daman and Diu	112	—	3	2.7
Lakshadweep	32	—	—	—
Pondicherry	493	—	—	—
Total	*3,287,263*	*765,210*	*633,397*	*19.27*

development of agriculture and heavy industries. The quality of the forests is also being degraded as indicated not only by the decline in the crown density, but also by soil erosion and lack of natural regeneration. Other serious problems are encroachment, grazing, forest fires, shifting cultivation and illegal felling. Most species of the flora and fauna are endangered which will also have serious economic consequences. A recent World Bank report has estimated that one million ha. per year were lost due to degradation and deforestation during the 1970s and 1980s. The rate of loss has somewhat slowed down after the promulgation of the Forest Conservation Act, 1980, but it still remains a cause for concern, indeed for alarm. It is, therefore, imperative to examine the strategies of forest management which have a significant bearing on the livelihoods of the rural people.

Table 15.2: Per Capita Forest Land in Asia-Pacific Region, 1990

Country/Geographical Area	*Per Capita Availability of Forests (in ha.)*	*Per Capita Gross National Product (in US $)*
India	0.08	360
Sri Lanka	0.11	470
Indonesia	0.64	560
Malaysia	1.02	2330
Fiji	1.17	1780
Tropical Asia	0.21	475
Total Asia-Pacific	0.17	602
Total Developing Countries	0.50	763
Total World	*0.64*	*4063*

Source: Food and Agriculture Organisation 1995

People and Forest Management

Forest management broadly refers to the organisation and control of access to and utilisation of trees, woodlots, plantations, natural forests and associated resources including benefits derived from them. It involves professional foresters, village-level organisations, non-governmental organisations (NGOs) and the rural communities.

Forest has essentially been the property of the State and its control over forests, particularly reserved forests, dates back to the colonial period. The Indian Forest Act of 1865 was the first attempt at establishing monopoly holding rights by the State. These rights were formalised and made explicit in the subsequent Act of 1878, and once more by the Act of 1927. Under these, the State was allowed to demarcate valuable tracts of forests and was entitled to its exclusive exploitation.

The inhabitants of these areas—mostly indigenous people or tribal communities—were deemed to derive their customary usage of the forest and its products not from a right of ownership but from a limited and contingent privilege. The State, in this framework, was thus able to assert its rights to absolute ownership, and this was done through the reservation of certain forest areas.

In this context, therefore, it is essential to understand the meaning of property. "Property is a right to a benefit stream that is only as secure as the duty of all others to respect the conditions that protect that stream. When one has a right, one has the expectations in both the law and the practice that their claims will be respected by these with duty" (Bromley and Cernea 1989). Thus it is the use of land or some other resource in relation to others that is central in defining property. The bare fact of ownership, then, is not as critical as the relationship with, and the expectation of, others who are associated with it. The right to use a property, or a resource, implies inclusion and exclusion, i.e. rights of access. Thus resources are a fundamental aspect of property use and property rights.

The forest area is shrinking considerably causing further poverty and misery in the rural communities in general and the tribal communities in particular. While in the recent period the scale of deforestation has emerged as a matter of widespread national concern, the substantive measures initiated for reversing the trend have been limited in scope and efficacy.

In view of these concerns, a debate is taking place on how forest area has to be viewed: whether it has to be treated as a state property, a private property, or a common property resource.

The case for state ownership or, at least, state management of forests hinges on a number of factors. First, forest management is associated with a wide range of externalities that impinge on not only the proximate producers but also on the economy as a whole and on the climate of the region. In general, it can be said that if they are maintained well, forests provide benefits to the rest of the eco-system. Any loss in the value of the benefit—a function of the rate of depletion—would, therefore, tend to exceed, often substantially, the loss in inter-temporal benefits experienced by the person or institution controlling the actual forest resource. Secondly, it can be argued that the management of forests requires a level of professional training and scientific competence that lies beyond the capacities of the potential private owners and the rural people. Thirdly, the time horizons for forest management and the spatial requirements for an efficient, conjoint exploitation of the resources through harvesting and replanting favour state ownership and investment. Private rights would either be too fragmented and hence inefficient or else they would need to be too large, thereby running counter to the general policy regarding land ceiling. Fourthly, the ecological variety of the Indian forests is likely to be preserved only if they are under state management. Private entrepreneurs would tend to replace diverse stocks by fast-growing varieties. Fifthly, state ownership allows for major economies of scale and a long-term planning framework. Sixthly, state ownership ultimately allows for a wider and more just distribution of revenues derived from forest products through the overall structure of government spending. Although this effect could be achieved through the taxation of private returns, it would imply a major revision of the basis of public finance in the country, let alone a more satisfactory control over "leakages".

Although each of these arguments is persuasive, and would appear to offer a strong case for state ownership when put together, the case remains strongly dependent on the degree to which the stated conditions are attained in reality and sustained. After all, state ownership is largely argued for as it leads to a more efficient outcome and not because its supposedly ethical superiority to private ownership. In this regard, all available evidence points unequivocally to the fact that the state has been unable to sustain India's forest resources. While some would argue that this has been because of a weakness in the construct of state ownership, consolidation of state monopoly is likely to run into difficult, probably insoluble, problems. To that extent, the very same issue that necessarily dominates any discussion of the demand for timber by indigenous communities comes to the fore in the general discussion of the relative virtues of state ownership. For it can be argued that in terms of both research and actual management practice, the Forest Department's monopoly has yielded poor and very limited results.

Tenurial Rights for Rural Communities

If state control over forests has proved to be an inefficient means for their management, let alone retention, attention needs to be given to the processes by which a set of different economic signals are transmitted to the potential exploiters of the resources. This requires, above all, a radical approach to the system of property rights itself. The aim of any reform must be to harmonise, to the extent possible, the social and private rates of return from forestry activity where time preferences is the key issue. This implies a more graded and subtle use of controls and contingent rights. In the era of globalisation, one argument would be to say that private property rights and a market in land and trees would provide the most simple and efficient outcome. There is ample evidence from Europe and elsewhere that forests can be maintained in a private ownership context and that the privatisation of rewards ensures a satisfactory enforcement of rights. The State, precisely because of its amorphous nature, is inherently a weak vessel for the physical, let alone psychological, enforcement of exclusive control.

This argument runs into a number of problems in the Indian context. First, private management of trees has customarily been associated with plantation or specialised husbandry. Secondly, given the political difficulties of establishing properties outside the usual land reform parameters, there are problems associated with the wrapping of rights. Forest management clearly has considerable potential for economies of scale and, given the ecology of most remaining Indian forests, the working area is relatively large. Thirdly, there remains the problem of the forest communities. Even if forestland was sold or leased to outside agencies, this would still raise the problem of what to do with the forest communities, which lack, in general, both capital and expertise. Both practical and ethical considerations strongly suggest that these communities must be actively included in any reform of the current system. This is clearly evident in the case of Madhya Pradesh (MP) which has a substantial forest area and tribal population. Wherever there is good forest cover there is also a heavy concentration of the tribal people. Some demographic features of MP are given in the following box.

MP: Some Demographic Features

Total population of MP	:	6.038 crore
Number of villages	:	51,806
Forest area	:	24.38%
Forest fringe villages	:	20,000 approximately
Tribal population	:	22% (90% live in forest fringe Villages)
Population below poverty line	:	37.43% (80% live in forest areas)
Cattle population	:	3.3 crore
Forest-dependent livestock	:	1.5 crore

Most *adivasi* or indigenous forest-based households in MP have the following resource endowments. Each household roughly commands on average between 2 and 10 acres. Although such holdings are large by Indian standards, the soil quality is often poor and the terrain hostile to successful husbandry. In almost all cases, the cultivated land is rain-fed and the intensity of landuse is low. Most commonly, a single monsoon crop of paddy (*dhan)* is raised, and this generates a high demand for household labour in the months of June-July and September-October. For the remaining nine months of the year, household labour is normally employed in the Forest Department's work, mostly in the collection of NTFP with *tendu patta* as a dominant item. They also work for other government departments. Often they migrate to other places.

Income from wage employment—largely from the Forest Department—can thus be complemented by a combination of remittances and other transactions. The latter are mostly through the sale of wood, either to urban traders/dealers or at the periodic *hats* (markets). Despite a long history of indebtedness to local *Sahukars (*money-lenders), low household income levels, and high rates of under-employment, the tribal economies have generally been marked by a relative affluence of the basic requirements—principally fuel and food—compared to the chronically income-constrained condition of many poor rural and urban households outside the forest areas. Yet, the denudation of the forest cover gravely undermines this condition of "primitive plenty". Loss of fuel-wood and tree cover are accompanied by a parallel loss in employment in the Forest Department work or in the collection of NTFP. The selected tribal areas of MP present a dismal picture in terms of development indices as shown in

Table 15.3. It is evident that any further loss of forest will impoverish the tribal people even more.

Table 15.3: Forest, Tribals, Poverty and Development Correlationship in Selected Districts of M.P.[#]

District	*Forest Area (in %)*	*Tribal Population (in %)*	*HDI* Rank*
Betul	39.0	37.5	30
Chhindwara	40.0	34.5	13
Mandla	63.0	54.8	16
Seoni	37.0	37.0	26
Shahdol	33.0	46.3	31
Sidhi	42.0	30.4	25
East Nimar (Khandwa)	26.8	46.0	21
Dhar	15.0	53.5	23
Barwani	50.0	64.8	44
Sheopur	43.0	20.1	33
Jhabua	19.0	85.7	45

[#]MP has 45 districts
* Human Development Index
Source: Government of Madhya Pradesh, 2002

A Case for Forest as a Common Property Resource

From the foregoing discussion it is evident that there has to be reform of the property rights in forest management if poverty is to be alleviated from the indigenous people. Sustainable forest management is the key to the sustainable development of the rural people.

Even in the age of liberalisation and globalisation, it has to be understood that there can be no financial assets if there are no ecological assets. Sustainable development is increasingly linked to environmental conservation. Here, it is apt to quote a tribal chief who said:

Only after the last tree has been cut down,
Only after the last river has been poisoned,
Only after the last fish has been caught,
Only then will you find that money cannot be eaten.

In this context, it is important to note that the National Forest

Policy of 1988 recognised that "the life of tribals and other communities living within and near forests revolves around forests. The rights and concessions enjoyed by them should be fully protected. Their domestic requirements of fuel-wood, fodder, minor forest produce and construction timber should be the first charge on the forest products" (Government of India 1988). Conservation and the people's livelihood are an integral part of sustainable development. Conservation of forests has to be balanced harmoniously with the development of indigenous communities through livelihood security.

The National Forest Policy, 1988, has been further strengthened by the June 1, 1990 circular of the Ministry of Environment and Forests, Government of India, which highlighted the need for and processes of involving village communities and voluntary agencies in the protection, development and management of forests.

The circular of 1990 together with the National Forest Policy has facilitated the formation of village-level committees known as village forest committees or Forest Protection Committees (FPCs). This strategy is known as Joint Forest Management (JFM) where the government and people are partners in forest protection and management. By the end of March, 2002, 27 States had adopted JFM as the main strategy, and 63,000 village FPCs had been implementing the JFM in 14 million hectares of forest area (Government of India 2002). The Government of India acknowledges that the JFM experience has had a positive impact. These changes are presented in brief (Government of India 2002).

Rehabilitation and Improvement in the Conditions of Forests

There is evidence that the JFM has rehabilitated the country's degraded forests. In the past few years, the overall forest cover of the country has increased by 3,896 sq. km.; the main reason for this rehabilitation and improvement is the successful implementation of the JFM programme. In areas under the JFM, incidents of illicit felling have sharply declined. It has been reported that in Rajasthan, unlike in the past, people did not resort to tree felling in the JFM areas even during droughts. A study carried out by the Andhra Pradesh Forest Department indicated that between 1996 and 1999, dense and open forest covers have increased by 18 and 22 per cent respectively, mainly due to the introduction of the JFM. Another study of Sabarkantha district and Vyara division of Gujarat has shown a significant improvement in the forest cover after the initiation of the JFM. One of the more immediately visible ecological effects of JFM has been the recovery of fodder resources in the JFM areas. The prolific growth of vegetation has led to increased biodiversity and relatively rapid increases in the wild herbivorous population in many instances.

Increase in Livelihood Options

JFM programmes have created livelihood opportunities in several places. The communities have benefited from the livelihood options under the JFM projects through micro-planning, sale of NTFP, share in the final harvest, etc. Further, the JFM has helped many FPCs to build up a substantial level of the community funds, which are used for local development activities.

Reduction in Encroachments

In several places, the JFM has led to the reduction in the area under illegal encroachment and lowering of the rate of fresh encroachments. In Andhra Pradesh nearly 12 per cent of the encroached forestland has reportedly been vacated after the JFM programme was initiated.

Involvement of NGOs

The JFM programme has led to a considerable involvement of NGOs in the forestry sector, although the extent of involvement varies significantly from state to state. This has facilitated interaction between communities and the government.

Change in Attitude and Relationship

One of the most significant impacts of the JFM programme has been the change in the attitude of the local communities and forest officials towards the forest and towards each other. For instance, members of Botha FPC in Buldhana, Maharashtra, even postponed a wedding in their village in order to fight a forest fire. This would have been unthinkable in the pre-JFM days. In several FPCs, traditional forest protection practices have been revived, for example, *kesar chhannta* (sacred groves) in Rajasthan. The large number of training and orientation exercises carried out in the different states has also contributed to a positive change in the attitude.

Despite such experience, the empowerment of the rural communities is far from satisfactory. The FPCs have no clear-cut tenurial rights. The Panchayat (Extension to Scheduled Areas) Act, 1996, also has a provision by which communities have ownership of NTFPs. And yet the tribal communities are deprived of the rights for management of forest products, which determine their socio-economic conditions.

Conclusion

In keeping with the philosophy of decentralised governance, people's involvement in the decision-making processes and their consequent empowerment are crucial. Therefore, tenurial rights for the rural people must be secured. The following factors may be considered for effective indigenous/local management control systems. The two main institutional issues are:

1. Provision for secure tenure rights to the rural people, and
2. Development of systems of regulation and enforcement based on local decision-making.

There is a need to formalise community-based management systems at both local and state levels. The culture of the indigenous people and the dynamics of social processes have to be understood properly since sustainable forest management is the key to sustainable rural livelihood. A sustainable alliance has to be forged among government organisations, NGOs, and local level organisations. There has to be an effective partnership of all the stakeholders for capacity building, monitoring and evaluation. Sociological and anthropological insights, perceptions and knowledge are, therefore, essential for bringing reforms in property rights for a sustainable development of the rural communities.

It is clear that improved forest productivity will ensure equity and livelihood for the rural poor. The rural livelihoods must be integrated with the management of forest as a common property resource (CPR), with the involvement of communities in the form of village forest committees or forest protection committees. Once they are involved, forest resource cycle will be completed as schematically presented in the Diagram.

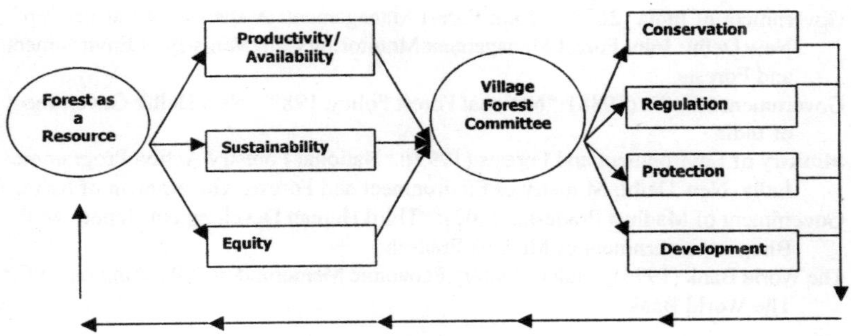

Diagram: Forest Resource Cycle

Source: Biswas 1993.

It is important to empower communities to take decisions on the management of forests. The JFM experience is already a decade old. On the basis of this, it is strongly recommended that the forest be treated as a CPR, implying greater legitimacy and more power to the communities. The government must facilitate the communities so that forests may be treated as CPRs. A memorandum of understanding must be signed between the forest community and the government. Legal recognition should be given to the FPCs.

The National Forest Policy, which essentially pleads for community empowerment, needs to be backed up by appropriate acts and legislations. There is also an urgent need for amending the various forest laws and acts to facilitate treating of the forest as a CPR. If done properly, environmental stability will be achieved which, in turn, will lead to sustainable rural development enhancing and strengthening rural livelihoods.

REFERENCES

Biswas, P.K. (1993): "Forestry-Based Sustainable Development: The Social Dimensions". *Indian Journal of Public Administration* 39(3).

Bromley, D.W., and Cernea, M.M. (1989): "The Management of Common Property Natural Resources: Some Conceptual and Operational Fallacies". World Bank Discussion Paper 57, Washington, D.C.: The World Bank.

Food and Agriculture Organisation (1995): "State of the World's Forests". Rome.

Government of India (2002): "Joint Forest Management: A Decade of Partnership". New Delhi: Joint Forest Management Monitoring Cell, Ministry of Environment and Forests.

Government of India (1988): "National Forest Policy, 1988". New Delhi: Government of India.

Ministry of Environment and Forests (1999): "National Forestry Action Programme: India. New Delhi: Ministry of Environment and Forests, Government of India.

Government of Madhya Pradesh, (2002): "Third Human Development Report, M.P." Bhopal: Government of Madhya Pradesh.

The World Bank (1996): "India, Country Economic Memorandum". Washington, D.C.: The World Bank.

16

Leadership in Community Initiated Forest Management

RUCHA GHATE

Even after two decades of research, the scholars of "commons" are still intrigued by the ground reality: while some communities organise themselves successfully to solve their "commons" problems by crafting institutions indigenously, others in similar circumstances do not. While searching for factors that are conducive to collective action, scholars have identified many such factors. This paper focuses on the *role of leadership,* considered an important factor in initiating and sustaining collective action in forest management. *Leadership in this paper is synonymous with the person or persons who have taken the initiative in bringing the community together for the common cause of managing surrounding forest.* It is an effort at building consensus, formulating rule structure, ensuring monitoring and equitable benefit sharing, and dealing with infractions. Since a successful leadership cannot always be articulated, identification of the elements leading to a successful leadership in collective action can lead to useful policy implications.

This paper is based on a study of three neighbouring communities from the Vidarbha region of Maharashtra state (Map 16.1), which was a part of the erstwhile Central Province and Berar (Map 16.2)[1]. Vidarbha has a high share of forest cover (more than 50 per cent) and indigenous population (almost 40 per cent) of the state. For the majority of population (more than 70 per cent) subsistence agriculture is the dominant occupation which increases their dependence on natural resources like forests. Due to the low share of industrial investment in the region, Vidarbha's share in the state's income coming from the secondary sector is low. However, the large forest area in the region

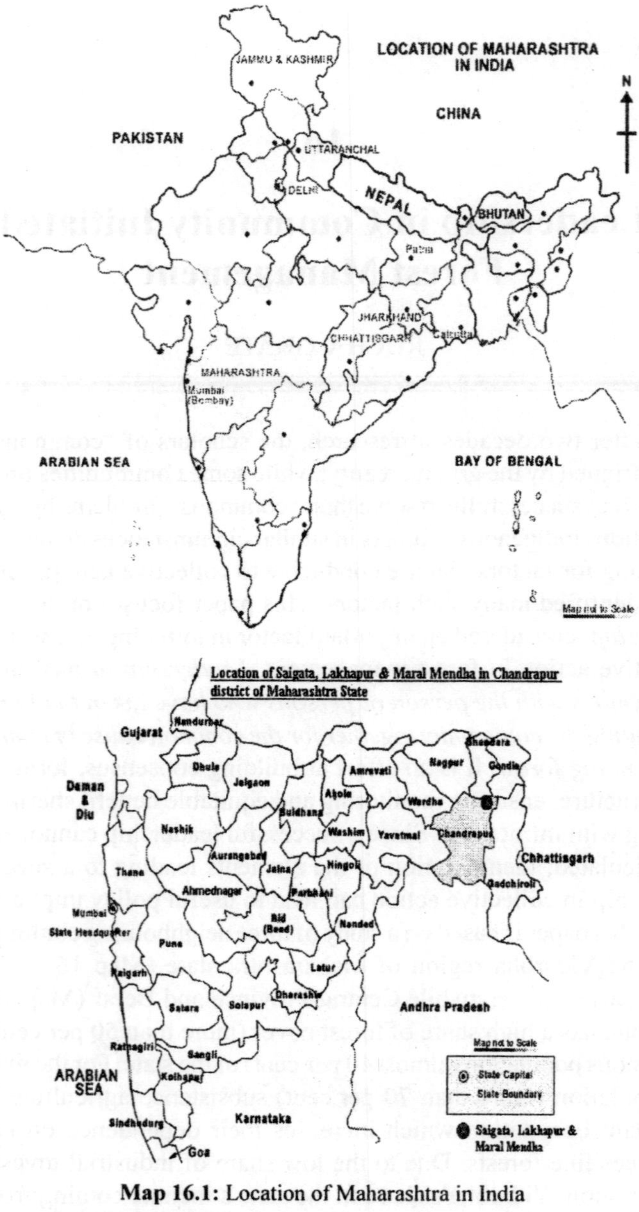

Map 16.1: Location of Maharashtra in India

Source: www.mapsofindia.com

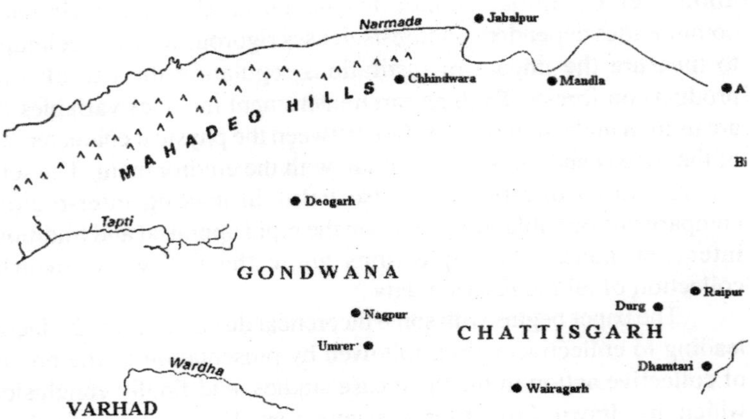

Map 16.2: Vidarbha

Source: Guha 1999, p. 123

has the untapped potential of income and employment generation. Yet, due to the exclusive ownership and management of the resource with the state, with no respect for traditional conservatory practices and community ownership, the forests have been continuously deteriorating for a long time. The participatory approach in forest management that has been recently adopted by the forest department could only partially succeed due to various reasons. The real challenge in this region is to turn the highly abused forests into income- and employment-generating resources. To achieve this, it is essential that communities participate in the endeavour in the real sense. From this point of view it is necessary to understand what induces some communities into collective action, and deters others.

This paper presents three case studies. One is the case of a community that came together two decades ago and is still protecting and managing its forest collectively. The second is that of a community whose unity was jeopardised because of an external influence. The third is a perfect example of "The Tragedy of Commons" where collective action was initiated but was abandoned soon. All the data required for the study were collected through a set of 10 research instruments developed by the International Forestry and Resources

Institutions Research Programme to facilitate collection of information about demographic, economic and cultural characteristics of communities dependent on forests. It uses rigorous forestry techniques to measure the impact of institutions regulating the use of forest products on forests. Each research instrument includes variables that are used to understand connection between the physical characteristics of the forests and human interaction with the environment. The set of pre-structured questionnaire also helps in making inter-regional comparisons possible. Relying upon the rapid appraisal and traditional interview method, the questions guide the fieldwork ensuring collection of all the relevant data.

The paper begins with some theoretical discussions on the factors leading to collective action, followed by presentation of the process of collective action in the three case studies, and finally conclusions which are drawn through process analyses. The purpose of process analysis is to understand how the communities or their institutions have developed, what were the aims and motives behind coming together, and how was the process initiated. In other words, it tries to understand the ways in which their objectives were achieved, aims were fulfilled, and if they were not fulfilled, why they were not fulfilled. The process helps one to understand the potential areas of intervention for achieving wider, common goals. The basic steps that are followed in presenting the six cases are: (1) perception of the problem (how and by whom); (2) rapport-building or means of communication used; (3) methods of dealing with differences of castes, classes, opinions and expectations; (4) development of the rule structure; (5) methods adopted for monitoring and execution of rules, flexibility and accountability; and (6) perceptions of the community about success.

The major conclusions of the paper are: (1) the leadership that ensures benefits in the short as well as long run, promotes coordination between formal and informal institutions, and (2) the leadership that uses indigenous methods that are acceptable to the larger community succeeds in collective action and, therefore, management of the Common Pool Resources (CPRs).

Theoretical Basis

The theory of collective action is considered one of the important components of the New Institutional Economics. It is generally believed that collective action is required for production as well as maintenance of a public good. The literature on the commons has travelled a long way since Olson's (1965) "zero contribution thesis" through Hardin's (1968) "tragedy of commons", to many scholars now taking cognizance of voluntary associations that are creating and enforcing rules that protect natural resources. Literature published in the past two decades provides ample evidence of this (Agarwal 1999; McKean 1992; Ostrom 1992). Field research has established that though the temptation to free ride on the provision of collective benefits is a universal problem, self-organised resource governance too has survived in multiple generations (Ostrom 1990; Poffenberger 1990).

As a next step, scholars have been trying to isolate and identify factors that are conducive to initiating as well as sustaining collective action. Adams, Brockington and Dyson (2001) mention that community-based natural resource management is successful only under very specific environmental, economic and social conditions. It is also found that when the users of a CPR devise the basic rules *themselves*, they tend to manage local resources better than when the rules are imposed on them externally (Tang 1992; Baland and Platteau 1996; Wade 1994). Wade (1994) has identified factors such as the size of the group, clear boundaries and ease in monitoring and enforcement as some of the conditions that determine the effectiveness of rules leading to successful management of the commons. Gary Libecap (1995) argues that the likelihood of collective action is influenced by the size of the aggregate expected gains, the number and heterogeneity of the bargaining parties, and information problems. It is a well-accepted fact that the factors that affect the biophysical forest conditions are demographic (population size, rate of change, etc.), economic (market demand, shifts in relative prices, size of land holdings), ecological (climate, soil characteristics, altitude, slope); and institutional (local institutions for resource management, government policies) (Poteete Ostrom 2002). Baland and Platteau (1996) too have emphasised the importance of the small size of user group, location close to the resource, homogeneity among group members, effective enforcement mechanism and the past experience of cooperation as factors necessary to achieve cooperation. In a later work Gaspart and Platteau (2001) have brought forth the importance of structural characters like market conditions, extraction-techniques that bear upon enforcement costs, inter-personal relationships and history-determined patterns of authority and leadership. They emphasise that the support of the State is often required to help communities manage their resources. Flexibility in the development of innovative schemes to confront unintended circumstances at the local level is another important aspect that can ensure full participation of the locals in conservation initiatives (Gazon 1997). Agrawal (2001) has argued that external factors such as markets, technology, the state and population pressure are important contextual factors. After studying numerous cases of collective action all over the world, with the help of 14 case studies, Ostrom (1990) has designed eight principles as "essential elements or conditions that help to account for the success of these institutions in sustaining the CPRs and gaining the compliance of generation after generation of appropriators to the rules in use" (1990; p.90). These are: (1) clearly defined boundaries, (2) congruence, (3) collective-choice arrangements, (4) monitoring, (5) conflict-resolving mechanisms, (6) minimal recognition of rights to organise and (7) nested enterprises. Later, she suggested (i) attributes of the resource and (ii) attributes of the appropriators that are conducive to an increased likelihood that self-governing associations will form (Ostrom 1999). The attributes of the resource are: (1) possibility of improvement of the resource, (2) availability of reliable and valid indicators of the condition of resource system, (3) predictability and (4) small spatial extent for the appropriators to have an appropriate knowledge of the external boundaries. The attributes of the appropriators are: (1) salience of the resource, (2) common understanding, (3) low discount rate, (4) trust and reciprocity, (5) autonomy and (6) prior organisational experience and leadership.

Krishna (2001) has stressed the importance of leadership for moving "stock of social capital" to "flow of benefits". His study involves 60 villages of Rajasthan, India, and has stressed that without the support of a capable leader a community cannot translate its collective action into benefits. According to Nabli and Nugent (1989), "because of the importance of group perceptions, the *communication* and *organisational skills* and *knowledge* of the *technology* of collective action on the part of group members and especially those in leadership positions may also contribute to success in collective action". It is possible that even if people question the appropriateness of the institution and its inefficiency, they may not have sufficient motivation to do anything about it if there is no leader. It is the leadership that attempts to bypass the constraints of existing institutions; at times create new institutions that match their interests. (Agrawal and Gibson 2001). Lapiere and Fransworth (1949) have mentioned that leadership is a behaviour that affects the behaviour of other people more than their behaviour affects that of the leader. They further add that, "leadership is a concept applied to personality-environment relation to describe the situation when a personality is so placed in environment that his will, feelings and insight directs and controls others in pursuit of a common cause". Leadership potential is critical. "Both, traditional leadership represented by influential persons from the local area, and modern leadership represented by college graduates, can play an important role" (Dick, Raju, Gulati, 2002). The process of consensus building, organising and maintaining collective action involves considerable transaction costs that leadership can reduce. Individuals may be influenced by leaders because they may have more faith in the information provided by them. If the leadership is from within the community, the members have the opportunity of watching their leader from close quarters. They can immediately know if she or he is disproportionately advantaged by the actions of the whole community. A charismatic leader can give greater assurances to the followers because they believe that the leader has wide influence, although such a leader may not be effective for a long time.

In this paper I have tried to assess the role of leadership in bringing people together for a common cause of protecting and managing forests within the jurisdiction of their villages. The three cases representing success, partial success and failure of collective action are located next to each other and, therefore, share similar geographical, historical, social, political and economic background. These factors are discussed before elaborating on the process of collective action in each case.

Background of the Three Case Studies

The cluster of three villages—Saigata, Lakhapur and Maral Mendha—is located in Bramhapuri Taluka (sub-district) of Chandrapur district of Maharashtra (Map 16.1). Located on the northeast side of the state, this region, now known as Vidarbha, was once a part of the state of Central Provinces and Berar (Map 16.2), with Nagpur as its capital. Central Provinces and Berar included the major portion of Madhya Pradesh and Chhattisgarh. Even after independence, the Vidarbha region remained a part of Madhya Pradesh till 1960. It was after the Samyukt Maharashtra movement was launched that the area with a majority of Marathi-speaking population came under the jurisdiction of the state of Maharashtra. Vidarbha has 11 districts.

Ownership of forests in this region has an interesting historical background. Ignoring the communal ownership structure of the pre-British era, the government of independent India continued the British legacy of government ownership of all forestland. It would be pertinent to briefly look at the post-independence developments in the formal institutions and the changing attitudes and priorities of the Forest Department to appreciate the actions of the locals.

If the causes of deforestation are traced, it is found that till 1955 large chunks of forests were under the *malgujari* system introduced by the British. They appointed a local rich land-holder, *malgujar,* to collect revenue on their behalf. The system was abolished in 1955. Before the forests were transferred to the Revenue Department, and subsequently to the Forest Department, a large number of trees were cut down by the malgujars within this short period of transition. The local population also utilised this period to plunder the forest resources. Even after the rights were legally transferred to the Forest Department, the local communities continued to enjoy some usufruct rights over the forests known as *nistar* rights. An area classed as protected forest was demarcated for the use of the locals. The rest of the forest area was classified as reserved forest. The Forest Department had its working plans (for the reserved forest) under which forest harvesting was done through contractors by auctioning of coupes. Irregularities practised under this system caused in most of the destruction. Even after the department took over the forestry operations, the attitude of revenue maximisation remained. Personal assessment of the forest officers was done, based on the amount of revenue their divisions could generate. Therefore, although the forestry work was done according to the Working Plans which had been developed scientifically, the discretionary power given to the officers was always used for maximisation of revenue. This is the major reason of deforestation in the study villages of Saigata, Lakhapur and Maral Mendha, where the forestland was already small and population pressure constantly growing.

Studying these communities is worthwhile because two of them did not resort to anarchistic solutions, but the third community of Maral Mendha did. Saigata and Lakhapur communities preferred sacrificing immediate benefits in order to preserve the resource for future. Local leadership seems to have played an important role in initiating (in Saigata and Lakhapur) as well as sustaining (in Saigata) the collective action. Geographical, demographic and socio-economic details are presented in Table 16.1.

CASE STUDY 1: SAIGATA COMMUNITY

Saigata once had a lush green forest with rich floral as well as faunal diversity. This was not very long ago, as many people living today narrate their encounters with tigers and other wildlife. Saigata is located in an area which was a once corridor connecting two wildlife sanctuaries, Andhari Sanctuary, which surrounds Tadoba Tiger Reserve, and the recently created Bhamragarh Sanctuary. The villagers do not have to dig deep in their memories to remember how the forest on the village boundary not only provided them with sufficient fuel wood, fodder, and timber for household use, but also generated excess—a source of income for the locals. However, the unsustainable use by the community, the revenue maximising approach of the Forest Department, and the growing number of settlements in the neighbourhood nearly wiped the forest out.

The process of degradation has had multiple dimensions. All the households in the community were migrants who had settled down not very long ago. Therefore, the community was not a cohesive group with shared past and developed mutual trust. Cultivation being the sole occupation of all the communities in the vicinity, encroachments on the forestland was not uncommon. Growing population pressure,

Table 16.1: Profiles of Study Villages

Features	*Saigata*	*Lakhapur*	*Maral Mendha*
I. Physical			
Geographical location	20°.36'53.2"N 79°47'07.4" EO	20°.37'17.4"N 79°46'42.9" EO	20° 37'41.9" N 79° 48'26.8" EO
Altitude	246 meters ASL	256 meters ASL	263 meters ASL
Forest type	Dry deciduous mixed forest	Dry deciduous mixed forest	Dry deciduous mixed forest
Total Area	566.44 ha	491.50 ha	281.49 ha
Area under Forest Department	280.00 ha.	269.86 ha.	78.12 ha. (officially)
Distance from market	8 km	10 km	5 km
II. Demographic			
Population size.	432	547	700
Total Male	219	292	380
Total Female	213	255	320
Number of households	88	110	125
III. Social			
Main religion(s)	1.Hindu = 77.31% 2.Bouddha = 22.69%	1.Hindu = 55% 2.Bouddha = 45%	1.Hindu = 72.14% 2.Bouddha = 9.29% 3.Mahanubhav = 18.57%
Three main caste groups and percent-age in population	1.Mahar = 15% 2.Gowari = 12% 3.Gond = 12%	1.Kunbi = 50% 2.Mahar = 40% 3.Gond = 2%	1.Mali = 50% 2.Mahar = 15% 3. Teli = 10%
IV. Economic			
Dominant Occupation	Agriculture	Agriculture	Agriculture
How many house-holds own land?	84	110	106
Land holdings	Small (less than 2 ha.)	Small (less than 2 ha.)	Small (less than 2 ha.), only legal.
Other occupations	Tenants, Shop-owner, Agricultural Labour	Agricultural Labour, Barber, Tailor,	Agricultural Labour, Brick Making, Shop owners
Dependence on the resource	For subsistence	For subsistence	For subsistence
Level of Income	Comparable with neighbouring villagers	Comparable with neighbouring villagers	Higher
V. Legal Status Legal ownership/ property rights regime.	Forest Department	Forest Department	Forest Department
Policy application	Indian Forest Policy	Indian Forest Policy	Indian Forest Policy

small size of land holdings and meagre incomes of the landless, all resulted in an unsustainable use of the resource. Since forests surrounding the villages were considered "public property", the community living at subsistence level looked at it as a source of cash income. The upcoming township in Bramhapuri, which was declared a sub-district centre, was only 5 km. away from Saigata (as well as from Lakhapur and Maral Mendha). This proximity accentuated the speed of forest degradation in the area. A lot of felling took place in Saigata forest for supplying timber for construction work in Bramhapuri. The rising number of houses and households meant growing demand for cooking fuel, bamboo, timber for furniture, etc. For all these activities, the nearby forest was an easy and cheap source. The suppliers of forest tried to maximise their profit produce in the wake of growing demands.

Initiating Collective Effort

One Mr. Suryabhan Khobragade, a resident of Saigata, was always uncomfortable with the continual degradation of the forest. He was disturbed by the fact that a part of the forest, which was once known as *andhari* (meaning darkness) because it had such a thick tree cover that even the sunrays could not penetrate, was now totally devoid of big trees.[2] He had witnessed the changes in the land-use patterns since the days of the *malgujars* for whom he had worked as a child. Between 1955 and 1975, the forest around Saigata had changed from a thick canopy forest to degraded land. But he was also aware of the fact that it would be difficult to dissuade fellow villagers to give up their income-generating pursuits without offering them an alternative. After holding many discussions with the like-minded people in the village, it became clear to him that asking the fellow villagers straightforwardly to stop anti-forest activities would not yield the required response. Instead, something positive needed to be done circuitously to bring the community together. It had to be an activity that gave positive returns to encourage people to come together in the first place. At that time, the state Agricultural Department had a scheme, *Krishak Prashikshan*, for training farmers to adopt improved techniques of cultivation. Under the scheme, there was a provision of setting up a *Krishak Charcha Mandal* (Farmer Discussion Forum) in any village that showed interest.

Mr. Khobragade had attended a five-day training workshop under the scheme where he was given a radio so that he could listen to the agriculture related programmes. He came back and spoke to the villagers about his experience and what he had learnt at the training programme. They all then got together and on October 7, 1973, as Mr. Khobragade distinctly remembers, set up a *Krishak Charcha Mandal* in Saigata.

At that time a radio programme discussing various agricultural techniques from all over the world was being broadcast by the All India Radio (AIR) on Mondays and Fridays wherein the farmers were encouraged to apply these techniques. All the men of the Saigata community regularly got together at 7:30 in the evening on the two days to listen to the programme. The programme was of half-hour duration but the Saigata community used to continue their discussion about the techniques presented in the programme for another half hour. In those days, this was the only occasion when the people of the village came together. As a part of the scheme, an award (at Zilla Parishad level) was announced by the Agricultural Department of the Chandrapur district for those communities who successfully applied the techniques taught through the radio programme. They were given a questionnaire for this, made available at the sub-district office of AIR. A group of inspectors from the Agricultural Department used to confirm the actual application of the technique and evaluate the genuineness of the effort. The farmers of Saigata started successfully applying these techniques and won an award for two consecutive years in 1974 and 1975. It proved to be a great morale booster for the villagers as their very first experiment in collective action had brought them recognition. The economic benefits that followed this successful experiment, together with the recognition of the collective effort in the form of the award, helped the community to get together for reasons beyond farming.

Extending Collective Action

Mr. Khobragade's discomfort with the degraded state of the forest turned into a crusade to rescue it from the brink of destruction when one morning he woke up to find his mother warming bathing water for him over cow-dung cakes (often used as fuel in rural India). This event brought to his mind the fact that the 300 ha. of abundant forest that once belonged to Saigata—not in a very distant past had reached this state of degradation. Those were the days when there was enough fuelwood available in the forest, and cow-dung was used more efficiently as farm manure. He shared his anguish with the community. The community had by this time already come together through the *Krishak Charcha Mandal* and a majority of them shared his concern for the deteriorating condition of the forest leading to scarcity of fuel-wood and fodder. All that they needed now was a plan to start the process to save the forest. Mr. Khobragade initiated an effort to first identify the dependence of each household on forests.

Dissuading the Expropriators

Under the leadership of Mr. Khobragade, the active group within the community found that there were three categories of activities that were seriously degrading the remaining forests. The first category consisted of community members who collected fuelwood for sale in Bramhapuri, delivering it literally on the doorstep of the households. They were gradually made to realise that they were actually losing out by doing so, since they were either not charging for the labour involved in the collection of fuelwood or for transporting it to Bramhapuri. Khobragade suggested that either the customers come to Saigata and buy fuelwood or the collectors should charge an extra price for transporting the headloads. This argument convinced the traders that they were making a net loss in the trade and that they would only be fools to continue this practice. This technique worked. The sale of fuelwood by the community members stopped.

The second category was of extractors, that is, charcoal makers. This was a very profitable business; it fetched more income than farming. Thus, it was difficult to convince this category of extractors without offering any immediate alternative. The pro-conservation group tried to reason with the charcoal makers and convinced them that their business would last only till the forest lasted. After that, they will have no source of income. They were also told about the other ill effects of forest degradation.

The third category consisted of all the households of Saigata, which were indiscriminately exploiting the forest products, not caring for the sustainability of the resource. Everyone had found that the water level in the wells and in the village lake had been lowering. Pests on crops had increased, severely affecting agricultural production and income. Women had to spend more time and energy in collecting fuelwood and fodder. Bamboo and other useful timber had vanished from the forest due to which people had now started buying it from the market. Therefore, the community had only to convince itself to impose restrictions on consumption. To encourage this, Mr. Khobragade adopted a unique and indigenous method. He used his skills in writing, directing and acting in skits (known as *dandaar* in the rural areas of this region) to spread the message. He feels proud when ever he mentions that the high-caste actors had to ask him to apply make-up to their faces, thus letting him touch them. The typical style of this folk art of taking a dig at the social ills in a lighter vein made people think more seriously about the future outcomes of their present actions.

Informal Organisation Comes up Formally

All these factors combined together and led the people to protect the forest by setting up a *Van Sanrakshan Samiti*, or Forest Protection Committee, in 1979. The common feeling was "if we did nothing to protect our own forests, who would?" The general body of the committee consisted of all the adults in the village as members, and an executive body was formed to regulate the day-to-day functioning. However, the Gràm Sabha (general body) framed all the rules regarding the use of the forest products. Suggestions were invited from all members. As a result, all the members participated in the rule-making and decision-taking activity. Every decision was taken unanimously,, and, therefore, it was binding on everybody. Initially the Samiti started supervising and controlling the various activities of its own community members inside the forest. There were only a few infractions. However, it was increasingly realised that without stopping the entry of outsiders in the forest, it would not be possible to protect the resource in the true sense. With this began a long period of struggle for the people of Saigata.

The revenue boundaries of the villages were not clearly demarcated. As a result, movements of people from the nearby villages into other community forests was a common occurrence. Especially, forests being *de facto* an open access resource, restricting anyone from illicit extraction was unheard of; it was also unacceptable. Kirmiti Mendha, a neighbouring village, did not have much forest within its village boundary. For all these years, it had met its forest needs from the Saigata forest. The Kirmiti Mendha community members did not appreciate the newly imposed restrictions by the Saigata community. The demand for fuelwood continued to rise in Bramhapuri, and now even other the nearby villages had started feeling the dearth of forest products due to continued denudation in the region. Despite a lot of pressure on the community members, Saigata continued to protect its forest by keeping vigilance day and night. The whole community shared the responsibility of watching the forest. Households took turns in patrolling. Many instances are narrated by Saigata villagers today about how women had to come forth to stop women timber thieves and physically seize their axes. This had to be done by the women of Saigata as a woman can easily lodge a police complaint of harassment if she is even touched by a man.

Going Beyond Protection

The uniqueness of Saigata lies in the fact that it did not stop at merely protecting the forest. The community gradually moved towards thinking in terms of improving the quality of the forest. The people had already come together for practicing improved methods of cultivation. This had helped reduce forest dependence to some extent. Rules and restrictions on harvesting forest products were already established. However, due to the paucity of funds few maintenance activities could be taken up initially. More emphasis was on the regulated use and strict guarding of forest from outsiders. As a result, the forest growth till then was only due to natural regeneration. Now, the community started thinking of managing the forest in addition to protecting it. After several brainstorming meetings, it was decided that different patches of the forest, traditionally known by different names like *Tiwas* (a tree species), *Kotwal* (is the lowest government official in the revenue department), *Mothya Devache Ran* (the forest of the main deity), *Kosran* (indicating a short distance from the settlement) and *Gavtache Beed* (the forest of grass) will be treated as management zones by the villagers. Thus, each management zone was closed for harvesting for a certain period on a rotational basis in order to allow natural regeneration to take place without any disturbance. *Gavatache Beed* since that time has been kept separately for the fodder and thatching needs of the community. Similarly, any fresh wood-cutting activity is completely prohibited from the *Andhari Van* (the dark forest). Only dead, dried wood is allowed to be collected as fuel-wood. All these years of protection and plantation are showing up as the forest is slowly regaining its lost characteristic of darkness (*Andhar*). In *Kotwal Raan* there are restrictions on the cutting of trees. Only restricted felling is allowed. *Mothya Devache Van* and *Kosran* are alternatively used by the community for extracting forest products. *Tiwas Van* is kept aside for *in situ* plantation for converting it into a mixed forest. It was closed for three years in order to allow the growth of a valuable species used for timber, like *Bija.* The community took up taking care of *Bija* after being challenged by the Forest Department that *Bija* never grows naturally. The villagers' argument was that by stopping the entry of animals in that area, and thereby preventing the crushing of *Bija* seeds under their hooves, the seeds could germinate. And they were right: within three years *Tiwas* had many *Bija* saplings. The then forest officer reportedly appreciated this piece of indigenous knowledge.

Inclusion in the Formal Participatory Structure

In 1992 the Forest Department asked its divisions all over the state to select two villages each for implementing the Joint Forest Management (JFM) programme. Seeing the good work done by the people of Saigata, the Bramhapuri Division of the Forest Department approached them to register under the JFM. But the people did not accept the invitation immediately because they did not trust the department officials. Long discussions took place on questions such as why had the department suddenly changed its stance, what was the guarantee that the revenue would be shared by the department 20 years hence, and what was the need for getting into the agreement since the community had already been enjoying *de facto* usufruct rights. The overall impression that the people had about the Forest Department was not very good due to their past experiences. They even blamed the Department for the degradation of the forest. The Department was initially interested in entrusting the work of convincing people to join JFM to Mr. Khobragade and even suggested it to him. But he flatly refused the suggestion and asked the Department to settle the matter with the people directly, saying that a decision would be taken only in the Gram Sabha. Finally, on June 27, 1993, this group formally organised itself as the Forest Protection Committee under JFM.

Present Structure of the Association

Despite joining JFM, Saigata community continues to have its own institutional structure for all practical purposes. At present, the forest association has an executive committee, consisting of three women and six men. The women have been a part of the executive committee for the past five years, but none of them has ever become the leader of the committee. The members of the association hold elections regularly to elect members of the executive committee. The executive committee members meet at least once a month. There is no specific tenure for the president, the vice-president, the secretary, or the treasurer. Their term depends on the number of votes given by the members. Since the inception of the association, three different individuals have led this forest association. They are: Mr. Suryabhan Khobragade, Mr. Vishwanath Gaikwad and Mr. Kishan Gaikwad. Those who have held positions in the executive committee have been forest users too. There has not been any competition for any position in the executive committee in the past decade. The committee has always chosen its leader unanimously. The members alone have the right to remove any member of the executive committee, and no external or higher-level authorities have the power to do so. No committee members receive any remuneration, in cash or kind. The education level of the members of the executive committee is the same as the average education level of the village. Ethnic and religious diversity exists among the members of the executive committee as it does in the community. Religions followed are mainly Hinduism and Buddhism.

Products Harvested

After the community came under the JFM wings the user group took up the regeneration activity of plantation, which could not be taken up earlier due to lack of funds. Now it is financed through the JFM funds. This is especially important as the Saigata community continues to depend heavily on the forest for its needs like fodder, fuelwood, timber, food, etc. The community's needs for fodder, fuelwood and timber (for house construction) are met by the community's forest – 100 per cent. Even their food needs are fulfilled to some extent by the minor forest products like awala, char and moha. The community cannot afford the expensive substitutes for fuel-wood, fodder and timber like kerosene and livestock feed. Nor can it afford to buy bricks available in the closest market for house construction. Thus, plantations like the 215 ha. bamboo plantation carried out under the JFM scheme are important for the community. Under the JFM programme, the community has a legal right to take a share of the forest products for self-use and also a share in the net profit from the sale of forest products when these are harvested.

Giving Teeth to the Association

The whole community of Saigata strives for the success of the association. The members of the forest association have carried out many activities over the years to achieve it. Activities coordinated and regulated by the community since 1996 are listed in the Box.

The forest association frames and modifies the rules and regulations continuously for the forest produce on the basis of suggestions given by the community members. It is one of the important features of the association. Four paid guards now guard the forest which was initially guarded voluntarily by the villagers. Payment is done from the association's coffer to which the members of the community contribute. The community has devised the structure of contribution, keeping in view the economic condition of each member. Rupees ten are charged from the landless, Rs. 20 from those who own less than five ha. of land and Rs. 30 from those who have more than five ha. of land.

In addition, in the past few years, the members of the user group have taken up many other activities like building a nursery to distribute seedlings for plantation, removing leaves and needles—litter—from the forest floor, and digging fire-lines. They have even sought help from external authorities to improve vegetation growth.

Activities of Saigata Community since 1996

- Plantation of seedlings
- Maintenance of the forest
- Harvesting of forest products
- Distribution of these products among users
- Sale of the harvested products
- Distribution of revenue from the sale of the products
- Determining the time of the harvest of the forest products
- Determining the quantity of the forest products to be harvested
- Determining the type of technology to be used to harvest the forest products
- Determining who is authorised to harvest these forest products
- Determining the use that these products can be put to including religious use
- Sale of the rights to harvest forest products that users can trade with others
- Renting of non-transferable rights to harvest forest products
- Monitoring the condition of the forest
- Monitoring conformance to rules
- Imposing sanctions on the rule-breakers
- Acting as arbitrators for the disputes among local users
- Interacting with higher authorities

Ensuring Acceptability

The Association has recorded its mission and objective as *achievement of self-sufficiency*. The emphasis on the villagers earning their living in the village itself reflects collective wisdom of the user group. The forest association has created the rules on its own; it has not followed the set of rules provided by the Forest Department. Members of the user group and officials of the associations enforce the rules. The association believes in cooperating with other associations especially the Forest Department and has signed a Memorandum of Understanding (MoU) to get help from the department. Nevertheless, they create and enforce rules independent of the department and do not like interference from the department on such matters. None of the rules created by the association has ever harmed the members in any way. Nor has any resolution been passed that would cut off a particular individual from obtaining benefits from the forest. The association tries to see that the economically deprived individuals get some support out of its activities. As a result, now the landless are working as agricultural labourers, while earlier they did not have opportunities to earn adequately and were involved in illegal cutting of trees. Even the gender disparity has gone down, and now more women are participating in the decision-making process.

There is a well-developed rule structure regarding forest products which includes rules on harvesting, processing and selling of fuel-wood, fodder and timber affecting the harvesting level and use of these products. There also are rules regarding timing and purpose of harvesting. The primary purpose of framing these rules is to ensure sustainable use of the forest by making sure that the forest products are harvested only for self-consumption. For this the required quantity is determined according to the need of each household based on the number of members in the household. These rules have not changed much over the past 10 years. Other than the restrictions or rules on the quantity harvested of these products, there are other restrictions also; for instance, these products can be harvested only from the designated locations within the forest. This rule has changed over the past 10 years according to the availability. Restrictions also exist on the form of the product that can be harvested, for example, in the case of fuel-wood, the harvesting is limited to dead wood only, and in the case of fodder, only mature grass can be collected. There are rules regarding the type of transport to be used to remove the harvested product from the forest. Either the members carry the harvested product on their persons or use bullock-carts. These restrictions have remained the same over the past 10 years. The members of the user group almost always follow these restrictions.

Dealing with Infractions

It was found that sometimes members did break the rule, for instance, people would not follow the restrictions about specified locations. These infractions have taken place more often during the daytime and mainly in the summer season in the case of fuel-wood and timber. For fodder, it has been noticed that, infractions take place in the winter season. The penalty structure is such that it progressively increases with every repetition of infraction. When a harvesting rule is broken for the first time, a fine, greater than a day's earning but not more than a week's earning, is imposed. If the offender breaks the rule for the second time, then the community has decided that the fine would be greater than a week's earning. If the rule is broken for the third time then the offender is made to apologise publicly and his case is reported to the Forest Department. This decision on penalties is taken through a vote of the executive committee. The fine once imposed is then collected by an official of the user group or the forest association. Most of the users in Saigata accept the penalties once imposed on them. The local forestry association records these penalties. All members of the user group are allowed to see these records. If a situation arises when the offender refuses to pay the fine, the committee members of the user group expose the offender to public rebuke, and a final request is made to comply with the penalty order. In an extreme case the offender loses his right to harvest the three products which can be restored only after a public apology. So far, the community itself has been successful in imposing the penalties and the users have complied with the decisions. As a result, no external government official had to be called in to enforce the penalty. Government officials were called only once in the year 1998, when some persons belonging to the neighbouring village of Kirmiti Mendha were caught for illicit felling of trees.

The main source of revenue is the amount of money collected by the association from the member-households, fines and voluntary contributions received from external agencies. Some households also contribute in the form of labour hours. The major item of expenditure is the amount spent on guarding the forest. All the members of the association together make decisions about expenses on various items without any interference from external authorities. No elaborate records are maintained. All financial records are available for the members of the community to see.

Transparency, Flexibility and Participation

There is complete transparency regarding the rules, functioning of the association, and other matters. All members take active part in all the activities of the association and attend meetings regularly. All the members of the associations are well aware of the rules which are clear and easy to understand. At the same time, some degree of flexibility has also been introduced in the rules for dealing with the situations of emergency or for handling unusual problems of any member of the user group. As a result, all members find that the rules are fair and legitimate. The decisions are taken in the general body meetings that are held at least once every year, and its implementation is ensured by the executive body which meets more frequently. There is a provision to call an emergency meeting or a special meeting to discuss immediate problems faced by the villagers. Such meetings have been called during the past five years, and the executive committee has made some changes in the rules of the association by considering the suggestions made by the members. A few years back some members had suggested that instead of allowing people to collect firewood whenever they wanted and at any time of the year, there should be restriction on the time period when firewood could be collected. Based on this suggestion the fuelwood harvesting rule was modified. In this manner the annual general body meeting of the association normally frames the rules or modifies them, decides on the location of harvesting, among other things. On the other hand, the executive committee normally takes decisions on the types of penalties to be imposed.

CASE STUDY 2: LAKHAPUR COMMUNITY

The message written on a board at the entrance of the village that welcomes all visitors to the village says in Marathi:

> *Equality and brotherhood – that is Lakhapur village. Our village is our God. Ask His permission humbly and then enter our village. We rule our village. Water, forest, and land are ours and will remain ours. This is our motto. No forest official is allowed to enter the village. No one can enter the village without the Gram Sabha's permission.*

The sequence of events that prompted such strong sentiments in the people goes back to the period when a transition in the management system of forests, from *malgujari* to the revenue department of the government, was taking place. As has been mentioned earlier, during this time large scale illicit felling took place. It took some time for the local communities to understand the practical implications of change in the management system and its consequences. Since they were told that the forest in the vicinity of their village was to be protected by the government henceforth, everybody worked to maximise individual utilities. The subsequent transfer of forestland from the revenue department to the forest department also did not matter much to the locals. Officials of the forest department visited each village only to conduct forest survey and threaten the communities of dire consequences if they extracted anything from the forest because the ownership of the resources was with the department from then on. At the same time the local population was witnessing a different phenomenon. Forests had continued to remain open to all, and indiscriminate felling was going on unhindered. The Lakhapur community members were perturbed by the situation and could foresee that in future there would be scarcity of forest products on which they depended so heavily. In order to stop this, the community approached the forest department for their help. Instead of support, the community received a message from the then range forest officer to mind their own business. This led to souring of relationships between the community and the forest department.

Leadership from "Inside"

The resource had already degraded to a great extent by the middle of 1970s. One Mr. Baburao Dighore from Lakhapur took it upon himself to bring the people together to make them aware of their rights on the forest products. The effort started informally, people usually assembled in the evenings and discussed the day-to-day happenings. Since every household was substantially dependent on the forest, discussions were centred on the forest. Growing concern over the continuous deterioration of the forest quality and unobstructed felling of trees by people from the nearby villages compelled the community to think about protective as well as restrictive measures. People began to realise that if they did not protect the forest at this stage of degradation, they would never be able to save it and the source of their daily needs would be permanently gone. They, therefore, organised themselves in the form of an informal association in 1979 and called it *Gram Swarajya Jungle Sanstha* (Forest Organisation of an Independent Village or Self-Ruled Forest Organisation). Since then they have been protecting their forest. Meetings of the organisation were held in which the villagers framed rules for the forest use for all community members.

Different patches of forests that were known by different names like *Ghodikhalche* jungle, *Padepati*, *Mothya Devache Raan* and *Mukaji Devache Raan*, indicative of either the status (like a sacred grove) or its location ("forest below the horse-like rock"), were treated for various purposes by the community. For the protection of the forest from outsiders, individuals from each household were sent as watchmen on a rotation basis.

Mr. Dighore handed over the reins of the association to Mr. Janba Shivram Tondare, who took active interest in the working of the association. The Forest Department continued to have an indifferent attitude. The officials were not concerned about the degradation of the resource, nor were they appreciative of the measures taken by the residents of Lakhapur. A complete lack of coordination has been persisting ever since. Even after the department adopted a participatory approach in managing the forests, the relations did not improve. The community of Lakhapur continues to believe and claim that it owns the forest and its products just as it owns all other resources within the village. They feel that the forest has degenerated over the years due to neglect, inefficiency and corruption among the forest officials. Therefore, they have taken the task of managing and regenerating the forest upon themselves. The community has similar feelings for other government officials as well. Recently, they have appointed their own teachers in the primary school run by the *Zilla Parishad* (a government agency at sub-district level).

The "Outside" Influence

The discordant note reached a higher pitch when the Lakhapur community came in contact with a charismatic leader, Sant (Saint) Tukaram Dada who came to stay in a nearby place known as Adyal Tekdi in the early 1990s. The community was highly influenced by his ideas, and the saint managed to overshadow the local leaders. With a firm belief in decentralised decision-making, he prompted people to claim ownership of the resources of their villages, and make their own decisions regarding resource-use, and distribution of benefits. This philosophy rather appealed to a large section of the community since they already had bad experience with the Forest Department. He appealed to the community in the name of judicial rights as well as social and religious responsibilities. Tukaram Dada continues to influence Lakhapur and other communities in the vicinity. His methods are religious, for example there are daily prayers and morality classes for children in the community on Gandhian lines. It is his teachings that led the Lakhapur community to consider itself the sole owner of the resource and thereby possessing the right to use its products as it pleases. The community became more defiant as well as adamant after it came into the *Gram Swarajya* (village autonomy) fold of Tukaram Dada in 1998. Lakhapur and Saigata had initiated forest protection work almost simultaneously, protecting their forests together. However, things changed with the entry of Tukaram Dada in the life of the Lakhapur community. Saigata did not accept Dada's philosophy because it believed in cooperation, not confrontation. The differences in the beliefs of the two communities separated them and the cracks still show.

Structure and Working of the Forest Association

Since the inception of the forest association, its formal set-up has had an executive committee of nine members. Till now no women members have found place in this decision-making committee. Appointment of the members of the executive committee normally takes place through elections, which are held every year in the annual meeting of the Gram Sabha, in which every member of the association participates. In the case of an emergency, a meeting can be called but it has not been done since 1996. The term of the members of the executive committee including the President, the Vice-President, the Secretary, and the Treasurer is fixed for a year, but the user group alone is authorised to remove these members. No external or higher authority is entitled to dismiss them. These members hold the positions in the committee on a voluntary basis, i.e. they do not get remuneration in cash or kind. The elected members meet when required. So far, there has been no tussle for any position of the executive committee. Since its inception, Mr. Bhaskar Patil, Mr. Ramkrishna Raut, Mr. Sakharam Patil, Mr. Ramchandra Thaore, Mr. Shravanji Panse and Mr. Sitaram Deshmukh (the current head of the association) have led the association.

All these members of the executive committee are also a part of the larger group forest users and have been ordinary members of the association at some time or the other. None of these executive committee members own any assets or capital that operates on raw material obtained from the forest. Most of the members reside in the village itself. The average education level of the members of the executive committee was found to be the same as the average level of education in other villagers, which was not very high. None of the members hold any position in other collective or government bodies except Mr. Sitaram Deshmukh who has been with the Malaria Eradication Department of the Government of Maharashtra for a considerable period of time.

The association has been carrying out forest protection activities continuously for the past two decades. The whole community of Lakhapur works voluntarily for the association. The members mainly interact with one another about the tasks to be undertaken within the forest such as harvesting, guarding, monitoring and maintenance. It was found that they could hardly take up any forest improvement or regeneration activities due to paucity of funds. They have rarely planted seedlings or trees or cleared undergrowth. They have not built any fence to protect the forest, although watchmen have been employed for guarding it. During the past few years, the members of the user group have not made any attempt to remove encroachments, create a nursery for seedlings, seek external help to improve vegetation growth, or reduce the harvesting levels of medicinal plants. This is mainly because the village does not have any financial assistance either from any private organisation—there are no private organisations functioning in this area providing this kind of help to the rural communities—or the Forest Department—Lakhapur community refuses to cooperate with it. Over the years, the only activity the village has undertaken for the forest has been clearance of dead wood and grass. In order to reduce their dependence on the forest and its products, the members of the user group have planted some trees that are good for fodder and fuel on an individually owned agricultural land. They have not tried to develop any local technology to reduce their dependence on the forest. In 2000 the community had taken up some teak plantation on their own. The two main forest activities that remain are regulating the use of forest products by the community members and guarding the resource from poaching by outsiders. The association has coordinated the activities related to the maintenance, determining time and quantity of the forest products to be harvested, monitoring the forest condition, and ensuring conformance to the rules framed and also deciding penalties in case of violation of the rules. The association now employs two paid guards throughout the year; earlier the community members used to perform this duty voluntarily. These guards are paid Rs. 600 per month from the amount collected by the members of the Lakhapur community.

Restrictive Rules

Although the association carries out limited activities in the forest, it has framed several rules by the majority vote in the Gram Sabha for its use. No cognizance is taken of the rules laid down by the Forest Department. The harvesting rules differ from product to product. For fodder there are no rules regarding the quantity or timing of harvesting. However, the community often selects the area of the forest from where it can be harvested. In the case of timber, locals do not have any *de jure* rights, but the Lakhapur community has certain regulations in this regard. The community members can harvest timber for house construction or for making agricultural implements only after the Gram Sabha's approval. In the case of firewood, the local rules conform to the rules recognised by law, but this has happened only by chance. Under the Indian Forest Act the local community has usufruct rights in the protected forests which are usually demarcated areas closer to settlements for meeting the day-to-day needs of the nearby community. They are to be managed by the Forest Department. But as stated above, the Lakhapur community does not accept the ownership rights of the forest department and has only disrespect its authority.

The main forest products that are naturally available throughout the year vary moderately in quantity from season to season. Fodder, though mostly available in the rainy season, is difficult to harvest in this season. The use rules permit harvesting of fodder only for six months in a year including the month of August when it is most abundantly available. Although these rules exist, the community admits that most of the time 410 heads of cattle and 1,000 goats are let free for open grazing in the forest everyday and this puts great pressure on the forest. Since all the members do it, it is not treated as an infraction of rules. Timber, on the other hand, can be harvested every third year, and fuel-wood, in three quarters of a year, including the month of May when its availability is the maximum. The community uses wood for fuel. Nearly 80 per cent of its fuelwood needs are taken care of by the forest. One rule that is diligently followed by the community is that all the products are used strictly for self-consumption. Nobody is allowed to sell these forest products in the market.

In the case of timber, the total quantity to be harvested or used during the year is determined by making an estimate of the total availability of the product each year. The actual quantity harvested is distributed equally among all the user households. In the case of fuel-wood, the total quantity is determined according to the requirement of each member household. These restrictions have more or less remained the same for the past 10 years for timber, but in the case of firewood there have been some changes. There are restrictions about the locations within the forest from where timber or firewood can be harvested. In the case of both timber and firewood a tree can be cut down only after it grows to certain minimum girth. This restriction has also not changed in the past 10 years. There are also restrictions on the means of transport for timber; the product cannot be carried on bullock-carts. It has to be carried personally by the members of the user group. No individual can go to the forest alone for harvesting any product, he has to be in the company of at least four people. This has proved to be a very effective measure for monitoring. All decisions are taken in the Gram Sabha after consulting all the members. The rule structure apparently looks robust but it does not deliver because of the growing discontent among a faction of people.

No Recorded Infractions

The community in Lakhapur reported that no infractions had been recorded so far. This is a little hard to believe looking at the growing discontent and internal conflicts in the association. Although no breaking of rules has been reported, penalties are there for any possible infraction. If anyone breaks a harvesting rule for the first time he pays a fine not greater than one week's work. For the second time, the fine would be a permanent suspension of his harvesting rights for the products, thus giving the offender no chance to repeat the offence. In the case of infraction, of other rules it has been decided that appropriate penalties would be decided by the vote of the executive committee and the fine thus imposed would be collected by an official of the forest department and would be treated as a source of revenue for the local association. The community is confident that if these penalties are imposed, the offenders will comply. Further if an offender does not pay the fine, the group has kept the provision of public rebuke to the offender and even social boycott. If however, the offender wishes to have his suspended harvesting rights restored, he has to publicly apologise and give an assurance to the community members that he would not repeat the offence in future. During the past ten years, no infractions have reportedly taken place. All the members of the association are well aware of the rules and find them fair and legitimate.

Tall Claim

Not everything in the village seems as perfect as it is claimed by the few respondents who spoke to us. During our meetings a small group of four or five villagers tried to give us the other side of the picture. But before they could tell us much, a heated debate ensued between the two groups. The dissatisfied group seemed to be against the philosophy of isolating the village from the government-funded development works. They believe that their association was not only protecting the forest but also taking decisions at the village level without also antagonising government officials before the arrival of Tukaram Dada. The dominant group, on the other hand, believes in total autonomy as far as the forest protection and improvement are concerned, and wants no interference whatsoever from the Forest Department. It is in constant disagreement with the other group which feels that assistance from the Forest Department would be useful for their forest. The dominant group, constituting mainly of people belonging to the Kunbi caste (cultivators), constituting 50 per cent of the total population, is highly influenced by Tukaram Dada. Of the remaining, 40 per cent Mahar are (former "untouchables"), and a few Gond (numerically the most dominant tribe of central India) and other caste groups who are not in favour of the saint's teachings.

This split in the community came out in the open in 1998. The Seventy-third Constitutional Amendment encourages decentralisation and promotes self-rule by the Gram Panchayats. It has provision for transferring the rights of decision-making about the resources of a village to the Gram Sabha. Lakhapur was quick in establishing its authority on its forest by cutting down trees in the name of resource management and land-use policy. This action was apparently prompted by the external leadership. Legal action was initiated by the Forest Department which arrested the culprits immediately. When Tukaram Dada could not help the arrested in any way, the community split into two: one of the groups no longer trusted the external leadership. This led to internal conflicts affecting monitoring and rule-compliance. The association has become weak from inside because of numerous infractions which are not reported. The rules for forest use have remained only on paper. The office-bearers, all belonging to the dominant group, claim that written records are being maintained regarding the history of the association, identity of the office-bearers, meetings and resolutions of the meetings, income and expenditure of the association, quantities of forest products harvested and their distribution among the users, a list of individuals who did not follow the rules of the association and were punished, and the conflicts of the association with individuals and other associations and the type of punishment imposed. However, the records are unavailable not only to outsiders like us, but even to the other community members.

The unjust methods of the office-bearers are apparent from the equal contribution principle adopted by them. The annual contribution by all the households towards the fund of the forest association is fixed at Rs. 100, irrespective of the economic status of the member—households that own land and the ones who are marginal farmers or landless pay the same amount. The amount to be paid may be *equal*, but *equitability* is missing from the whole plan. Incidentally, all the office members of the association own land. The dissatisfied group, being in minority and belonging to the economically backward class, can neither protest within the community nor can it approach the formal governmental agency like the Forest Department or the police. As a result of following the tradition of not allowing outsiders to intervene in the village matters the accounts are not audited and the minority has no influence since decisions are taken by a majority vote.

An Uncertain Future

It all began well. The villagers considered the forest as a sacred and valuable economic resource. The significant dependence of the villagers on the resource and shrinking of the forest cover made them learn the value of the forest but after it had already paid a high cost. This initially prompted them to protect the forest. The community accepted a self-imposed discipline of restrictive use, invested time and effort in the protection activity and resisted commercial exploitation. But in the absence of support from the formal institution (the Forest Department), it lacked both, expertise and funds for development. Thus, Lakhapur is a clear example of what can happen if there is no coordination between formal and informal institutions. Though it claims to be a follower of the Gandhian concept of *Gram Swaraj*, it seems to be following it in a distorted manner. Defiance in the case of Lakhapur has come as a reaction to the inefficient management by the then forest officials. However, continued non-cooperation has resulted only in loss of income generating employment and opportunity to improve the forest quality. The Forest Department did show an inclination to include Lakhapur under the JFM programme in 1992, but the villagers refused to cooperate with the department. Today, the *Gram Swarajya Jungle Sanstha* has neither ensured sufficiency of forest products to the community nor has it succeeded in keeping the community as a cohesive group.

CASE STUDY 3: MARAL MENDHA COMMUNITY

Lack of initiative for self-governance can be a result of various factors. At times, some people may be simply unaware of the environmental or CPR problems. Others may be aware but not convinced that they can do anything about it or if the effort is worth a in a given situation. In some situations the problem may lie in the inability of the community to come up with solutions that are reasonable and acceptable to all the members of the community. Lack of required funds could be a problem in a few cases. Then there could be other competing obligations or fear of reprisals from those with other interests, and inability of the community to resolve this conflict. The Maral Mendha community is an extreme case of lack of collective action. It is difficult to believe that in fact the community was the first to get together, even before Lakhapur and Saigata, and had even formed an association for protecting the forest in its vicinity. But the effort was soon given up because there was an open access, but no effective controls on the access to and use of the resource. Such situations lead to competitive and unrestricted entry and exploitation of the resource by all parties, which usually result in too-rapid exploitation and resource rent dissipation (Libecap 1995).

Maral Mendha seems to be a typical example of this phenomenon. It is a village that has 71.46 ha. of land as forestland within its village boundary which was once wooded with many precious trees. But just in three decades it is all virtually gone. Excepting 2 ha., all the forestland has been encroached upon and at present is under cultivation. It is difficult to believe that the open land used for grazing was initially a vast rich forest. Undoubtedly, it is an extreme case where the community has done away with its common property completely by competitive exploitation and encroachment within a brief period of two decades. It seems as if the community has succeeded in collective action for ruining the commons!

As is true about Saigata and Lakhapur, very little is known about the history of Maral Mendha since written or published records are not available. From the accounts of the villagers it seems sometime in the early 18th century, people in search of fertile agricultural land had settled down close to the water tank. The settlement got its name Maral Mendha as it was dominated by the *Marar* (*mali* – a caste of vegetable growers) community. Along with the subsistence crops, the community, at that time, was able to grow onions and sugarcane; two crops that need a lot of water. This became possible as Maral Mendha had sufficient irrigation water available in its huge 600-ha. tank. Since vegetable crops brought them immediate cash income, the community started encroaching upon the forestland, converting it into agricultural land, thus discounting the future heavily. Those who owned land, cleared the adjoining forest to increase their farm size, and those who did not, simply cleared a piece of forestland and started cultivating it. Their vision was myopic regarding the long-term benefits from the existence of the forest. They were more interested in the immediate gains from agriculture compared to the distant and unsure benefits associated with forest protection. This self-interest encouraged them to systematically clear every piece of the forest of the village. Even after practising this for many years, they were still left with some forest (including the forest area of Saigata and Lakhapur) that provided them with their daily necessities of fuel-wood and fodder for the animals.

According to the forest map of 1977-78, out of the 71.46 ha. of the total forest area under the village territory, 70.83 ha. was protected forest and 00.63 ha. was shrub forest. The villagers remember the forest, which at that time had many valuable wood timber and fruit species. The elderly residents of Maral Mendha remember having valuable species like teak in its forest, although there is no physical evidence for it now. They even boast that although the total forest area was smaller than that of Lakhapur and Saigata, the quality of the forest was much superior. They feel that it is this feature of the forest that attracted more timber smugglers to Maral Mendha, contributing to its degradation. Irrespective of this, no measures were taken to protect the forest from the encroachments by the user group, nor was any attention paid towards saving it from external harvesters. It is true that the two villages, namely, Uchali and Kalita, that share common boundaries with Maral Mendha had a very small forest area allotted to meet their forest-based needs and, therefore, it is very likely that Maral Mendha had to face the pressure of this excess requirement. The present reality, however, is that most of the land demarcated as forest in government records is encroached for cultivation, and not a single tree is found on the remaining 2 ha.

An Attempt at Getting Together

The systematic cutting of the forest continued until the mid-1970s. While more and more forest area was being brought under agriculture, the community started facing greater difficulties in obtaining fuel-wood and fodder. It was around this time that the neighbouring communities of Saigata and Lakhapur villages started protecting their forests, thereby denying access to Maral Mendha. A small patch was still under forest cover in Maral Mendha at that time. This led a few villagers to raise the question of forming a forest association in 1979. As a result, an informal forest association was set up to make forest-related decisions and save whatever was left of the forest. But the effort failed miserably and within two years of its inception, the association became defunct. In this community, a majority of the farmers were used to taking two crops a year, and saw a huge potential in converting forest land into an immediate income generating resource, and so it was extremely difficult to convince them of the benefits of conservative use of the forests. There was no unanimity in the decisions because there were fundamental differences regarding the very objectives of the association. The villagers today claim that the neighbouring villages followed their example in forming a forest protection committee and succeeded in doing so, while Maral Mendha, the pioneering village, had failed in its effort.

A Great Setback

The process of destruction was accentuated in 1988 when the construction of the Gosikhurd Dam on the river Wainganga was initiated by the Government of Maharashtra. It was an irrigation project, and a canal to be built under this project was to pass through Maral Mendha. Since most of the land to be taken over by the government for the canal was forestland, villagers encroached upon it, hoping to receive cash compensation from the government at the time of its requisition. The irrigation project was also expected to enhance substantially the prices of its agricultural land due to its proximity to the irrigation canal. This too encouraged the residents of Maral Mendha to encroach on the forestland. These encroachments in Maral Mendha do not seem to have taken place out of necessity; they were strategically planned, keeping in mind the possible enhanced future value of land as well as the possibility of being compensated by the government. This can be substantiated by the fact that some of the landowners in Maral Mendha sold off the small pieces of land that they possessed and, using this money, made massive encroachments on the forestland. More than two decades after the declaration of the irrigation project, neither the land has been requisitioned nor has any compensation come to the Maral Mendha community. The only thing that has happened is total destruction of the forest. Maral Mendha village looks distinctly different from Saigata and Lakhapur. It has concrete houses with tiled roofs, better clothes and more food, larger land holdings to till, and more cash in hand. Yet, the women from the village have to travel long distances for fetching fuel-wood, and men have to buy ploughs and other wooden implements from the nearby market at high prices.

Failure of Formal Leadership

One wonders at the total passivity of the Forest Department in the whole process. It is difficult to believe that the department officials were unaware of the not-so-gradual destruction of the resource. Apparently, the economically powerful people in the village have corrupted the formal owners of the forest. Like in all villages, the village level institution of Gram Panchayat is present in Maral Mendha, but it has no vision regarding the sustainable use of forests. Today Maral Mendha is guided by short-term gains that clearly reflect on the state of its forest. But the social problems arising out of the situation became visible when our discussions led to heated debates among the villagers, indicating a clear rift between the rich and the poor, as well as differing perceptions of men and women. Conflicts were clearly on class and gender lines.

Apparently, the poor sections of the community are not satisfied with the state of affairs wherein a few have cornered all the gains of illegal encroachments. Women also complained that the men folk think only about increasing their income by acquiring more land. They did not realize that since there was no forest left for the village use, the women had to collect fuelwood from the neighbouring forests and were subjected to embarrassments if caught. Conflicts also became evident between the landed and the landless. The landless cannot afford to encroach upon the forestland because they do not have the resources to make it cultivable. This class is disadvantaged from both the sides, neither do they have any income from agriculture to enable them to buy forest goods, nor are they left with commons to take care of their day-to-day needs (fuelwood and other minor forest products). The poorer sections of the village wanted restoration of forestland and asked us to urge the Forest Department to act firmly against the encroachers and rebuild the forest. They do not have confidence to go and approach the department officials, nor do the officials come to the village to find out their requirements, or to check the state of the "forest".

The community is clear about the internal conflicts and diversity of opinions. It is difficult even to call it a "community" since it has no shared understanding, no common norms, or no active forum to share common concerns. It is only a group of individual households living within a village where each household is trying to maximise its utility irrespective of the impact it has on the whole community. During our discussions, someone from the community said, "We too could have saved our forests only if we had someone like Mr. Suryabhan Khobragade (the leader of Saigata) to lead us and show us the inevitable outcome of our short-sighted actions". Since there cannot be a Suryabhan Khobragade in every village, the public institutions like the forest department or the Gram Panchayat are expected to provide the necessary leadership and future directions. Both these institutions had failed completely in the case of Maral Mendha.

Looking Back—Introspection

The environmental consequences of clearing the forestland are visible as no woody species can any longer be found in the forest area and the land has become highly degraded. The impact of heavy grazing and damage by the pests is visible. High temperatures and exposed surfaces have adversely affected the quality of soil. Sugarcane, a crop that requires lots of water, was grown in the village not very long ago. Sufficient water was available then in the village wells and in the irrigation tank. With all the trees cut off, the soil is not able to retain water. Therefore, water levels in the wells have gone down, and many wells go dry during the summer. For fuel, either the standing trees on individual agricultural fields are cut down or cow-dung that could have been used more productively as manure to agricultural fields is burnt as fuel. Another significant consequence is an increase in the number of insects and pests in their fields. Many villagers accept that this is due to the destruction of the forest. "When there was forest, insects got their food from there, where will they go now if not to our fields?" is what they say.

The failure of the early attempts at conservation and unchecked cutting of the forest can be attributed to a number of factors that are all endogenous. Lack of an effective leadership, caste composition with predominance of the Maral population that saw cash crops as a source of immediate income and preferred to grow these at the cost of the forests, and passing of an irrigation canal through the village increasing the prospective prices of agricultural land as well as the likelihood of being compensated by the government once the land was requisitioned seem to be the major factors that led the community to destroy its forests. Initially it was the high dependence of the neighbouring communities, which did not have their own forestland, which added to the pressure of demand on Maral Mendha's forest.

The later large scale and systematic encroachments made by the villagers with an eye only on the short-term gains seems to be the most important factor leading to the present and state of affairs in Maral Mendha. The preference of the present over the future has resulted in this "tragedy of commons".

Recent Developments

The villagers do not know how, but the local Member of the Legislative Assembly (MLA) recently (July 2002) made some funds available for taking up plantation on a 25 ha. patch in Maral Mendha's forestland. Bramhapuri Division Office of the Forest Department was entrusted with the execution of the project. It is interesting to note that the Department did not consult the community regarding the choice of the species to be planted, nor did the villagers show any interest in the work. Neither did the villagers go for plantation work nor are they guarding the plantations now. For the plantation work labour from Saigata was employed, who were paid slightly lower than the wages earned by agricultural labour during the sowing season. Even the guards employed by the forest department come from other villages. When we specifically asked some villagers what their feelings were about the activity and how would it help them, the respondents disinterestedly said, "Once the trees are big enough, they will be cut down for timber". Even today the community does not believe in protecting forests for future benefits, thereby discounting the future heavily.

A Fascinating Query

What motivates humans to act in such diverse ways, apart from the natural or accidental differences, makes an interesting query. It is fascinating because many times communities have to bear a substantial cost in the form of time spent, efforts put in and postponement of current consumption for preservation of a resource (in this case the forest resource). The cost in terms of how much people have to give up today for uncertain future benefits, especially the communities which are officially referred to as "below the poverty line", is awesome. Saigata is an example of this. Two decades ago, before entering the JFM agreement with the forest department, when Saigata villagers decided to take things in their own hands and took a conscious decision to leave their forest alone for natural regeneration, it had many immediate consequences. The women had to travel a long distance for fetching fuel and fodder, or buy them at a price in the nearby market. Men had to stay awake at nights to protect the forest from intruders. Sometimes even women had to join men in guarding the forest. There were several occasions when they were hurt (physically) by the timber smugglers while protesting against thefts. The whole community of Saigata has been so motivated that it has remained unaffected by the apparently prosperous neighbouring community of Maral Mendha all through.

Lakhapur community has not been very successful in improving the quality of its forest mainly because it has refused to accept any help from the Forest Department labelling it as a corrupt department with *mala fide* intentions. It is paying heavily for its collective action in the form of forgone developmental funds. This is a stark example of the inevitable when there is lack of coordination between formal and informal institutions.

Importance of Coordination

In a democracy, neither total defiance of a formal structure is possible, nor is it advantageous to ignore the existing (informal) leadership that has been accepted by all under the institutional arrangement prevailing at the local level. Sustainable use of the forest resources is one of the primary objectives of the present National Forest Policy. Decentralisation is thought to be a key to that end. Thus, the 73rd Constitutional Amendment, which encourages decentralisation in the form of transferring some rights and functions to the local Gram Panchayats, is a step in that direction. Keeping this in view, the present study has dealt primarily with the successes and failures of the community-initiated institutions in the sustainable use of the forest resources. Lack of coordination between formal and informal institutions invokes two types of reactions: defiance of the statutory framework or a self-initiated activity, which may not necessarily be contradictory to the broader objective. In either of the situations, both the institutions have to bear a heavy cost. Usually there are institutions informally working in a village. Some provide incentives to the forest users to engage in a sustainable use of the forest, often resulting in development of the resource. These institutions generally prescribe a low discount rate, giving more importance to the ecological and bequest value of forests. But there also are institutions, or rather lack of institutions, where the members of the community act as individuals (and not as a group necessary for collective action) for their own benefit, irrespective of their impact on the surrounding CPRs. Such actions could be compelled by poverty and lack of income generating employment opportunities, or it could be strategic and consciously taken. The present study has incorporated each of these types in its sample of villages.

Common and Uncommon Factors

While looking for factors conducive to collective action, one comes across several factors mentioned by the scholars of commons. To identify the impact of institutional factors, including that of *leadership*, I have tried to control some of these factors. As the three communities are located just next to one other, the type of forest, climate, soil, altitude and slope are similar. Each community has a forest adjacent to its village. The population size and mix (heterogeneity of caste) are comparable and occupational structures are similar with agriculture being the dominant occupation. All the three communities come under the jurisdiction of one Forest Division, and one revenue division, therefore the administrative structure is the same for them and the boundaries are clear. All the three settlements have come about at similar times (two to three hundred years ago), and no community has had any previous experience if organising or has had a traditional Panchayat. Economic factors such as land holding size, distance from market and techniques of product extraction are comparable. It is the existence and working of informal institutions, or lack of it, that is dissimilar. Therefore, in this study institution is the independent as well as the determining variable. In the case of Saigata, the process analysis clearly brings out that its indigenously developed rule structure and participatory decision-making has played a major role in bringing acceptability and discouraging infractions. Saigata community, and to some extent Lakhapur community as well, traditionally did not possess organisational skills, but they gradually and laboriously built a common understanding, created a cheap and easily available conflict-resolving mechanism, and evolved a participatory monitoring mechanism. Due to the basic agrarian structure of all the three communities, forest has been a salient resource for all. But the element of sacrificing present benefits for ensuring future benefits in the initial periods, and allowing a highly degraded resource to regenerate, was successfully inculcated as a shared norm in Saigata and Lakhapur. The three communities initiated collective action for protecting the fast degrading forest resource, almost simultaneously, in the 1970s. While Maral Mendha gave up the collective effort soon, Lakhapur community started facing problems from within due to shifting of norms, which has fractured the community. It is only in Saigata that the community was able to evolve an acceptable rule structure (institution) in the absence of any autonomy, and maintain it even through the transition to Joint Forest Management (JFM) giving them participatory rights in benefit sharing. This achievement can be attributed to the coordination between the formal organisation, the Forest Department and the informal institution of Saigata community. Good communication among the community members due to regular interactions in the general body meeting for taking each decision has played a major role in bringing congruence between the two institutions. And it is undoubtedly the success of leadership of Mr. Suryabhan Khobragade which has ensured the sustainability of the collective action by nesting of the two enterprises.

Role of Leadership

Emergence of a leader as well as his acceptance by a community depend on various factors. This leadership can be informal/traditional or formal. The latter is provided by larger constitutional structure like the Panchayat system or the Forest Department, as is the case in the present context. According to a leading sociologist, Srinivas (1972), sources of power, as manifested in leadership, could be traditional due to caste dominance, economic dominance, or numeric dominance. Numeric dominance often leads to political clout and thereby access or closeness to power. And this affinity with power can be used for economic advantage, and resultantly in more political power. The nature of group activity, for which leadership is being considered, is equally important for determining leadership.

Leadership in Saigata refutes this theory to some extent. The leader here belongs to a low caste, a caste that does not outnumber other castes in the village. Nor does he belong to the economically dominant class. On the other hand, Lakhapur community has leadership from outside. The community is highly influenced by a charismatic religious leader, Tukaram Dada, who has appealed the community in the name of judicial rights, and social responsibilities in the name of God. Unlike Saigata, Lakhapur adopted a defiant approach. In Saigata, and also initially in Lakhapur, the leaders and his followers were facing similar problems of scarcity and, therefore, there was no ego or status complex. In addition to this, Mr. Khobragade never assumed the role of a leader. In an unconventional and informal manner, he propagated social outlook. His success in the form of total acceptability has its roots in the sincerity of purpose, indigenous methods of spreading the message, and clear, transparent functioning. It is also rooted in his readiness to share vital information with his fellow villagers that was useful for their upliftment. He realised right in the beginning that it was not possible to dissuade the poachers without giving them an alternative source of income. He first tried to improve the productivity of farms, increase income levels marginally, create labour opportunities for the landless, and started talking about the need to protect the forest surrounding their village. Only after providing for a short-term objective, the broad objective of the sustainable use was adopted by this community as a value.

Good leadership is often stated to be the requirement for a successful collective action; yet, it cannot achieve high levels of institutional performance single-handedly (Israel 1987, p.34). Most practitioners believe that leadership is the most critical, if not the only critical factor for the successful development of institutions. A leader is generally perceived by the followers to have vision to lead them into a safe future, and also has the capability of providing solutions to the present problems. In the absence of any one of the two qualities, the likelihood of success is meagre. But for policy formulation, what is to be done if there is no good leadership to work with? It is difficult to find a leader in every village who has vision, the ability to influence others, is benevolent, and accepts equity as an important criterion in the working of groups.

Concluding Remarks

The most obvious conclusion of this study is that the communities are capable of organising themselves for common purpose. They can benefit from the existing social capital, or can even build it consciously, although social capital is accumulated very slowly (Putnam 1993, p. 179). An efficient and acceptable leadership may not exist in all the communities, but it is the responsibility of either the formal agency to provide it, or develop it from within the community. A leader need not be charismatic. In fact, a leader who is not well versed in the situation faced by the community or whom the community does not consider as its own may not be acceptable. A leader, who can provide solutions with immediate effect in matters of day-to-day concern for the community and fulfil the needs that are close to survival, is more welcome than the typical political leadership that has mass appeal. In the wake of the participatory approach adopted by the Forest Department, it is important to take into consideration the fact that participation of communities does not depend so much upon the programme (JFM and similar programmes) as it does on the level of social capital. Therefore the formal developing agencies should make use of the social capital that already exists, or consider investing in it (Grootaert and Narayan 1999).

One cannot ignore the fact that majority of the forest area in India belongs to the state. Although the results of the study reveal that self-initiated efforts are more effective as well as sustainable, in the given situation it is very unlikely that communities will gain exclusive rights over forests and be the sole decision-makers. At the same time one cannot expect that a very large number of communities will take up forest conservation on their own without any right to tenure. The study shows that Saigata did not become a role model for Maral Mendha. To assume, that Maral Mendha will never become a model for the younger generation of Saigata would be highly risky. Nor can the society afford to wait for all the forest-dependent communities to take up the protection and management of the fast degrading forests of India. Therefore, the best solution lies in blending of the two, the formal and informal institutions, with congruence of objectives. The Forest Department needs to take the lead here; they have to identify and respect the communitie. that are already protecting their forests or are ready to participate in forest management. It has to be a catalyst, provider of expertise as well as funds wherever required, and supply appropriate leadership where the need arises. We need to accept that self-initiated efforts cannot become a pattern or a rule. At the same time, local leadership may prove to be ineffective if it fails to reach out and track additional resources in the state (Krishna 2001). Local leadership can prove to be most efficient in resource management if groomed properly by the state because social capital is not a historically fixed endowment. If the formal agency tries to integrate its efforts with the existing informal efforts, it might be possible even to build upon the existing stock of social capital within a relatively short span of time (Hall 1998). Coordinated efforts of the two institutions have the maximum potential of being feasible as well as effective on a wider scale. It is best put in the words of Ostrom (1992, p. 351):

> Without some specialists who monitor, record information and interpret the rules in a consistent way, the shared community of understanding can so erode that the rules become meaningless. If the specialists are not themselves subject to review by the others – including all the members of the community – their shared understanding of the rules can also disintegrate and be replaced by local despotism. Thus, I would argue that neither community ncr enforcers are sufficient. Both are needed and both can enhance each other.

NOTES

1. This paper is based on a research project (1999-2000) funded by the Workshop in Policy Analysis, Indiana University, USA.
2. Permission was taken from all the persons named here to mention them by their real names.

REFERENCES

Adams, B. D.; Brockington, J.; and Dyson, B. Vira (2001): "Common Choices: Policy potions for Common Poll Resources". Personal Communications, Department of Geography, University of Cambridge.

Agrawal, Arun, (1999): *Greener Pastures: Politics, Markets, and Community among a Migrant Pastoral People*. Durham, NC: Duke University Press.

Agrawal, Arun, (2001): "Common Property Institutions and Sustainable Governance of Resources". *World Development* 29(10): 1649-72.

Agrawal, A., and Gibson, C., (2001): "The Role of Community in Natural Resource Conservation". In Agrawal, Arun, and Gibson, Clark. (eds.) *Communities and the Environment.* New Jersey: Rutgers University Press.

Baland, J., and Platteau, J., (1996): "*Halting Degradation of Natural Resources: Is There a Role for Rural Communities?*" Oxford: Clarendon Press.

Gaspart, Frederic, and Platteau, Jean-Phillippe (2001): "Institutional and the efficient management of Environmental Resources". Personal Communication.

Gazon, L. (1997): "Institutional Structure and the Effectiveness of Integrated Conservation and Development Projects: Case Study from Madagascar". *Human Organisation.* 56(4).

Grootaert, C., and Nararyan, D. (1999): "Local Institutions, Poverty and Household Welfare in Bolivia". Washington, D.C.: The World Bank.

Guha, Sumit (1999): *Environment and Ethnicity in India 1200-1991.* Cambridge: Cambridge University Press.

Hall, C. (1998): "Institutional Solutions for Governing the Global Commons: Design, Factors, and Effectiveness". *Journal of Environment and Development.* 7 (2): 86-114.

Hardin, G. (1968): "The Tragedy of Commons". *Science*, 162: 1243-48.

Isreal, (1987): *Institutional Development: Incentives to Performance.* Baltimore: The Johns Hopkins University Press.

Krishna, A. (2001): "Moving from Stock of Social-Capital to the Flow of Benefits: The Role of Agency". *World Development* 29(6): 925-43.

Lapiere R.T., and Fransworth, P.R. (1949): *Social Psychology.* New York: Mcgraw Hill Book Co.

Libecap, G.D. (1995): "The Conditions for Successful Collective Action". In .Keohane, Robert O., and Ostrom, Elinor. (eds.) *Local Commons and Global Interdependence: Heterogeneity and Cooperations in Two Domains.* London: Sage Publications. pp. 161-90.

McKean, M.A. (1992): "Management of Traditional Common Lands (*Iriaichi*) in Japan". In Bromley, D. (ed.) *Making the Commons Work: Theory, Practice and Policy*. San Francisco: Institute for Contemporary Studies. pp. 63-93.

Meinzen-Dick, Raju, and Gulati (2002): "What Affects Organisations and Collective Action for Managing Resources? Evidence from Canal Irrigation Systems in India". *World Development* 30(4): 649-66.

Nabli, M.K., and Nugent, J.B. (1989): "Collective Action, Institutions and Development". In Nabli, M.K., and Nugent, J.B. (eds.) *The New Institutional Economics and Development: Theory and Applications to Tunisia*. Amsterdam: Elsevier Science Publishers.

Olson, M. (1965): *The Logic of Collective Action: Public Goods and the Theory of Groups.* Cambridge, MA: Harvard University Press.

Ostrom, Elinor (1990): *Governing the Commons: The Evolution of Institutions for Collective Action* . New York: Cambridge University Press.

Ostrom, Elinor (1992): "Community and the Endogenous Solution of Commons Problems". *Journal of Theoretical Politics* 4(3): 343-51.

Ostrom, E. (1999): "Formulating the Commons". In Burger, Joanna; Norgard, Richard; Ostrom, Elinor; Plicansky, David; and Goldstein, Bernard. (eds.) *The Commons Revisited.* Washington, D.C.: Island Press.

Poffenberger, M. (ed.) (1990): *Keepers of the Forest: Land Management Alternatives In Southeast Asia.* West Hartford, CT: Kumarian.

Poteete, A., and Ostrom, (Forthcoming): "An Institutional Approach to the Study Of Forest Resources". In Poulsen, John (ed.) *Human Impacts on Tropical Forest Biodiversity and Genetic Resources,* Centre for International Forestry Research (CIFOR). New York: CABI Publishing.

Putnam, Robert D. (1993): *Making Democracy Work: Civic Traditions in Modern Italy.* Princeton, N.J.: Princeton University Press.

Srinivas, M.N. (1972): *Social Change in Modern India,* New Delhi: Orient Longman Limited.

Tang, Shui Yan (1992): *Institutions and Collective Action: Self-Governance in Irrigation Systems.* San Francisco: ICS Press.

Wade, R. (1994): *Village Republics: Economic Conditions for Collective Action in South India,* San Francisco, CA: Institute for Contemporary Studies Press.

17

A New Paradigm of Development Based on Afforestation of Wastelands Through Tree Growers' Cooperative and Other Village Institutions

KATAR SINGH

India has vast tracts of wastelands, which have been lying barren for ages for a variety of reasons. Wastelands are normally defined as degraded lands that are currently not cultivated, but which can potentially be brought under vegetative cover with reasonable efforts and cost, and lands, which are subject to degradation on account of natural causes. This definition was first mooted by the National Wastelands Development Board of India (Gautam and Narayan 1988) and is now widely accepted. Wasteland can result from both its intrinsic attributes such as location, environment and chemical and physical properties of the soil from human-made circumstances.

There are a number of estimates of wastelands in India, varying. from 75 million hectares to 200 million hectares (mha) (Government of India, 1976; Vohra, 1985; World Bank, 1988, Chambers *et al.* 1989). A recent survey by the National Bureau of Soil Survey and Land Use Planning revealed that 66 per cent of India's total geographical area (around 192 mha) was at varying stages of degradation (quoted in Haque 1997).

There are no reliable estimates of wastelands in India that could suggest be rehabilitation of these wastelands through economically viable afforestation projects. However, according to one such estimate made by Chambers *et al.* (1989) 84 mha of wastelands comprising private cultivated lands (field bunds and boundaries), degraded forest lands and private and common uncultivated degraded lands are available for tree growing in India. These wastelands can broadly be divided into two categories according to ownership – privately owned wastelands (35 mha) and government owned wastelands (49 mha). The government owned wastelands also include the village common (grazing) lands and other open-access lands, which are owned by the Forest Department, or the Revenue Department, or by other government agencies such as the Indian Railways and the National Highways Authority of India. In our opinion, this estimate seems to be reasonable and good enough for all practical purposes until we have a more reliable one.

It would be pertinent to state here that most of the wastelands in India irrespective of their ownership are accessible to local people without any restrictions and are used without any rules and regulations. In this sense, they may be called Open Access Resources (OAR). All OAR suffer from what Hardin (1968) called, albeit erroneously, "the tragedy of the commons". The problem should correctly be termed as "the tragedy of the commons". The problem should correctly be termed as "the tragedy of the open access". Most OAR are degraded, eroded, denuded of vegetation, encroached and polluted. Tree plantation on such lands by the Tree Growers' Cooperative Societies (TGCS) or other types of people's organizations offers a practicable alternative to improve their status and productivity and avert their tragedy. It, therefore deserves the highest attention and priority in terms of allocation of resources.

In India, the western and central States of Gujarat, Madhya Pradesh, Chhattisgarh, Maharashtra, and Rajasthan have relatively large tracts of wastelands (Table 17.1). It could be seen from the Table that the extent of wasteland in each of these states as a proportion of the total reporting area varies from nearly 18 to 29 per cent. This means that these states offer higher scope for tree plantation on such lands than most other states.

Under a variety of social forestry and social welfare programmes, many state governments are now granting government-owned wastelands to the rural poor, or the TGCS or other types of people's organizations on a long-term lease for tree-growing. The TGCS have been organized in seven states of India, namely, Andhra Pradesh,

Gujarat, Karnataka, Madhya Pradesh, Orissa, Rajasthan and Uttaranchal.

Table 17.1: Estimates of Wasteland in Selected Western and Central States of India by Category

	Type of Wasteland	*Gujarat*	*Madhya Pradesh*	*Mahara-shtra*	*Rajasthan*
1	Gullied and/or ravenous land	736.97	7924.40	1548.07	4473.59
2	Upland with or without scrub	12228.20	31920.88	20359.55	16753.92
3	Waterlogged and marshy land	164.94	49.96	296.12	1.29
4	Land affected by salinity/ alkalinity/coastal/inland	3028.99	162.81	78.50	2279.11
5	Under-utilized degraded notified forest land	2776.16	17527.87	10168.75	10815.64
6	Shifting cultivation area	0.00	0.00	0.00	0.00
7	Degraded land under plantation crops	31.84	914.43	687.43	100.39
8	Degraded pastures/ grazing land	209.75	145.19	1349.40	9243.82
9	Mining industrial wastelands	9.79	118.95	6.37	64.00
10	Sands-desertic coastal	76.09	24.57	50.61	13303.64
11	Steep slopping area	323.92	180.49	1389.57	182.28
12	Barren rock/stony waste/ sheet rocky area	1402.48	2600.11	2388.84	3190.23
13	Snow covered and or glacial area	0.00	0.00	0.00	0.00
14	Total wasteland	20989.13	61569.66	38323.21	60407.91
15	Total reporting area	118878.00	337871.00	208893.39	205869.00
16	Wasteland as % of the total reporting area	17.66	18.22	18.35	29.34

Source: The National Wastelands Identification Project (NWIP), NAEB Home Page

In this paper, we attempt to examine (i) the economic rationale of tree plantation on wastelands, (ii) briefly review the major policies and programmes of afforestation of wastelands in India, (iii) analyse the experience of the TGCS and other types of people's organizations with tree plantation on wastelands, and (iv) explore the problems and prospects of scaling up and sideways this innovative institutional model.

We limit our study and analysis to Gujarat, Madhya Pradesh, Maharashtra and Rajasthan, where the TGCS and other forms of people's organizations are currently engaged in tree plantation on wastelands.

Rationale for Afforestation of Wastelands and Averting their Tragedy

In this section, we first examine the economic feasibility of afforestation of wastelands and then explore the theoretical basis for averting the tragedy of wastelands through changing their status from open access to cooperative property of co-users.

Economic Rationale for Afforestation of Wastelands

Baloni (2002) reviewed 21 studies on the economics of afforestation undertaken in the past two decades in India and found that the wastelands afforestation projects in India were financially feasible even when non-market benefits of afforestation projects are not taken into consideration. Further, it was also found that the Financial Internal Rate of Return (FIRR) from the afforestation projects was more than the prevailing interest rate on the long-term loans for the forestry projects in India. This means that afforestation projects are financially viable and bankable.

Afforestation activities generate substantial employment opportunities as 70- to 80 per cent of the expenditure incurred on plantations was in the form of wages paid to labourers. In view of this, the Government of India is encouraging the afforestation of wastelands, through various programmes, the afforestation of wastelands to generate employment opportunities in rural India. This is substantiated by the fact that 20 per cent of the funds under various rural development schemes of the Central Government are earmarked for afforestation.

At the macro-economic level, afforestation projects provide a number of backward and forward linkages to various sub-sectors of India's economy. Kadekodi and Ravindranath (1997) have estimated the forward and backward linkage indices of the forestry sector in India to be 1.13 and 0.6088, respectively. New afforestation projects might further enhance these linkages. For example, the recent spurt in *poplar* plantations in the State of Haryana in Northern India has led to the emergence of *poplar*-based veneer industry in the region; veneers are used for the production of plywood and different types of composite woods.

It seems that afforestation of wastelands is going to would emerge as a big enterprise in the coming years in India to meet rapidly the increasing demand of raw material for wood-based industries. This is mainly because the supply of wood from the government-owned forests has been declining over the years owing to the forest conservation strategies adopted by the government. The new Indian Forest Policy, 1988 stipulates *inter alia* that the wood-based industry should collaborate with farmers to grow trees on their private lands or to establish their own captive plantations; in the past, wood-based industry in India was provided wood at a subsidized price from government-owned forests. On the other hand, the government is promoting farm forestry and community forestry programmes on private and community lands, respectively to meet the wood and fuel food needs of the rural poor in India. Thus, in view of the increasing importance of tree plantation on wastelands and their contribution to the Indian economy, there is a need for stepping up the pace and scale of afforestation programmes in the country.

The Theoretical Rationale for Averting the Tragedy of Wastelands through TGCS

Given their open-access nature, wastelands are bound to be degraded/ overexploited and given their finite extent, their use is subtractable, competitive, i.e. if one of the co-users uses more of a piece of wasteland, the less is left to that extent for the other co-users. In resource economics, this phenomenon is known as interdependence of the underlying appropriate/production functions or existence of externalities in appropriation/production. An externality is defined as an unintended and uncompensated side effect of an activity. When an externality is present, the competitive equilibrium of use of the resource (open access) is socially inefficient. We illustrate this with an example of a village grazing land, which is *de facto* an open access resource for the villagers.

We presume that there are N identical households in a village households owning together 100 animals and interested in grazing their animals in the village grazing land, which has a carrying capacity of only 50 animals. Under this assumption, each rational (profit maximizing) animal owner will try to graze all the animals owned by him/her. In doing so, he/she would reduce the quantity of forage grass available to the other animal owners. There exists a problem of a negative externality that which reduces the availability of grass stock, which in turn leads to an increased cost of stall-feeding the animals to compensate the reduced quantity from the pasture. Therefore, there is a loss of net revenue to all the animal owners. Every rational animal owner behaves in the same manner. The consequence of this rational behaviour on the part of individual animal owners is disastrous for all of them as a group or community in the sense that the grazing land is overexploited and every animal owner's revenue goes down. Why this happens can be explained in terms of the divergence between the private marginal cost and the social marginal cost of grazing, i.e. the existence of an externality. Each animal owner considers only his/her (private) costs of grazing and not the cost of overgrazing (an externality), which he/she is inflicting on the other animal owners. This results in the private marginal cost of grazing being less than the social marginal cost of grazing and therefore, the competitive equilibrium level of grazing being higher than the socially optimal level of exploitation. This is illustrated in Figure 17.1.

As shown in the figure, the competitive equilibrium level of grazing is attained when the level of extraction is X_2 where the private marginal cost is equal to the marginal revenue. The socially optimum level of extraction is X_1, where the social marginal cost is equal to the marginal revenue. Thus, the open access equilibrium is attained at a higher level of grazing and hence a higher level of exploitation than the socially optimum level of exploitation, i.e. $X_2 > X_1$.

To avert the tragedy of the common village grazing land, it is necessary to change its status from an open access to a competitive property of its co-users. This could be done by organizing the co-users in some form of formal or non-formal organization and vesting in their organization the usufructuary rights to the grazing land on a long-term lease basis. If this could be done, the level of exploitation of the wasteland involved will be socially optimum as the externality involved in its use is now internalized by the organization of the co-users. This is the rationale underlying the TGCS or any other form of co-users' organization as an instrument of averting the tragedy of common wastelands.

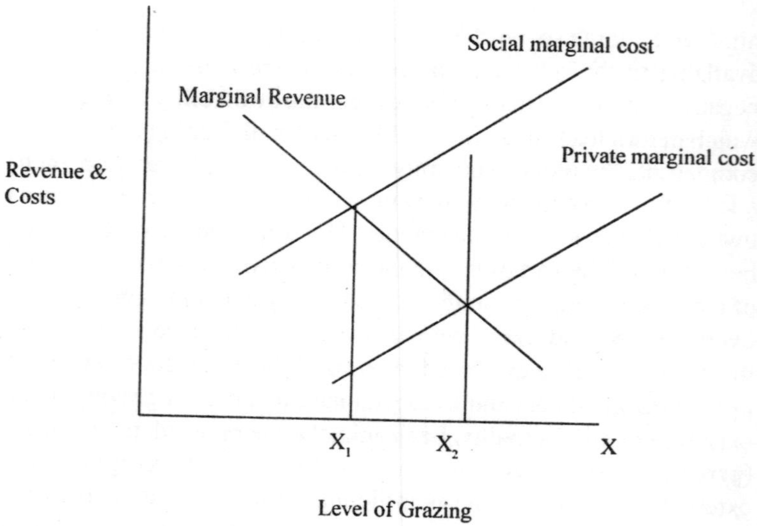

Fig. 17.1: Competitive (open access) Equilibrium Level and Socially Optimal Level of Grazing in a Common Village Pasture

A Review of Policies and Programmes of Afforestation of Wastelands

Although the practice of growing trees by Indian farmers is as old as the cultivation of crops, it was in 1976 that the National Commission on Agriculture first articulated the need for government involvement in this activity on a significant scale. Consequently, social forestry projects were started by many of the state governments in India in the late 1970s and the early 1980s. Later, the National Forest Policy of 1988 also emphasized the role of social forestry as a source of raw materials for forest-based industries.

The State Forest Departments (SFDs) in India are the most important and resourceful of all the organizations engaged in tree plantation on wastelands. As stated earlier, they launched social forestry programmes in the late 1970s and early 1980s with the objectives of arresting and reversing the depletion of India's forest resources and to meet the biomass needs of the rural poor. The programmes laid emphasis on community participation. They got a big boost in the early 1980s when several international development and financing agencies started co-financing with the SFDs social forestry projects in India. Consequently, during the decade of 1980—1990, some 14 externally aided social forestry projects were underway in as many states of India. The funding agencies included the World Bank, Food and Agriculture Organisation (FAO), United States Agency for International Development (USAID), Canadian International Development Agency (CIDA), Swedish International Development Agency (SIDA), Overseas Development Administration (ODA) and Danish International Development Agency (DANIDA).

The National Forest Policy 1988 has changed the face of the Indian forestry. It is both conservation-and production-oriented. The basic objective of this policy is to maintain the environmental stability through preservation of forests as a natural heritage. It also emphasizes the need for increasing substantially the forest/tree cover and the productivity of forests in the country to meet the essential national needs. However, the distinctive feature of this new policy is its plea for "creating a massive people's movement with the involvement of women for achieving its objectives and to minimize the pressure on the existing forests". In this sense, it is a complete departure from the previous National Forest Policy of 1952. The new forest policy is a harbinger of "management change", i.e. from Government management to people's management of forests. As a follow up to the new policy, the Government of India has issued orders and guidelines for joint forest management (JFM) from time to time in the last ten years or so.

In a recent development, the Ministry of Environment and Forests has issued fresh operational guidelines for the formulation of National Afforestation Programme for the Tenth Five Year Plan (2002-2007). These guidelines seek to promote a participatory approach to the development of forests for the Central Government sponsored afforestation schemes. The afforestation schemes operational during the Ninth Plan have been merged under the new National Afforestation Programme so as to "avoid multiplicity of schemes with similar objectives" and to ensure "uniformity in the funding pattern and implementation mechanism".

One of the major features of these guidelines is that all the new centrally sponsored afforestation schemes will be implemented by a two-tier-set-up consisting of Forest Development Agencies (FDAs) and JFM committees to facilitate greater participation of the community in planning and implementation. The FDA is a new institutional set-up, which will be a registered society under the Societies Registration Act., constituted at the territorial wildlife forest division level. Other than JFM Committees, the already existing village institutions with a different nomenclature will be the implementing agency at the grassroot level. The FDAs will work in tandem with JFM committees by signing a Memorandum of Understanding. On the one hand, the FDAs will strengthen the existing JFM Committees and on the other, they will create new JFM Committees. To be concise, the purpose of the National Afforestation Programme will be to make the JFM a "central integral part" of all the afforestation projects in the country.

Recently, the Government of India came up with a Greening India Programme, which proposes to cover 43 mha of degraded forest and non-forest land under the watershed approach in a 10-year timeframe. This includes regeneration of 15 m.ha of degraded forests under the JFM. The government has proposed to set-up a Green India Authority and Green India Fund to undertake this programme. The implementation of this programme requires Rs. 4,800 crore annually against the current availability of Rs. 1,615 crore through the Government of India's budgetary resources (Balooni and Singh, 2003). Given the limitation of budgetary resources for forestry activities, the government will have to seek funding from other sources. One such source is "institutional finance", which has not yet been fully tapped for forestry activities in India.

The National Bank for Agricultural and Rural Development (NABARD), an apex development bank in India, supports and promotes agriculture and rural development including tree plantation on private and community lands. NABARD provides refinance facility to certain category of financial institutions in respect of the loans advanced by them to the ultimate beneficiaries: individuals, forest-based industries, state forest development corporations and NGOs for undertaking tree plantations and other development activities. Since the inception of NABARD in 1982, its contribution to tree plantation activities has been paltry (Balooni and Singh 2003). Moreover, in recent years also, the amount disbursed by the financial institutions to afforestation programmes, mostly for farm forestry programmes, has declined considerably (Balooni and Singh 2003). It was INR 90 million in 1998-99 as compared to INR 290.5 million in 1990-91.

Experience with TGCS and Other Forms of People's Organisations

Depending upon the form of organization involved in the activity, one could classify the agencies engaged in afforestation of wastelands in the following five categories:

(i) State Forest Departments (SFDs),
(ii) Non-Government Organisations (NGOs) including Gramya Jungle Committees, Forest Protection Committees and Watershed Associations,
(iii) Tree Grower's Cooperative Socieities (TGCS),
(iv) Private Companies, and
(v) Individual Proprietors.

The TGCS are of a relatively recent origin in India. The Fadaval Tree Growers' Cooperative Society organized in the mid 1970s in Surat district of Gujarat state is probably the first such society established in India. A bold initiative was taken by the National Dairy Development Board (NDDB) in 1986 to organize TGCS under a pilot project in selected states of India. For this purpose, a national-level cooperative organization, National Tree Growers' Cooperative Federation (NTGCF), was established with its headquarters at Anand. It is a cooperative institution registered under the Multi-State Cooperative Societies Act. The NTGCF initially selected five Indian states of Andhra Pradesh, Gujarat, Karnataka, Orissa and Rajasthan for organisiing TGCS. Later, two more states, namely, Madhya Pradesh and Uttaranchal, were included in the project. In February, 2001, a new organization called the Foundation for Ecological Security (FES) was created. With effect from April, 2001, the responsibility for implementing the TGCS project of the NTGCF was transferred to it. The FES is an autonomous non-governmental organization registered under the Societies Registration Act XXI of 1860. It has a broader mandate than the NTGCF in the sense that it seeks to work with and facilitate the promotion of a wide range of democratic village/people's institutions, besides, of course, the TGCS. Its mission is ecological restoration and conservation of land and water resources in the eco-fragile zones of India (FES, 2002).

By the end of March 2002, NTGCF/FES had organized 879 village institutions including 507 TGCS in these seven states. The TGCS had altogether 105,598 members and had planted 21,771 ha of government-owned wasteland and village panchayat grazing land. Nearly 14.2 million trees had been planted on common and private lands. The average expenditure incurred on tree plantations varied from as low as Rs. 3,901 per ha in Orissa to as high as Rs. 25,293 per ha in Uttaranchal depending on the location and physical characteristics of the land. The overall average expenditure for all the seven states taken together was Rs. 7,258 per ha (FES, 2002: 22 and Table 17.2). The total expenditure incurred on tree plantation by the TGCS and other village institutions in India as of March 2002 was Rs. 158 million.

Table 17.2: Some Selected Indicators of the Status of TGCS and Other Village Institutions in India as of March, 2002

Particular	*Gujarat*	*Madhya Pradesh*	*Andhra Pradesh*	*Karna-taka*	*Orissa*	*Uttar-anchal*	*Rajas-than*	*All*
Year of launching of TGCS/ village institutions	1986	1997	1987	1987	1987	1992	1986	1986-97
No. of TGCS/ village institutions set-up	138	37	146	103	154	88	213	879
No. of members of TGCS village institutions	14384	5932	8615	13449	30185	5582	27451	105598
Area planted by TGCS/village institutions (ha.)	2428	1737	4257	3811	2445	722	6371	21771
Average expenditure per hectare of planted area (Rs.)	4126	6849	5368	4169	3901	25293	10919	7258

Source: Personal communication with Shri Jagdeesh Rao, Executive Director, Foundation for Ecological Security, Anand, and Shri Dinesh Reddy, Managing Director, National Tree Growers' Cooperative Federation, Anand.

In India, over the past decade, there has been a tremendous growth in the number of NGOs and other forms of people's organizations involved in social forestry projects. It is estimated that at least 500 NGOs are engaged in this activity in India. The Gujarat State Forest Department is one of the pioneers in India in involving NGOs in social forestry projects. At present, some 54 NGOs in the State are directly or indirectly implementing various social forestry projects.

The Government of India through its social forestry programmes (including farm forestry) has tried to involve local people in the afforestation projects on private as well as community lands. However, the implementing agencies in most cases have failed to involve people in the social forestry projects. Nevertheless, social forestry programmes have provided an opportunity for the Forest Department personnel to begin a dialogue with village communities, which laid one of the foundations for the Joint Forest Management (JFM) programme, which was launched later in India.

The main objectives of the TGCS is to enable villagers to grow trees and grasses of suitable species on their own agricultural lands and degraded village revenue lands to meet the local needs of fuelwood, fodder and small wood. The ultimate goal is to improve the socio-economic condition of the members and the quality of local environment (Singh 1994). Any 11 or more adult persons belonging to different families can form a TGCS by making an application to the District Registrar of Cooperative Societies. A TGCS is registered under the Cooperative Societies Act. Any person is entitled to be a member of a TGSC if she/he is residing within the area of its operation, has completed 18 years of age, is growing trees and/or grass, has been given a tree-lease, and has agreed in writing to sell his/her produce only to the TGCS. The governance structure of a typical TGCS consists of a general body (GB), a management committee (MC), an honorary chairperson and a paid secretary. The GB comprises all the members of the TGCS and has the supreme powers conferred on it under the Cooperative Societies Act and Rules and its own byelaws.

Sale of shares and the entrance fee are the main sources of funds for the TGCS. Every member has to buy at least one share of Rs. 10 and pay an entrance fee of Re. 1. Loans, donations, subsidies and grants constitute the other major sources of revenue for the TGCS. Initially, NTGCF used to provide a loan of Rs. 458,000 to each TGCS established under its auspices for the initial period of five years for planting trees on 40 ha of village wastelands. The NTGCF, in turn, receives funds and grants from many national and international agencies including the Canadian International Development Agency and Swedish International Development Authority. The bylaws of the TGCS stipulate that out of the profit earned by the cooperative from the sale of fodder, timber and other tree produce, 25 per cent be transferred to its reserve fund, a certain amount determined in accordance with the Cooperative Societies Act and Rules is set aside for the cooperative education fund, and a sum not exceeding 12 per cent of the paid-up share capital is earmarked for payment of dividend to the share holders. Of the balance and after statutory deductions 65 per cent is distributed as bonus to the members in accordance with the value of trees/grass and any other produce sold by the members to or through the society; 5 per cent is set aside for community development work; 10 per cent for bonus to the society's staff, 15 per cent for soil, water and energy conservation and wasteland development fund; and 5 per cent for cooperative propaganda fund.

A case study of a village TGCS in Kheda district of Gujarat is discussed below (Box 1). It is too early to assess the performance and sustainability of the TGCS that have been established under the auspices of the NTGCF/FES. But on the basis of the data on the actual costs and intermediate benefits and estimates of the final harvest, we found that a typical TGCS can be found financially viable over a period of 15 years or so. Singh and Balooni (1997) estimated the average cost of tree plantation for a sample of three TGCS in Kheda district of Gujarat to be Rs. 13,523 per ha at the 1995-96 prices over a period of five years. The costs included the cost of plantation of trees and after-care; cost of land development and soil and water conservation; and overhead costs of the TGCS. The costs incurred in earlier years (before 1992-93) were compounded at the rate of 10 per cent to express them at the 1995-96 prices. The BCR at the 15 per cent discount rate varied from 4.46 to 5.35 over a period of 16 years on the basis of projected benefits (Balooni 1997).

Box 1: The Vatra Tree Growers' Cooperative Society: A Case Study*

Vatra is a medium-sized village in Kheda district of Gujarat. In 1996, it had a total human population of about 3,965 distributed in 566 households. Of the total population, about 63 per cent were farmers, 22 per cent landless labourers and the remaining 15 per cent were engaged in other non-farm activities. The total geographical area of the village is about 722 ha of which about 522 ha (72%) was arable (cultivable) and about 142 ha was *gauchar,* i.e. village common grazing land, in 1987. A TGCS was organized in the village by a spearhead team of the National Tree Growers' Cooperative Federation (NTGCF) and formally registered on July 20, 1987, under the Multi-State Cooperative Societies Act, 1984. As of 1996, the TGCS had 560 members of whom 311 (56%) were landless, 190 (34%) marginal farmers having less than one ha land, and the remaining 59 (10%) were small farmers having 1-2 ha land. The TGCS got 40 ha of degraded land from the Revenue Department of the Government of Gujarat on lease for 15 years for tree plantation.

The TGCS planted some 121,745 saplings of 21 different tree species on 40 ha land over the period 1987-1992. The survival rate was about 89 per cent. The major tree species planted were *ganda baval (Prosopis juliflora) deshi baval (Acacia nilotica), and neem (Azadirachta indica*). The saplings were raised by the members in their own nurseries and were sold to the TGCS at the rate of Re. 0.43 per sapling. Women were given preference by the TGCS for raising saplings.

The total employment generated over the period, 1987-1992, was 11,464 man days of which women accounted for 61 per cent. The average cost of tree plantation was R. 9,369 per ha at the 1995-96 prices and the projected net present value of benefits to the members at 15 per cent discount rate and the 1995-96 over the 16 year period, 1987-88-2002-03, was Rs. 162, 240 per ha. The benefit cost ratio at the 15 per cent discount rate was 5.35 and the Financial Internal Rate of Return 61.95 (Balooni, 1997: 240). Thus, the tree plantation was economically and financially viable and benefited the landless labourers and marginal and small farmers who were members of the TGCS. In addition, the TGCS restored the productivity of the degraded land on a sustainable basis, improved the micro-climate and empowered its members through education, training and participation in the management of its affairs (Saxena, (1996:57).

* Adapted from Saxena (1996) and Balooni (1997: 190-204)

The TGCS seems to be the most appropriate form of organization for promoting social forestry as it is member-centred and its primary goal is to serve its members while having a high degree of social responsibility. If the poor people including the landless interested in social forestry are organized in the TGCS, they could have access to institutional finance, technical advice and training, managerial support, production inputs and national and international markets. The TGCS can bargain better than individual tree growers with those whom they asell their produce and from whom they buy their production inputs.

Constraints Encountered, Lessons Learnt and their Policy Implications

The TGCS have experienced several problems in their organization and operations. They include the time-consuming and complicated procedures for acquiring degraded land owned by the government, delays in sanctioning and disbursement of bank credit, low (non-remunerative) prices for tree products, and flawed public policies and programmes (Balooni and Singh, 2001). We briefly describe some of the major problems encountered by the TGCS, lessons learnt and their policy implications based on our own study as well as the work done by other scholars.

Lack of Information and Problems in Acquisition of Degraded Land for Tree Plantation

The information needed for assessing the potential of non-forest and cultivated lands like ownership, extent and type of degradation, and present and future uses, has never been collected on a systematic basis for the entire country (Romm 1981b). This has dampened the progress of tree plantation through the TGCS. Besides, there are inordinate delays in the acquisition of such lands due to complicated bureaucratic procedures involved. For example, on an average, there was a time lag of 309 days between the registration of cooperatives and the leasing of village common lands by the state governments to the cooperatives (NTGCF 1996).

The hassles in the acquisition of degraded lands are further aggravated by the encroachment of such lands by the local people as well as the lack of a clear demarcation of the boundaries of such degraded lands. The NGOs, forest and revenue departments generally prefer to allocate resources according to the administrative boundaries determined in the settlement plans. These settlements were done during the 19th century. The ground realities of use and management of these resources have since changed quite considerably. These changes need to be incorporated for proper management of the plantation areas and a negotiated settlement between different villages, or, and hamlets within a village, need to be arrived at for an effective implementation of the JFM (Balooni and Ballabh, 2000).

Information on Credit Availability

Most of the tree growers in India are poor, small-scale operators, unorganized and illiterate. They do not have access to information on the availability of credit for tree plantations provided by the financial institutions under the various government schemes. This is one of the reasons why the Government of India's Margin Money Scheme in collaboration with NABARD (designed to provide assistance to farmers as a component of credit for tree plantation on degraded lands) could not achieve its targets.

There is no doubt that tree plantation in India has increased to around 27.62 m ha during 1980-1999 due to various social forestry programmes like farm forestry and community forestry (ICFRE, 2000). This could be achieved also due to the widespread dissemination of information among the farmers and techniques of cultivating about fast-growing species like eucalyptus sp., *poplar* sp., and *acacia* sp. A combination of dissemination of information on the availability of institutional credit and active collaboration between State Forest Departments and NGOs can help speed up the pace of afforestation through faster disbursement of institutional credit. These measures will also help NABARD and the financial institutions refinanced by it in increasing the flow of institutional financing for afforestation programmes.

Institutional, Organisational Legal Constraints

The State Governments in India need to take some concrete steps for the benefit of tree growers like modifying the legal provisions so that tree growers can freely harvest trees grown on their own farms. In several states, provisions of the Forest Law discourage farm forestry by imposing restrictions on felling and transportation and sale of timber standing on private lands. For example, in Gujarat, there are restrictions on felling of 26 tree species including teak (PRADAN, 1990). Further, the farmers have to seek the permission for felling trees from the

Revenue Department before harvesting trees on their private lands. It could take a year or two before the farmer gets the requisite permission (NTGCF, 1998). The Andhra Pradesh Forest Produce Transit Rules of 1970 regulate the transit of forest produce into or from or within any area in the State of Andhra Pradesh. According to Balaji (1997), "at policy level [in the State of Tamil Nadu] the cultivation of trees is inhibited by a number of archaic Acts and rules that restrict felling and transport of timber". These restrictions erode the value of produce for the farmers and dissuade them from taking up plantations.

According to Guha (1994), even the proposed new forest Act, which is to be called the "Conservation of Forests and Natural Ecosystems Act" and is to replace the Indian Forest Act of 1927, stipulates unnecessary and irksome interference by the state in the affairs of the tree growers. It claims that it will facilitate tree farming, but at the same time it places numerous hurdles in the path of farmers who might actually want to plant trees on their own lands. It also requires that every tree grower registers with the local State Forest Department, and informs it when trees planted and nurtured by him are to be felled or sold. This would be a great deterrent to farmers who might otherwise like to plant trees on their land. This draft Act, which generated a lot of debate, is still to be presented in the Indian Parliament. In the meanwhile, the old Indian Forest Act of 1927 with subsequent amendments continues to be in operation (Kulkarni, 2000).

Non-Remunerative Prices and Lack of Marketing Facilities

Poor infrastructure and the lackadaisical approach to the marketing of farm forestry products followed in the past has led to tree growers receiving non-remunerative prices for their products. This has dampened the interest of present tree growers as well as potential tree growers in planting trees and approaching financial institutions for loans even when many schemes for tree plantation are available (Chambers *et al.* 1989; Saxena, 1992). This situation has been more or less the same for decades now. In many places where transport and communication facilities are lacking, middlemen and local entrepreneurs pay very low prices to the tree-growers and often cheat them. This can be attributed to the lack of knowledge on the part of tree growers regarding the prevailing market prices and their inability to go to the distant markets. This problem is further aggravated by the monopoly market situations, described by Balaji (1997) as "the problem of myopic suppliers and gigantic buyers", which weakens the bargaining power of the individual tree-growers.

There is a need for the state governments' intervention for provision of requisite information about markets and prices and for purchase of harvested produce at a remunerative price, if necessary. We illustrate the role of prices in promoting tree plantation by an example of the rise and fall of the farm forestry on private lands promoted by the various agencies of the Government of India during the late 1970s and early 1980s. During this period, *eucalyptus* (a fast-growing tree species) plantations on private lands were undertaken in many parts of the country on a large scale as it was highly profitable at the then prevailing prices. However, later on, preference for *eucalyptus* as a plantation species withered due to its overproduction and consequently the crash in its prices. The government did not intervene to stabilize the eucalyptus wood market prices.

Concluding Remarks

India has vast tracts of wastelands, which have been lying barren for ages for a variety of reasons. Most of such lands are physically suitable for growing trees, which is also economically viable. But this requires massive investment of funds and an appropriate institutional/organizational structure, both of which are lacking in India. Both the private investment and the budgetary allocations of the government for afforestation are inadequate vis-à-vis the requirement. Most of such lands are owned by the government and village panchayats and are *de facto* open access resources. They are degraded, denuded, encroached and misused. There is, therefore, a need for exploring alternative ways of afforestation of such lands. One of the institutional innovations, which has been successfully tried in seven States of India, is organizing the TGCS and involving several other types of people's organizations in tree plantation on such lands.

The experience with the TGCS and other types of people's organizations with tree plantation on wastelands has been a mixed bag of success and failures. There are a number of constraints in promoting TGCS and other village institutions as instruments of wasteland afforestation. It is argued in the paper that the constraints could be and should be removed as soon as possible so that the wastelands could be put to more socially productive use and help improve the micro-climate, besides creating lots of employment opportunities and producing raw materials for the wood-based industries. Given the limited government budgetary resources and the large extent of wastelands in India, the author highlights the need for the government to facilitate promotion of TGCS and other forms of people's organizations and to mobilize more funds including institutional credit for wasteland afforestation in India.

REFERENCES

Balaji, S. (1997): Forestry Extension in Tamil Nadu – Approaches and Challenges Ahead, In: Proceedings of the 2nd IUFRO Forestry Extension Working Party S6.06-03 Symposium, Nairobi, Kenya, 7-12 September. Available at http:/ iufro.boku.ac.at/ iufronet/ d6/ wu60603/proc1997/balaji.htm

Balooni, Kulbhushan (1997): Financing of Afforestation of Wastelands, unpublished Ph.D Dissertation, Department of Economics, Sardar Patel University, Vallabh Vidyanagar, India.

Balooni, Kulbhushan (2002): "Economics of Wastelands Afforestation in India, A Review", New Forests (forthcoming).

Balooni, Kulbhushan and V. Ballabh (2000): "Managing Village Plantations through Tree Growers' Cooperatives: Emerging Issues and Policy Implications" *Agricultural Economics Research Review* 13(1), 54-70.

Balooni, Kulbhushan and Katar Singh (2001): "Tree Plantations for Restoration of Degraded Lands and Greening of India: A Case Study of Tree Growers' Cooperatives", *Natural Resource Forum*, 25(1), 21-32.

Balooni, Kulbhushan and Katar Singh (2003): "Institutional Financing of Wastelands Afforestation in India: Some Issues and Options", *Natural Resource Forum*, 26 (Forthcoming).

Chambers, R., N.C. Saxena and Tushaar Shah, (1989): *To the Hands of the Poor: Water and Trees*, New Delhi: Oxford & IBH.

FES, (2002): Foundation for Ecological Security Annual Report 2001-2002, NDDB Campus, Anand.

Gautam, N.C. and L.R.A. Narayan, (1988): *Wastelands in India*, Mathura: Pink Publishing House, India.

GOI, (1976): Report of the National Commission on Agriculture, Part IX, Forestry, Government of India, Ministry of Agriculture and Cooperation, New Delhi.

Guha, R. (1994): "Forestry Debate and Draft Forest Act: Who Wins, Who Loses"? *Economic and Political Weekly*, 29 (34), 2192-2196.

Haque, M.S. (1997): "Development of India's Wastelands through Institutional Credit—A 15-Year Plan" In: T.K. Sarkar, R.C. Vaish, V. Verma and S.P. Gawande, (Eds.) *Advances in Wastelands Development*, Soil Conservation Society of India, New Delhi, 155-159.

Hardin, G. (1968): "The Tragedy of the Commons", *Science*, 162: 1243-8.

ICFRE (2000): "Forestry Statistics, India," Indian Council of Forestry Research and Education, Dehradun, India.

Kadekodi, G.K. and N.H. Ravindranath (1997): "Macro-economic Analysis of Forestry Options on Carbon Sequestration in India", *Ecological Economics* 23(3), 201-223.

Kulkarni, S. (2000): "The Flight of the Tribal", *Seminar* (Protecting Nature—A Symposium on Some Legal Issues Concerning the Environment), August, 492. Available at http:/www.India-seminar.com/semframe.htm

NTGCF (1996): Mid-term Review, National Tree Growers' Cooperative Federation Limited, Anand, India.

NTGCF (1998): Annual Report 1997-98, National Tree Growers' Cooperative Federation Limited, Anand, India.

PRADAN (1990): Access to Government Wastelands for Afforestation: Legal Provisions in Andhra Pradesh, Bihar, Gujarat, Karnataka, Madhya Pradesh, Maharashtra, Orissa, Rajasthan, Tamil Nadu and Uttar Pradesh, Professional Assistance for Development Action, New Delhi.

Romm, J. (1981a): The Uncultivated Half of India (Part-I), *Indian Forester* 107(1), 1-23.

Romm, J. (1981b): The Uncultivated Half of India (Part-II), *Indian Forester* 107(2), 69-85.

Saxena, N.C. (1992): "Farm Forestry and Land Use in India: Some Policy Issues", *Ambio* 21(6), 420-425.

Saxena, Rakesh (1996): "The Vatra Tree Growers' Cooperative Society", in Katar Singh and Vishwa Ballabh (eds.) *Cooperative Management of Natural Resources*. New Delhi: Sage Publications.

Singh, S. (1993): "Policy of NWDB regarding Tree Growers' Cooperatives", In: Shashikant, and R. Saxexna. (eds.) *Proceedings of the National Seminar on Tree Growers' Cooperatives,* ISO/Swedforest, New Delhi, pp. 66-69.

Singh, Katar (1992): People's Participation in Natural Resources Management, Workshop Report 8, Anand: Institute of Rural Management, Anand.

Singh, Katar (1994): *Managing Common Pool Resources: Principles and Case Studies*. Delhi: Oxford University Press.

Singh, Katar and Kulbhushan Balooni (1997): "Tree Growers' Cooperatives: Farm Forestry in India", *Journal of Forestry*, 95(10).

Vohra, B.B. (1985): "The Greening of India", In: Bandyopadhyay, J.N.D. Jayal, U. Schoettl, and C. Singh (Eds.) *India's Environment: Crisis and Responses*, Natraj Publishers, Dehradun, pp. 26-40.

World Bank (1988): India: Wasteland Development Review, World Bank, Washington D.C.

18

Land Ownership Patterns

Implications for Natural Resources Development and Governance

NEELIMA KHETAN

This paper attempts to share the experiences of Seva Mandir in undertaking natural resources development over the past 15 years in southern Rajasthan. The chief realization for Seva Mandir has been that the potential for a sustainable natural resources development and community participation is significantly defined by the nature of the land tenure in that area.

Rajasthan remains one of the least developed states in India because of its limited industrial infrastructure, rural electrification, paved roads, literacy, public health facilities and level of household income. The Aravallis are its major mountain system, which divides it diagonally into two parts. The Aravallis are linked to the larger ecosystem of forests, rivers and desert, but now that it is almost completely deforested, the balance of the entire system has been disrupted. Before independence the Aravallis were densely forested with 50-60 per cent deep forest cover. Today only 10 per cent of the total forest cover remains. This has happened due to overuse for commercial logging and mining enterprises, increased population pressure and local mismanagement of the forest resources. As a result there has been an excessive soil erosion and the groundwater level has dropped significantly. The Aravallis are a natural watershed system with rivers and streams which are only seasonal and which disappear soon after the monsoons. Some observers claim that the rainfall intensity and frequency has dropped in direct correlation to the decreased forest cover. Deforestation in the area is also linked to the increasing level of desertification, as the natural barrier of the hills, which controlled the eastward spread of the Thar desert, is now barren.

Udaipur and Rajsamand districts lie in the southern part of the Aravalli hill region of the state. The rural population of this area is 2,395,382, which is 83 per cent of the entire population, of which 8.32 per cent are Scheduled Castes and 36.7 per cent are Scheduled Tribes. Further, in Seva Mandir's area of work (which constitutes a large part of the 6 of the 18 blocks in these districts) the tribal population is 68 per cent. Udaipur district has been subjected to recurrent drought, epidemic and famine throughout history. The average rainfall in the district during the monsoon months (June to September) in 625 mm/year.

The historical social context of the region was set in the erstwhile princely state of Mewar, which was feudal and resistant to development and modernization. During the Raj the district was dominated, politically and economically, by the landowners, who consisted primarily of the Rajput princes and their nobles, and socially by the existing caste affiliations. The hierarchy was reinforced by the parton-client relationship between the lower castes, the large tribal population of Mewar, and the landlord class, including the functionaries of the state. The economic systems were such that they led to an ever-expending debt cycle, bonded labour, slavery, etc. The economic dependency of the poor tended to be reproduced as debts were passed on to subsequent generations, so much so that indebtedness now seems to have become a distinguishing and enduring feature of the existence of the contemporary Bhil (the major tribe of the region). Under the old regime the peasants enjoyed very few rights and their lives were circumscribed by the lack of state initiative in its development and enhance the people's capabilities. The patron-client relationship was based on strict and even oppressive hierarchy. The post-independence period, in some respects, weakened the rural poor, even though it abolished feudalism. The value and the extent of the resources available to the rural people diminished greatly due to overexploitation by the state for purposes of generating revenues and promoting industrial development. Being severely handicapped in terms of education and the skills relevant to the organized sector, the rural poor could not benefit from the development of the organized sector, and the state continued with the custodial policies of the feudal/colonial area.

Most of the villages Seva Mandir works in are predominantly tribal and comprise poor peasants. While there is less economic stratification and considerable cultural and social homogeneity, the people are not organized and empowered to achieve their common interests. The lack of own resources and concentration of authority in the state has disempowered people and their institutions.

The district's primary economic mainstay used to be agriculture and forests. However, over time, with the increasing deforestation and overall degradation of land, labour, incomes are the most important contributor to family earnings – contributing between 60 to 80 per cent, depending on the rainfall and the agricultural crops. Income from forests is only a marginal third, though dependence on these lands for sustaining lifestyles – farm fodder, fuel-wood, etc. still continues to be very high.

Land Ownership in the Region

Seva Mandir is working in six Blocks of Udaipur and Rajsamand districts. The land ownership classification in these blocks is given below:

Sl. No.	*Block*	*Public Lands*				*Private land*	*Total area*
		Forest	*Pasture*	*Others*	*Total*		
	Badgaon	5,485	5,938	16,117	27,537	36,665	64,202
	Gogunda	25,231	9,627	20,588	55,546	34,547	90,093
	Girwa	31,916	10,531	58,896	101,342	35,517	136,860
	Kherwara	26,496	8,203	33,201	67,900	41,191	109,091
	Jhadol	77,410	4,095	27,541	109,046	35,054	144,100
	Kotra	164,415	5,565	40,777	210,752	31,480	242,237
Total area		330,953	43,959	197,217	572,129	214,454	768,583
Percentage of total		42.07	5.59	25.07	72.73	27.27	100.00

Forests are the dominant category of land. In some blocks, e.g. Kotra, the forest lands constitute over 70 per cent of the total geographical area. While some patches are still densely forested, majority of these lands are deeply degraded. Other public lands, pastures for instance, are also degraded and contested. In the years after independence, while access to these lands was denied legally, it was provided to individuals on an informal and arbitrary basis at the behest of derelict state functionaries, power brokers and elected representatives. Such persons were allowed to privatize these public lands without there being legal provisions for such arrangements. Occasionally this transparency was inherently arbitrary. These arrangements, rooted as they were in the arbitrary and wantonly informal and illicit arrangements, had two significant consequences. One, they forced the communities into ties of extreme dependence on and vulnerability to the patrons, and two, they led to fragmentation amongst the villagers, and created a normless society in its wake. The process also made it near impossible to put in place institutional arrangements for sustainable landuse, leading to large-scale deprivation, especially among the sections dependent on these public and common lands.

The extent of the nature of this problem can be gauged from the following. A study conducted in this region in the year 2000-01 showed that in certain areas up to 80 per cent of the forest area was "not available" for protection or afforestation. While the study principally focused on identifying areas that were still open and were available for forestry activities, it also brought out the area which, as of now, was not available for such activities. These estimates of "area not available" are very high, and range from 40 to 85 per cent of the gross forest area. All of this, of course, cannot be attributed to direct encroachments. However, given the terrain of the region, dispersal of habitation and landuse practices, where hamlets are dispersed and agricultural activities are undertaken in the valleys, encroachments of this kind over even limited areas can render a large area unavailable for undertaking regeneration efforts.

Subsequently, another study, done in three Forest Blocks of Udaipur district to find out the actual encroached area, found the encroachment to be very high – ranging from 47 to 100 per cent.

Similar is the situation of the pasture lands. A study done in one administrative block of Rajsamand district found 8 out of 13 pastures heavily encroached. This is quite worrying but what is even more worrying is that laws provide no possibility of regularizing encroachments on pasture lands, as opposed to forest lands, where political compulsions have often led to land titles being handed out to encroachers on forest lands.

Seva Mandir's Experience

When Seva Mandir started its afforestation and natural resources development programme, it was unaware of most of the above land ownership patterns – it knew the *de jure* status but did not fully comprehend the *de facto* status. In the early 80s Seva Mandir was successful in implementing a watershed project to cover a cluster of three villages. A series of water storing structures were built which significantly improved the water regime of the concerned villages and raised their overall agricultural productivity. With this niche success and its large outreach through its adult education work which was spread over five blocks of Udaipur district, Seva Mandir responded positively to the challenge posed by the National Wasteland Development Board (NWDB) in 1985 to create a people's movement to afforest degraded lands (excluding Forest Department lands, to which access was denied at the time). Seva Mandir shared the view that poor peasants who depend on natural resources for their livelihood would be willing to participate in its rehabilitation and sustainable management. The NWDB provided Seva Mandir with a large grant to build up a people's movement to plant trees and green the landscape. These funds were used to provide to over 5,000 peasant families small monetary incentives to plant trees on their private wastelands.

In order to encourage cooperative effort at land development, Seva Mandir also provided incentives to farmers to pool their private lands and develop these in a cooperative way. Two models of cooperative efforts at private land development were crystallized. One model was called "mini-chak" model, where two to five farmers on pooling their lands were entitled to 50 per cent subsidy on the total estimated wage costs for fencing the land and afforestation work. The other model that evolved was for more than six farmers to come together and pool their land for development purposes. Here the level of support was to the extent of 80 per cent of the full costs. The level of subsidy was raised because it was felt that fencing for a larger piece of land needed to be more durable and would, therefore, require greater compensation for the opportunity cost of doing this work. In the case of pasturelands the extent of support was 90 per cent of the total cost of the land treatment work.

Since the mid-80s when Seva Mandir accepted the challenge to create a people's movement to rehabilitate the degraded resource base it has been fortunate to find the funds to honour its commitments to the village people to come together and rehabilitate their land and forests. It was also able to communicate to a large body of the village people through its network of village foresters and a growing number of reasonably well-executed land treatment works which as and when the villagers came together to rehabilitate their degraded lands, would be available to them for this purpose. But despite the adequate provisions of support and consistency of its applications across the large area, there was striking lack of demand for developing the CPRs. Of the 10,000 ha of land treated so far, less than 20 per cent is on common lands. While the people did come forward in large numbers for treatment of their privately owned lands, the demand to develop lands that were either pooled, private or common such as pastures and forest lands has been slow to pick up.

When we analyse the response to the schemes for wasteland development, it becomes apparent that the demand for community land development is significantly lower than the demand for private wasteland development, even as the incentives for the former are greater than for the latter. Within the category of private wasteland development, the demand for large pooled plantations consisting of 10 to 15 farmers is significantly less than the demand for mini-chaks, i.e. smaller units of pooled private lands and purely private homestead plantations. The incentive for large *chaks* development, while smaller than for community land development, is greater than the incentives for mini-chak development. As against a contribution of 20 per cent for the former category of land development work, in the case of mini-chaks the minimum contribution is 50 per cent of total cost. Incentives for purely individual homestead plantations are possible in the case of individual plantations based on the saplings planted and their subsequent survival, as opposed to the quantum of soil and conservation work done in the mini-chaks.

The data on the pattern of scheme utilization *prima facie* suggests that it is difficult for people to come together and act on community lands, let alone act on a watershed basis. In the case of community lands the reason is two-fold. One, most community lands are heavily encroached and therefore not available for purposes of rehabilitation as community lands. Two, the slow progress on these types of lands is due to the absence of institutions and social capital needed to manage such properties. The reasons for this can be traced to the pattern of governance, land and social relations that define rural society. By and large people feel that the state and its institutions are discretionary and arbitrary. The state is powerful not only because of its law and order functions but also as the arbiter in matters relating to private land ownership. A *Patwari* can play havoc with landowners by arbitrarily altering land records kept in his possession. This fact apart, the state itself is the custodian and owner of huge pieces of land. Local people both covet and are dependent upon these for their livelihood. The immense authority available with the state has not worked to strengthen the local institutions and add to the social capital. Because of the arbitrary and discretionary nature of governance, peasants have tended to lose their associational capacity and instead have willy-nilly accepted the patronage role assumed by the state and its representatives. For those who protest their subordinate and dependent status the price can be severe. Seva Mandir's research and experience validate this. Access to state-owned lands despite a positive policy framework has been next to impossible. The FD has dragged its feet on giving permission to do JFM work. The DRDA has been equally resistant to promoting watershed development, notwithstanding the National Watershed guidelines and the large outlays provided by this scheme.

The factor of arbitrary and derelict governance apart, the lack of social capital also has to do with the lack of education and economic security that characterizes the bulk of the poor in the area. Very few people are able to provide leadership because they lack the means to do so given their own vulnerabilities and handicaps. In these circumstances where people don't have access or ownership rights on the land that constitutes the watershed, and their own cohesion and capability base is thin, it is difficult for them to relate to an integrated or holistic concept of land development. For such a concept to take root the multiplicity of constraints have to be addressed. There is need to establish a social base for land rehabilitation along side a leadership to spearhead this work. At another level there is need to get the state to change its approach to land management. So long as the state uses its patronage to fragment the people's collective stake in land rehabilitation, it is difficult to get villagers to develop a collective stake in an integrated approach to land development. So far neither the Forest Department (FD) has nor the Revenue Department shown any interest in disciplining their staff to ensure that common property resources are not privatized and that land access is provided as an entitlement.

The current approach of Seva Mandir of providing a multiplicity of opportunities for land development gives people a chance to participate and gain some experience in cooperative land rehabilitation work. By occupying the interstice of the private spaces and some common property resources that remain for participatory land development, small beachheads are established from where people can debate the values of their recovering a fuller stake in an integrated land management. The available evidence suggests that this strategy is paying dividends. Villagers are showing interest in establishing a more transparent regime for property management and also coming together to stake a claim for managing the CPRs as permitted under programmes like the JFM, Watershed guidelines and pasturelands. What is critical is to revitalize the village people's interest in NRM. This is possible if we can build on their existing stakes in land and leverage this engagement for addressing the more contested areas of NRM. Hopefully, this will lead to an integrated land management.

19

Institutional Renovation for Pastureland Development in a Village of Rajasthan

SUNIL RAY

Development of local institutions has been receiving increasing attention in the ongoing development discourse on the management of local resources by the community. Several studies have analysed the strengths and weaknesses of this approach (Leach, Robins and Scoones 1997; Ballabh and Balooni 2002; Wade 1988). The underlying purpose of these studies is to examine whether the local institutions have the potential to manage local resources in heterogeneous communities. However, while social and economic differentiation is a stark reality, complete reliance upon the homogeneity assumption may be misleading for the construction of a development approach especially for the poor (Baland and Platteau 1996). In fact, that heterogeneity also acts as a divisive variable in the hands of the powerful which is then used for weakening the solidarity between individuals and thwarting collective action. There are several instances that show how social heterogeneity and intra-village conflicts and inequality impede collective action (Bardhan 1999). Despite these difficulties, it may be worthwhile to probe under what conditions local institutions have the potential to offer a development approach for all including the poor and the disadvantaged.

Inquiry then begins with the nature and form of social embeddedness of the individual that has a firm impact on his/her choice or behaviour (Veblen 1919). But, can choice formation of individuals be devoid of specific social, cultural and historical context in which individuals are embedded (Harris 2001). The development approach, as the present paper shows, may run the risk of being flawed if the analytical importance of such context is reduced. For, it is this specific social, cultural and historical context that has motivated the inhabitants of Chhota Saradhana village in Rajasthan to create a new form of social embeddedness, attune their self-goal choice in accordance with the new institutional choices for development, conservation and management of common pastureland.

The paper based on a case study of Chhota Saradhana village seeks to analyse how institutional renovation has helped the village community to grow and conserve their natural resource-base, grassland, and gain from it. The first part of the paper briefly describes the social context in which institutional renovation was sought and underlines the changing social processes. The second part traces how the village institution renovates itself for the conservation and development of common pastureland. The third part analyses the benefits that accrue to different groups of households including the poor. The fourth part presents conclusions.

THE SOCIAL CONTEXT

Chhota Saradhana is a non-descript village in the Jawaja Block of Ajmer district. A decade ago, nobody could have imagined that the village would be able to meet its increasing requirements for fuel and fodder by developing their own natural resource-bases. The gradual loss of vegetative cover led to scarcity of fodder and fuel in the village. Its severest manifestation was seen during the drought of 1987. Only then did the villagers of Chhota Saradhana realise how important it was what Dhaneswar Acharya, founder of the Magra-Mewar Vikas Sanstha (MMVS), an NGO, was trying to do. All along he had been trying to motivate them to conserve their natural resources through pastureland development. Acharya, the motivating force behind development in all the eight villages of the Jawaja Block, suggested to them that they should develop the pastureland of the village, which was much degraded, long before 1987. It was a programme to develop awareness initiated by Acharya through non-formal education that eventually turned degradation of pastureland into regeneration. One of the significant aspects of the awareness development programme was to bring people together and persuade them to jointly prioritise the common problems that they were facing, work out the means for their redressal, and find out if external assistance was available to solve them. The villagers arrived at a consensus: they decided to restructure production of fuel and fodder. It was a consensus for what one may call "institutional renovation".

The Village Dynamics

The early history of Chhota Saradhana goes back to the Gurjar community, which was the first to settle down in the village. Gurjars are traditionally pastoralists. Hence, they had a major attraction for vast grazing lands and vegetative cover. They took up livestock rearing as their principal occupation and agriculture as a secondary one. However, the next settlers in the village were members of the Jat community which had agriculture as their primary occupation. Initially, their occupations were distinctly different. And so were their concerns. Livestock was Gurjars' concern and the Jats worried about agriculture. However, the village community was never riddled with conflicts about sharing of resources. Abundant availability of natural resources compared to the need for them never allowed the village economy that was positioned closer to what one may call "natural economy" to lose its stability. While the members of the Gurjar community stepped up their activities in agriculture over the years, members of the Jat community expanded their household activities towards livestock rearing.

Chhota Saradhana witnessed several other changes. Apart from occupational diversification, there had been expansion in the range of caste groups. As many as seven caste groups including Jats and Gurjars live in the village now. One of the notable features of the caste groups is that livestock rearing has become equally indispensable for all. Dependence on it increased over the years due to uncertainties in agriculture as a consequence of persistent droughts. Competition for grass to feed the livestock became very intense. This was accompanied by competition for fuel-wood for human subsistence. Scarcity conditions began to pervade the village economy of Chhota Saradhana gradually and the economy turned very volatile. The intensity of scarcity pushed the villagers to a point of no return in 1987—one of the severest drought years in the recent past. It is this objective condition that created a space for institutional renovation in the village community. Before examining how institutional renovation could succeed in bringing about a new regime in the management, conservation, and growth of natural resources, it is important to learn about the social structure of the village and its correspondence with the ownership pattern of land resources. It is also vital to examine whether power relations contribute to the shaping of institutional renovation.

Social Structure and Land Holding Pattern

In a period of three decades, the number of households living in Chhota Saradhana has almost doubled—from 47 in 1971, it has increased presently to 83. As mentioned earlier, there are seven caste groups; the largest number of households belongs to the Gurjar caste (Table 19.1).

Table 19.1: Distribution of Households across Different Caste-groups and Landholdings

Caste groups	*Landless*	*Marginal*	*Small*	*Medium*	*Large*	*Total*
Gurjar	15	24	3	3	—	45
Jat	—	—	4	17	1	22
Megwal	5	—	—	—	—	5
Bawri	—	2	—	—	—	2
Kumhar	—	2	—	—	—	2
Rawat	—	—	2	—	—	2
Sadhu	—	5	—	—	—	5
Total	*20*	*33*	*9*	*20*	*1*	*83*
Percentage	*24.10*	*39.75*	*10.84*	*20.09*	*1.20*	*100.00*

Source: Field survey.

It is shown in Table 19.1 that only 21 per cent of the households have medium and large holdings while the rest are landless or have small and marginal landholdings. The majority of the Gurjar community falls under this lower landholding category. Eighteen out of twenty-two households belong to the higher category of land holdings primarily belonging to the Jat community. Households that belong to other caste groups are numerically weak and, therefore, they traditionally do not have any significant voice in the decision-making process in the informal institutional arrangement of the village. However, in the current context, social forces seem to have polarised across social groups vertically and tend to reinforce a balance in the social forces between the two dominant communities—Jat and Gurjar. Although the Gurjar community is numerically the largest their ownership of agricultural land is much lower than that of households of the Jat community, majority of whom are medium and large farmers. However, Gurjars own the largest number of animals in the village (Table 19.2).

Table 19.2: Ownership Pattern of Livestock across Social Groups

Caste	*Total no. of*	*Total number of animals*				
	Households	*Cow*	*Buffalo*	*Sheep*	*Goat*	*Bullock*
Meghwal	5	3	1	—	51	—
Sadhu	5	2	1	—	2	—
Jat	22	12	33	—	35	4
Kumhar	2	1	—	—	1	—
Rawat	2	1	4	80	20	—
Bawri	2	1	2	—	2	—
Gurjar	45	27	49	155	322	5
Total	*83*	*47*	*90*	*235*	*433*	*9*

Source: Field survey.

The significant element of this social context that seems to have contributed to the polarisation of all social groups was the uniform material conditions that all social groups encountered when there was drought. This provided a homogeneous base for all to renovate the institutional practices for consumption and conservation of grassland resources. As a consequence, power relations in whichever form they exist could not weaken the norms of mutual trust and reciprocity. The alternative credit delivery system as developed by the villagers themselves, on the contrary, has created a larger social space for deepening them further. The traditional money-lending system that is known for its instrumental role in shaping the rural power relations seems to have been replaced by this alternative. It may be noted that there are seven active women Self-Help Groups (SHGs) in the village. The total number of members is 115 with an annual collection of Rs. 1,38,000. Any member requiring credit pays interest of 2 per cent per annum. Similarly, menfolk of the village has formed three groups with 20 members each and has an annual collection of Rs. 4, 80,000. These groups have developed norms on their own for delivering credit to their members at a minimum cost. In such a social context, the awareness development programme as mentioned earlier lent credible strength to the social capital of this village community for institutional renovation for development and management of pastureland.

The nature of reciprocity and mutual trust changed the nature of social embeddedness of the village community. All social groups were then prepared to respond to renovation of the traditional institutional practices for collection of fuel-wood and fodder as suggested by the MMVS. Of course, it was a response out of sheer necessity for sustenance of both livestock and human beings. But, one cannot underestimate the outcome of institutional renovation achieved through deepening of social capital. It may be noted that this has no correspondence with the capacity building of the village achievable, as normally understood, through education.

Chhota Saradhana exemplifies an extreme form of educational backwardness. A cursory glance at Table 19.3 shows that 80 per cent

Table 19.3: Educational Background of the Village

Age groups	*Illiterate*		*Primary*		*Secondary*		*Above Secondary*		*Total*	
	M	*F*	*M*	*F*	*M*	*F*	*M*	*F*	*M*	*F*
< 5 years	17	15	4	5	—	—	—	—	21	20
6-14	1	10	22	25	15	4	—	—	38	39
15-20	2	16	4	4	17	3	3	—	26	21
21-30	9	20	4	1	6	—	—	—	19	21
31 years and above	36	51	10	3	8	—	1	—	55	54
Total	*65*	*112*	*44*	*38*	*46*	*7*	*4*	—	*159*	*155*

M = Male; F = Female
Source: Field survey.

of the members of the sample households above 30 years are illiterate and around 56 per cent of all the members in the age group 21 to 30 years of the sample households taken together are illiterate. The saddest part is that of those who begin their education, a very few of them could proceed only up to the secondary level. While the absence of adequate incentive from the village community constantly impinges upon the educational enrichment, necessity for occupational engagement for eking out a living assumes greater importance in the trade-off at the household level.

If capacity building is understood in the light of improvement of social capital achievable through enhancing people's sensitivity and ability to articulate their aspirations, Chhota Saradhana definitely sets an example of ingenuity with regard to collective initiative of the village community. Villagers developed not only the land that was classified as permanent pasture but also some parts of the land that was neither available for cultivation (barren) nor classified as permanent pastureland. For example, as shown in Table 19.4, during 2001-02 only 39 hectares of land was available as culturable waste that included both permanent common pastureland and land under tree crops and groves. Now, what the villagers did. They took out 92 hectares from 114 hectares of uncultivable (barren) land, merged it with 39 hectares of permanent pasture as mentioned above and fenced the entire 131 hectares of land as their own community pastureland. It may be noted that at the early stage of community initiative, it was 106 hectares of land that was fenced and developed. Subsequently, villagers enclosed 27 hectares of uncultivable (barren) land with the permission of the Revenue Department, Government of Rajasthan.

Table 19.4: Land Use Pattern of Chhota Saradhana (land in hectares)

No. of Households	*1981-82*	*1991-92*	*2001-02*
	54	*80*	*83*
Reporting area of the village	269.0	243.63	267.00
A. Forest	—	—	—
B. Irrigated land	43.00	2.43	16.00
C. Unirrigated land (including fallow)	49.00	127.48	97.00
D. Culturable waste (including permanent pasture and tree crops and groves)	57.00	27.92	39.00
E. Area not available for cultivation	120.00	85.80	114.00

Source: Census of India, Directorate of Census Operations, Rajasthan, 1981-82 and 1991-92. Data pertaining to 2001-02 were collected from Tehsil office, Bewar (Ajmer district).

The lesson that one may draw from this experiment is that the state and village community can jointly explore the possibility of bringing barren and uncultivable land under the management and control of the latter. The state was endowed with as much as 4.98 million hectares (14.56 per cent of the reporting area) of culturable wasteland in 2000. If the other categories of uncultivable land including permanent pasture that were reported to be 4.30 million hectares are added, land available for cultivation was estimated to be 27 per cent of the total reporting area of the state (Government of Rajasthan, 2000). Even if some parts of such a huge stock of natural capital are restored through protective means at the initiative of the village community as done in Chhota Saradhana it may boost the rural economy of the state in general and livestock economy in particular.

But there are a few implications of protection of pastureland from all sides. First, it directly stops encroachment on the common land that would probably take place in the absence of fencing. Second, it gives a sense of ownership to the villagers and strengthens institutional commitment of each individual member of the village community to sustainable management of grassland. Third, very importantly, it directly or indirectly calls for renovation of the socially inefficient village institution and allows it to break away from the traditional practices or habits related to the use of grazing land and fuel-wood collection.

INSTITUTIONAL RENOVATION

The traditional practices or habits that are historically specific and referred to as culture are central to institutionalists (Veblen 1919). Traditional agricultural practices, livestock rearing, use of grazing land, food habits, etc., intensified their close contact over time with the commodified exchange system that works within the basic model of utility maximisation. While such a system appreciated traditional practices of using grazing land guided mainly by self-goal choice, it never encouraged the village community to improve the conditions of grazing land and renovate the traditional grazing practices. But at the same time, it could not undermine the basic cultural traits of individuals such as a sense of belonging, mutual trust and reciprocity that constitute social capital and provide instant legitimacy to the village institution to retain its collective character (Mohapatra 2001; Warren *et al.* 2001). This seems to have encouraged the villagers of Chhota Saradhana to jointly internalise external intervention through social mediation and decide to renovate the traditional institutional practices of using grazing land. Social capital, thus, must be looked upon as an input into the process by which an institution is created at the local decentralised level for development. In order to ensure sustained development of the common pastureland, an increasing stock is a necessary condition (Chopra 2002).

Social Mediation

Social mediation that has crystalised social capital for an improved outcome gained considerable momentum in Chhota Saradhana village under certain specific material conditions that must not be overlooked. Of course, intense drought conditions of 1987, as mentioned earlier, had made a definite contribution to facilitating social mediation. Factors, external to the village such as likely encroachment by people from neighbouring villages and the fear of allotment of the common land to retired army personnel by the government, were perceived as threats to their control over the common land. The instrumental value of all these is enormous for social mediation that facilitated the villagers to internalise the need for institutional renovation and accept collaborative intervention of an external development agency such as the MMVS for development of pastureland. The first step was to form an informal group. Then the following steps were taken.

Raising of Village Nursery

In order to meet the fuel-wood crisis, the immediate task of the informal group was to raise a village nursery with the active support of the MMVS and the Society for Promotion of Wasteland Development (SPWD). The notable feature of this initiative was that the womenfolk of the village were brought to the centre of this activity not only for raising plantations but also for protecting saplings. The second most important aspect was that complete care was taken to protect the local species including those that were gradually disappearing. The once dominant plants in terms of the area covered were *Kumpla, Daand* and *Gaigan Kheenp* (all local names). These plants disappeared completely while *Arunja, Khejri, Deshi Babool* and *Thor* (all local names) were almost on the verge of extinction. Efforts were made to restore these plants in addition to growing new plants. The new plants included *Prosopis juliflora* and *Acacia hillocacea* and plants locally known as *Lemon, Neem, Anar, Ber, Bamboo, Subabool, Jamun,* etc. However, due to lack of adequate care and scarcity of water, most of the plants failed to survive. The only exceptions were *Prosopis juliflora, Thor, Baradi, Khejri* and *Deshi babool* that could manage to survive even without regular supply of water. The entire land that was not fit for cultivation and was considered as "wasteland" was now full of these species that virtually brought complete relief to the villagers in terms of meeting the fuel-wood crisis.

More importantly, the womenfolk, who used to walk everyday for miles together to collect fuel-wood, had some respite from this time-consuming chore. This boosted the self-confidence of the villagers and gave them a sense of identity but it saw its gradual erosion in the days of their struggle for eking out subsistence in drought conditions.

Grassland Development

The second most important step taken by the informal group was grassland development for meeting the fodder crisis that was prioritised by the villagers as next to the fuel-wood crisis. Steps taken by the informal group for grassland development are as follows.

Land Preparation

First, 106 hectares of land was earmarked and fenced with locally available materials such as stones. They had the option of wire fencing which was selected due to its cost-effectiveness. An anicut was constructed inside the pastureland for conservation of rainwater and retention of soil moisture. The cleaning of land and its levelling were taken up immediately. This was followed by the construction of staggered trenches and contour bunds for rainwater percolation and soil conservation. Three significant aspects of all these activities need to be underlined. First, women's participation was overwhelmingly large. Women from all social groups were divided into several groups with four to five members in each group. Every group was assigned different jobs to complete. Second, there was complete dependence of the villagers on the locally available materials for fencing. Third, the unique combination of the local knowledge with the knowledge imparted by the scientific organisations invited from outside for preparation of land and conservation of soil and water.

Organisational Networking

There were several technical aspects related to the revival of grassland ecosystem that needed special attention for ensuring sustainability. The informal group held several discussions with the MMVS and invited several organisations to train the villagers in various aspects of grazing land management without causing any harm to the natural process of growth. For instance, scientists from CAZRI trained villagers in seed treatment and production of grass. They cultivated grass on an experimental basis in three soil-nutrient conditions in three plots to examine under what conditions grass grows better with low investment. Seed of the *Dhaman* variety of grass was sown in one of the plots with fertiliser, another one without fertiliser and the third plot was rocky in which fertiliser and plenty of water were provided. The second plot showed encouraging results against the backdrop of water scarcity. This prompted the villagers to sow seeds of *Dhaman* grass in the entire land that was fenced. Training provided by the SPWD for the construction of check dams, contour *bunds,* etc., proved extremely fruitful. Other non-government organisations from where assistance was sought included CECOEDECON for the development of *Nadi*, Inter-Cooperation for seed testing, OXFAM for women's empowerment, and UNNATI for strategy formulation. All these organisations played a role at different points of time and at various stages. The interesting aspect of the entire exercise was that no assistance was sought from the government. However, the government did play a positive role when it allowed the village community to incorporate some part of the revenue land into pastureland already prepared. It was in this context that an informal group that constituted the Village Development Society (VDS) earlier was formalised.

Formalisation of VDS

The VDS that was formed informally gained formal status when it was registered under the Societies Registration Act. Earlier, villagers never felt it necessary to do so. However, it turned out that it was compulsory to register their group when they confronted the Revenue Department, Government of Rajasthan. The villagers wanted to incorporate 24 hectares of uncultivable land lying adjacent to the 106 hectares of land that they had already fenced. Since this adjacent land was revenue land, permission was sought by the villagers for incorporating the same into the pastureland. It was finally given by the Revenue Department. However, for the grant of permission, it was obligatory on the part of the villagers to have the legal status of a VDS.

Whether formal or informal, the VDS is basically correlation of the social forces of Gurjar and Jat communities that determined the outline of the activities of the farmer. The Gurjar and the Jat communities have maximum members in the VDS, while the representation of the other social groups is marginal (Table 19.5). While one may have no reason to resent it, in view of the lower numerical strength of these social groups, there is no evidence to suggest, as the field survey reveals, that they are taken into confidence in the decision-making process. For example, the number of members increased from 16 to 19 for it was imperative for the VDS to induct women. Three women members were drawn from the numerically small social groups but were hardly given space for articulating their opinions in the decision-making process. However, it is also true that no decision went against them since the poor households like them belong to the Gurjar and Jat communities also.

Table 19.5: Composition of VDS

No. of	*Social Group*							
Members	*Gurjar*	*Jat*	*Rawat*	*Sadhu*	*Bawri*	*Bhambi*	*MMVS*	*Total*
Initially	7	6	1	1	—	1	—	16
Presently	7	7	—	2	1	1	1	19

Source: Field survey.

The second most important aspect of the VDS is that the community leaders selected VDS members. The village community never exhibited interest in the election and primarily depended upon mutual trust and social network. The composition of the VDS was readily accepted and gained legitimacy in the meetings that take place with the entire menfolk of the village community twice a year. Women's role in the decision-making process was as peripheral as that of other marginalised social groups. However, their contribution to the growth and conservation of grassland development, as we shall see later, can hardly be discounted.

Framing of Rules

Rules framed by the village community determined the external limits of an individual's rational conduct. They are essentially meant for regulating the behavioural pattern of every individual household for growth and conservation of the common pastureland. The rules that were framed at the initial stage were as follows:

1. Nobody was allowed to cut plants and collect tree loppings from a pastureland. Nor should fuel-wood be collected from the same.
2. Grass, fuel-wood and tree lopping would be sold through the open auction system as instituted by the VDS.
3. Meetings between the VDS and the village community would be held twice during *Holi* and *Deepawali* each year. Discussions related to the management of pastureland would be held in such meetings. The VDS would implement the decisions taken therein.
4. Anybody found violating the stipulated rules would have to pay a penalty of Rs. 500. However, one had to pay a penalty of Rs. 51 per animal in case it was found grazing in the pastureland.
5. No common road should be laid inside the pastureland.
6. Each household had to provide at least one labour unit for any development work, for instance, construction of a wall or anything else for pastureland. In case a household failed to do so, it had to pay Rs. 50 to the VDS as labour charge.
7. Grass that was produced in the pastureland would be distributed (free of cost if distribution of grass takes place) equally to all households.

8. Some portion of the common land would be utilised for the cultivation of green grass only. Cultivation would be taken up on a contract basis. Any individual household may receive such a contract depending upon whether the household meets the conditions as laid down by the VDS.

It may be noted that enforcement of these rules took place without discrimination. The system of penalty was accorded such importance that everybody in the community was cautious about the protection of pastureland. As a result, no free riding took place. Another important aspect was the built-in flexibility of the rules that seemed to have given considerable space to the village institution to amend rules if necessary, as a part of coping mechanism.

Changing Rules: Institutional Flexibility

The open auction system followed for selling grass to the villagers created discontent among many villagers. For, it encouraged inequity in accessing grass grown in the land. This led the village community to replace the open auction system by direct sale of grass when it matured. In this system, individual households interested in purchasing grass had to enter into a contract with the VDS. The contract identified the area within the protected pastureland from which grass might be collected and the price of grass to be paid to the VDS (as fixed by the VDS). The household had the responsibility of cutting the grass. This arrangement continued till 1994 without any interruption. However, during 1994, demand for the green grass increased steeply due to the rise in the buffalo population in the village. The improved conditions of the village pastureland under the new institutional arrangement provided considerable incentives to the villagers to increase the buffalo population for more income. In this new context, the earlier system of grass collection was found to be a mismatch, which was why "headload' system was introduced.

Headload System

Under this system, First, only one member of each household was allowed to cut as much green fodder as she/he could carry on her/his head. However, if the production of grass was found to be good, one was allowed to carry two headloads a day. Secondly, one had to carry the headload from the pastureland directly to the household through the route as specified by the VDS. Five persons who violated this rule were fined Rs. 51 each. Besides, anybody carrying a headload without making an entry in the register had to pay a penalty of Rs. 51. Thirdly, nobody was allowed to enter the pastureland after 12 noon. And fourthly, one had to pay charges per headload as fixed by the VDS. These charges were fixed from time to time on the basis of the yield of grass in the pastureland. Table 19.6 shows the varying rate per headload of grass between 1995 and 2001.

Table 19.6: Charges per Head-load of Grass

Year	*1995*	*1996*	*1997*	*1998*	*1999*	*2000*	*2001*
Rate (Rs.)	2.0	2.0	7.0	3.0	5.0	5.0	5.0
Reason	HY	HY	LY	HY	LY	LY	LY

Note: HY: higher yield; LY: lower yield.
Source: Field survey.

No rate, however, was fixed per headload after 2001. For the grass grew only in small quantities due to persistent droughts. At the time of the field survey, which has been completed recently, households were allowed to take their animals inside for grazing. The villagers told us that it was part of a coping mechanism followed by the village institution at the time of fodder crises.

Coping Strategy

Along with the development of pastureland, the VDS and the village community together decided to cultivate green fodder at least in some parts of the pastureland throughout the year. This decision was taken against the backdrop of the suffering animals had to undergo during the drought of 1987. One may consider this as an innovative coping strategy. It was innovative in the sense that it encouraged private initiative for fodder cultivation while management and supervision remained under the control of the village community or the VDS. This again exemplifies institutional flexibility of the village community of Chhota Saradhana. It shows how people can evolve their coping strategy by combining both private initiative and community ownership in the field of grassland management.

Immediately after the decision was finalised, a bore well was installed in the common protected land with the sole purpose of creating an extra facility to be used for watering the plants in the common land, producing fodder and providing drinking water to the villagers when it was required, especially in the event of drought. Besides, this may provide water for production of a fodder during the lean season, from January to June. Of course, in the drought period there is no lean or peak seasons and hence it would be operational throughout the year. In view of the limited capacity of the bore well installed, it was also decided that not more than 20 *bighas* of the protected pastureland should be brought under fodder cultivation.

The village community, along with the VDS, decided to cultivate a variety of grasses such as Lucerne, *Kasni* and *Oat* in the Rabi season and sorghum and *Chari* in the kharif season on this common pastureland which was brought under grass cultivation. Initially during 1989, the community brought only three bighas of land under grass cultivation on which they cultivated only *Kasni* crop on an experimental basis. The entire job of crop raising to harvesting was given on lease for a year to one of the villagers. The village community and the VDS together decided the terms of contract for the job . These were:

1. The entire cost of cultivation, including electricity, will have to be borne by the person who finally gets the contract.
2. Selling or auctioning of grass, if necessary, will have to be conducted by the same person.
3. Villagers should contact the same person directly for procuring grass through the system of exchange as suggested by the VDS.

It is important to note that the area under fodder cultivation was no longer fixed. Initially, it was three bighas of protected pastureland that was earmarked for fodder cultivation. Subsequently, around 1995-96, pressure on feed and fodder increased significantly due to a steady increase in the animal population, especially of buffalo. This led the VDS to extend the area under fodder cultivation to thirty bighas.

The village community took considerable pains in preparing the land that was rocky and unsuitable for cultivation of fodder. Cultivation continued until 1998 when the area began to face a severe water shortage due to the onset of drought. The VDS was then forced to reduce the area of the land for fodder cultivation to eight bighas. However, it did not stop fodder cultivation.

Distribution Mechanism

- While the entire land that is being brought under cultivation for green fodder (whether it is 30 or 8 bighas) is given on contract, the fodder produced in a quarter of the land is exclusively owned by the VDS and the grass produced in the remaining three quarters is meant for selling to the villagers.
- The terms of contract with the VDS are different from those of the contract made with the villagers for grass distribution. The grass produced in the quarter of the land which is meant for the VDS is not given or sold to the VDS by the person who has the contract. Instead, as per the contract, he pays some charges as fixed by the VDS in four instalments to the latter for the grass produced in this plot. He auctions the same to the villagers. It may be noted that the charges increased at different rates over the years. Besides, the contractor also is changed from time to time as decided by the VDS and the village community.
- The system that exists for sharing of grass by the village community is slightly tricky but appears to be innovative in a variety of ways. The entire land is demarcated in terms of what is locally called *Biswa* (a measure of unit of land, 20 biswa =1 bigha of land). Any household of the village can contract for grass from either one *biswa* or more depending upon his or her requirements. He has to pay some charges fixed per one-time grass collection from each *Biswa.* Earlier Rs. 30 was charged per cutting of grass in one *biswa.* The rate, however, increased later to Rs. 300 . The rate per cutting of grass in each *biswa* is jointly decided by the VDS and the contractor depending upon the input costs of both materials and wages.

The venture seems to be a profitable one even for the contractor. The net income (gross income less cost of inputs plus wage costs) that he earns per *Bigha* of land is currently estimated to be Rs. 9,335. The size of the net income per *Bigha* should not necessarily lead one to conclude that in all eight *Bighas* of land which is under cultivation of grass at present, the same amount can be earned. There are certain varieties of grasses such as "Oat" which gets exhausted after two cuttings or so. Besides, there is a good amount of variation between the grasses in terms of yield as reported by the contractor. In any case, this is a venture, which is relatively risk-free and the farmers have continuous demand for green fodder. This is an incentive that directly or indirectly encourages any individual farmer of the village to take the contract and provide grass to the villagers as and when they require. However, it is risk-free so long as there is no water scarcity. The bore well and continuous support received from the village community mean that there is no water scarcity. In addition, animals from other villages should not be allowed to move into this land and eat away what all is grown. Those who are motivated by earnings may find the management of grass production a little risky, especially during the drought period when animals are free to move inside.

The system as explained above shows how institutional renovation is sought for evolving coping strategies. The unique feature of this renovation is that the village institution never allows the market forces to determine the production and exchange of grass. It allows the same to the extent it is required for facilitating a smooth exchange to take place and remove the uncertainty regarding fodder availability to a certain extent.

Institutional Renovation or Failure?

Although institutional renovation has made a significant change in the livestock economy and grassland eco-system during the past one decade or so, the present state of management of the pastureland seems to be sending confusing signals. The common pastureland is now divided into six equal plots without internal fencing and is allocated to six groups of households of the village. The groups were formed through a lottery system designed by the villagers themselves. Each group has its own leader who, along with the members, will be responsible for the management and development of "its" plot of land. Only members of the group have the opportunity to harvest grass and fuelwood from the same. The group will have its own norms of management. One may consider this as another form of institutional renovation that may have serious ramifications on the sustainability of grassland in future. As the field survey reveals, the village community went for this option in order to cope with serious financial difficulties. The VDS was finding it difficult to maintain and properly protect the pastureland because the common village funds have been depleting continuously in the last three drought years.

During 1988-99, the investment made for the development and maintenance of pastureland was Rs. 9.21 lakh. While the share of the villagers and income earned from the pastureland was Rs.3.60 lakh (39 per cent of the investment), the balance was received from the external sources. The total earnings from the pastureland through the charges received for providing dry and green fodder and selling of fuel wood was Rs. 1.89 lakh during the same period.

While one understands the difficulties in maintaining pastureland due to lack of funds, the villagers are not convinced that there is a need to divide management of the land. The overriding importance given to what is called "group rationality" over "collective rationality" of the village community is likely to weaken the social capital. In such a situation, one may be apprehensive that institutional renovation may lose its direction that ensures equity and sustainable management of the pastureland.

GAINS FROM INSTITUTIONAL RENOVATION

One of the significant aspects of the change that has come about in the village due to revitalisation of degraded pastureland is that it has reduced uncertainty regarding fodder availability. This, in turn, has acted as an incentive to the farmers to expand the size of their livestock. The assured stock of fodder that the village community had never seen in their recent past has given, as the field survey reveals, enormous confidence in the way they have been managing the grassland resource base. But the question is whether the poor are able to gain equal access to this resource base and improve the status of their livestock. Besides, the improvement in the grassland ecosystem, which is central to institutional intervention, is a direct gain that needs to be accounted for.

Access to Resources

Several studies have indicated that the poor are deprived of institutional outcomes due to a lack of access to the improved resource base. It is again power relations that the traditional institutional arrangements nurture which do not allow the poor to gain equal access to the resource. However, in a village like Chhota Saradhana, as mentioned earlier, power relations in whichever form they exist could never turn institutional renovations in their favour and make accessibility to this resource base inequitable. Access of the poor to the common protected pastureland can be gauged on the basis of the extent to which they could meet their requirement from the same. There are four sources of fodder available to farmers. These are: (i) Common protected pastureland, (ii) Common open pastureland, (iii) Own land and (iv) Other private sources.

The collection of grass from different sources by farmers is shown in Table 19.7 and Figure 19.1. No payment is made for collecting grass from the open common pastureland, but it is made if collected from other sources. The difference between the prices

Table 19.7: Fodder: Types, Sources, and Quantities, 2000-01

(per household, in quintals)

Category of Land Holdings	*Common Protected Pastureland*	*Common Open Pastureland*	*Own Land*	*Purchased from Private Sources*	*Total*
Landless	20.0 (76.57)	1.00 (3.83)	2.20 (8.42)	2.92 (11.18)	26.12 (100.0)
Marginal/ Small	25.5 (65.70)	1.44 (3.71)	8.59 (22.13)	3.28 (8.45)	38.81 (100.0)
Medium/ Large	33.6 (55.73)	1.38 (2.29)	16.89 (28.09)	8.40 (13.94)	60.25 (100.0)
Average per household	26.2 (63.54)	1.32 (3.20)	9.21 (22.31)	4.52 (10.95)	41.28 (100.0)

Note: Figures in parentheses are percentages of quantity of grass collected from a specific source to the total quantity of grass collected.

Source: Field survey.

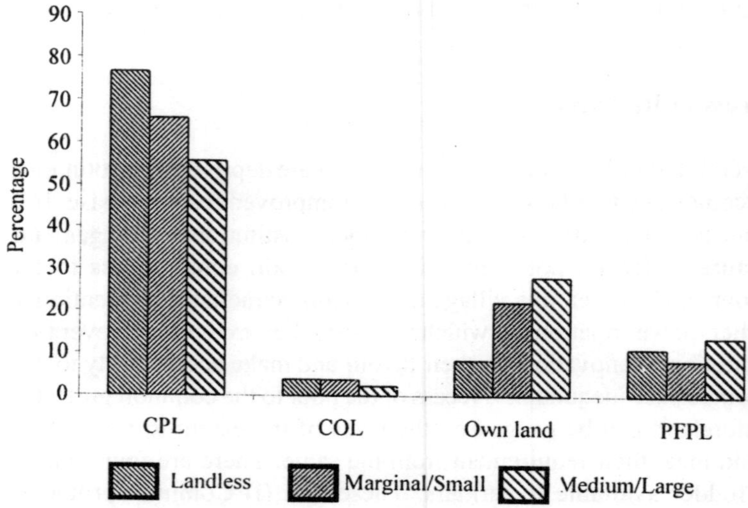

CPL = Common protected pastureland; COL = Common open pastureland; PFPL = Purchase from private land

Fig. 19.1: Collection of Grass from Common Pastureland and Other Sources

charged for grass\green fodder collected from the common, protected pastureland and the private land was substantially high: Rs. 25 per quintal in the case of the former and Rs. 100 per quintal in the case of latter. The landless and the marginal and small farmers gain more from the common protected pastureland than the other category of farmers (Table 19.7). Each landless household in the sample is estimated to have collected as much as 20 quintals of grass on an average during the year under consideration from the protected pastureland. It was around 77 per cent of their requirements. Although each sample household of the medium and large farmers collected the same from the same land to the tune of 34 quintals, it was around 56 per cent of their requirement. Grass/green fodder purchased from the private sources also includes some plots of the common, protected pastureland that are given on contract by the VDS to individual farmers of the village. It may be noted that the landless farmers lease in land from the medium and large farmers and also collect the grass grown naturally there. If all sample households are taken into consideration, on an average, about 63.5 per cent of the total requirement of grass per household is met by the common protected pastureland.

The dependence of the landless households of the village on the common protected pastureland for fuel-wood is no less. As it can be seen from Table 19.8 and Figure 19.2, 1.19 quintals of fuel-wood, or 52 per cent of the total requirement of fuel-wood of the landless

Table 19.8: Fuel wood: Sources and Quantities, 2000-01(per household, in quintals)

Category of Land Holdings	*Common Protected Pastureland*	*Common Open Pastureland*	*Own Land*	*Purchased from Private Sources*	*Total*
Landless	1.19 (52.0)	1.10 (48.0)	—	—	2.29 (100.0)
Marginal/ Small	1.38 (30.13)	2.47 (53.93)	0.73 (15.94)	—	4.58 (100.0)
Medium/ Large	—	1.62 (45.13)	1.97 (54.87)	—	3.59 (100.0)
Average per household	0.98 (25.9)	1.92 (50.8)	0.88 (23.3)	—	3.78 (100.0)

Note: Figures in parentheses are percentages of quantity of fuel-wood collected from a specific source to the total quantity of fuel-wood collected.
Source: Field survey

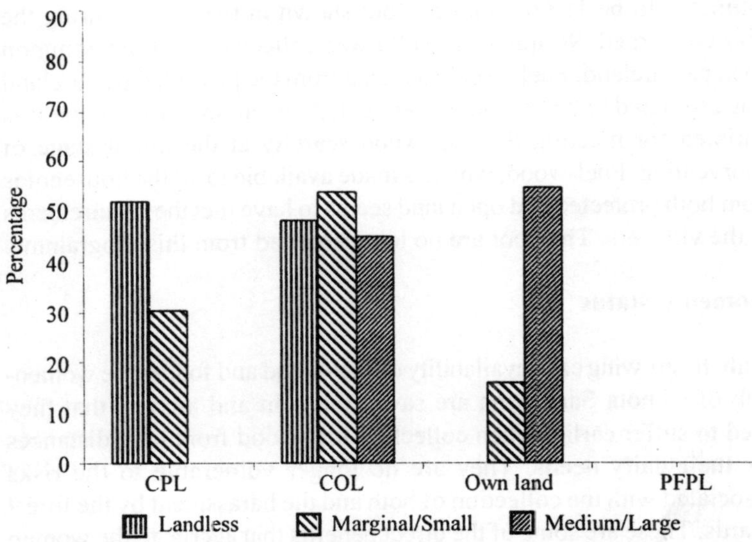

Fig. 19.2: Collection of Fuel-wood from Common Pastureland and Other Sources per household

households came from the common protected pastureland during the year under study. In the case of small and marginal farmers, it is 30 per cent. The medium and large farmers, however, largely depend on their own sources. As much as 55 per cent of the total requirement of fuel-wood of each sample household is met from own land and the rest from common open land. They do not appear to depend on the protected pastureland for fuel-wood. Tree have eaten the lopping made available from the protected pastureland is used as fuel-wood once the animals leaves. Dry plants available from the same protected pastureland are also used as fuel-wood. However, villagers have to pay for it.

It may be noted that the total requirement of both grass and green fodder of all the sample households together was estimated to be 2,064 quintals (not shown in the Table) during the year. The largest quantity, 1,311.50 quintals (63.54%) was collected from the common protected land alone. Only 66 quintals of grass (3.20%) were collected from the common open pastureland by all the sample households. However, the role of the common open pastureland in mitigating the fuel-wood crisis of the villagers is significant. Of the total fuel-wood requirement of the entire sample households together which was estimated to be 188.65 quintals (not shown in the Table) during the year concerned, 96 quintals (51%) was collected from the common open pastureland. Fuel-wood collected from the protected pastureland was estimated to be around 26 per cent. A plantation programme was initiated for meeting the fuel-wood scarcity at the initial stage of intervention. Fuel-wood, which is made available to all the households from both protected and open land seems to have met the requirements of the villagers. The poor are no less benefited from this programme.

Women's Status

With the growing easy availability of fuel-wood and fodder the women-folk of Chhota Saradhana are saved the pain and anxiety that they used to suffer earlier when collecting fuel-wood from long distances for their daily needs. They are no longer vulnerable to the risks associated with the collection of both and the harassment by the forest guards. These are some of the direct benefits that accrue to the women of all social groups in the village. However, one does not know how such benefits can be incorporated in the analysis of commensuration (O' Neill 2001; Espeland 2001).

Women now collect fuel-wood grown by the village community right in the vicinity of the village. Often, they take their camel-carts and collect both for three to four months and store it. This has made considerable difference to the lives of the women of the village in a few different ways. First, women now can allocate more time for productive household activities, having been completely freed from the drudgery. Secondly, they are more confident about positive institutional outcomes related to fuel-wood and fodder. This has enormously boosted their sense of ownership, although ironically, they are hardly taken into confidence in the decision-making process. Thirdly, and most importantly, girl children can now go to school instead of going to collect fuel-wood and fodder.

Improvement in Livestock

In order to gain an insight into the improvement in the status of livestock, especially of the poor, it is necessary for one to understand the nature and trend of expansion of their animal stock vis-à-vis that of relatively affluent farmers. The data of the sample households of this village were collected for three different years under three different conditions. The data for 1991 were collected from the MMVS to indicate the status of the stock position during the initial years of intervention. While the year 1997 was a normal year and the farmers had already reaped the benefits of management of their grazing land, the year 2002 was hit by the worst drought.

Two important aspects of the livestock position for all the landholdings of Chhota Saradhana may be noted from Table 9. First, landless households witnessed a considerable rise in the stock of their animals. During 1991, the initial year of intervention, not all sample households of the landless category had cows, buffaloes and goats. All of them reared sheep. However, the average stock of each type of animal rose steeply by 1997. It appears that each sample landless household had, on an average, two cows, three buffaloes, thirty sheep and five goats. The stocking rate of animals of the medium and large farmers also increased steadily during the same year. However, this may not be unusual in view of their landholdings and the capacity to rear animals.

Second, there was a sharp increase in the average stock of all animals of the landless households and medium and large farmers, while the stock of sheep and goat declined in the case of marginal and small farmers. Although there was a decline in all types of animals during 2002 for all households, the average stock of animals of the landless was not as bad as one expects it to be in drought conditions because many of these households had non–farm wage employment in the mines located adjacent to the village.

It may be difficult to establiṣh the corresponding impact of the improvement in the degraded pastureland on the stocking rates of animals of all varieties on the basis of the analysis of data of three time periods as given in Table 19.9. For, the stock of animals at a given point of time depends upon a variety of factors even under normal climatic conditions. As the field survey reveals, animals especially the small ruminants, are sold off at times in order to meet the financial needs and purchased when households are capable of doing so.

Table 19.9: Average Number of Animals across Landholdings

Category	*Year*	*Cow*	*Buffalo*	*Sheep*	*Goat*	*Bullock*
Landless	1991	0.42	0.92	12.50	0.25	—
	1997	1.75	2.75	29.75	4.92	0.33
	2002	0.75	1.25	16.08	4.83	0.25
Marginal/Small	1991	0.36	0.24	11.76	5.04	0.08
	1997	1.48	1.40	7.20	4.84	0.24
	2002	0.60	0.80	3.20	5.16	0.08
Medium/Large	1991	1.46	0.38	—	3.46	0.77
	1997	5.31	6.69	4.62	7.23	1.08
	2002	0.69	2.92	—	1.69	0.54

Source: Field survey.

But one must recognise that the stocking rate may be higher in a situation where pastureland is regularly protected. For the carrying capacity of the land may not decline as steeply as one expects in the absence of regular protection in adverse climatic conditions. The effect of adverse conditions on the grass production may be outweighed to a certain extent by way of increasing land productivity. This is what the community management of Chhota Saradhana village shows. The close correspondence between the carrying capacity and land productivity may confirm the sustained development as maintained by the traditional theory of rangeland development (Chopra and Kadekodi, 1999).

The exercise that is followed here does indicate a positive aspect of stocking of animals. Despite persistent droughts for the past three consecutive years, even the poor households are capable of retaining the stock of animals at a reasonable level. The perception of the households surveyed regarding the role of improved pastureland in improving the stocking rate of animals confirms this (Table 19.10).

Table 19.10: Improvement in the Status of Livestock: Response of the Households

Category	*Increase in the number of animals*	*Increase in the production of milk*
Landless	8 (67.8)	7 (58.0)
Small / Marginal	13 (57.0)	17 (68.0)
Medium / Large	8 (61.0)	12 (92.0)

Note: Figures in parentheses are percentages of the sample households of the respective category of land holdings.

As shown in Table 19.10, 68 per cent of the sample households of the landless category saw their direct benefit in the form of their increased ability to expand the size of their livestock due to the improvement of pastureland. In fact, medium and large farmers too benefited in the same way. But they perceived their gain more in the form of an increase in the yield rate of milk as expressed by 92 per cent of the sample households of this category of farmers.

Although the stocking rate especially of milch animals declined in a drought situation, it played a significant role in ensuring the nutritional security of the landless, marginal and small category of farmers. As given in Table 19.11, as much as 45 per cent of the milk produced in a drought year was retained for domestic consumption. The same poor farmers could retain only 31 per cent milk for domestic consumption five years ago when there was no drought. This seems to go against the popular perception that the poor tend to sell more milk under distress conditions. The retention of milk to almost half of what was produced during the drought year shows how it could ensure nutritional security of the poor households in the event of an insignificant agricultural production. Besides, the poor households retained more milk than did the medium and large farmers during the

Table 19.11: Average Production, Consumption and Sale of Milk per Household across Different Landholdings per Year

(in quintals)

Category	*2001-02*			*5 years ago*		
	Production	*Consumption*	*Sale*	*Production*	*Consumption*	*Sale*
Landless	12.76 (100.0)	5.70 (44.67)	7.06 (55.33)	27.14 (100.0)	8.33 (30.69)	18.81 (69.31)
Small/Marginal	9.01 (100.0)	4.07 (45.17)	4.94 (54.83)	21.95 (100.0)	6.85 (31.21)	15.10 (68.79)
Medium/Large	21.48 (100.0)	7.85 (36.55)	13.63 (63.45)	56.26 (100.0)	13.98 (24.85)	42.28 (75.15)
Average per Household	13.15 (100.0)	5.45 (41.42)	7.71 (58.60)	32.12 (100.0)	9.06 (28.21)	23.06 (71.79)

Note: Milk of cows, buffaloes and goats is taken into consideration.

drought year (Table 19.11). Thus the pastureland which is developed, protected and maintained by the village community makes a definite contribution in reducing uncertainty regarding fodder availability especially of the poor who, in turn, are capable of ensuring the nutritional security of the household. Although the sale of milk fetches more income to all households as compared to other sources of income from livestock, income from the sale of manure, the sale of animals themselves, etc., cannot be ignored (Table 19.12). One has to recognise the importance of these sources of income from livestock too, especially during the drought years.

Table 19.12: Average Gross Household Income from Livestock, 2001-02 (in Rs.)

Category	*Milk*	*Wool*	*Manure*	*Animal Sale*	*Gross Income*
Landless	12853 (84.80)	250 (1.65)	1213 (8.00)	842 (5.55)	15158 (100.00)
Marginal/Small	9211 (75.12)	89 (0.72)	1318 (10.75)	1644 (13.41)	12262 (100.00)
Medium/Large	21070 (73.11)	115 (0.40)	4058 (14.08)	3577 (12.41)	28820 (100.00)
Average per household	13169 (76.29)	134 (0.78)	2005 (11.62)	1954 (11.32)	17262 (100.00)

Note: Figures in parenthesis are percentages of gross income from livestock.

If the gross income from livestock is compared with the gross income from other sources such as agriculture and non-farm, livestock appears to have contributed 38 per cent of the gross income of the landless households, and 29 per cent for the small and marginal farmers (Table 19.13). It may be noted that the gross income from agriculture is estimated for 2001-2002, which was one of the drought years. Field survey reveals that both agricultural production and herd size of the livestock witness a considerable rise in normal years. Here, agricultural income includes both agricultural production and wage income of those who work as agricultural labour. Income earned by the sample households through non-farm activities is mainly wage income from mining. Earnings from business, manufacturing and service sectors are insignificant.

Table 19.13: Source-wise Average Household Income, 2001-02

(in Rs.)

Category	*Agriculture*	*Livestock*	*Non-Farm*	*Total*
Landless	4940 (12.38)	15158 (37.99)	19800 (49.63)	39898 (100.00)
Marginal/Small	6815 (16.08)	12262 (28.92)	23316 (55.00)	42393 (100.00)
Medium/Large	23228 (28.83)	28820 (35.77)	28515 (35.39)	80563 (100.00)
Average per household	10633 (20.56)	17262 (33.38)	23824 (46.06)	51719 (100.00)

Note: Figures in parenthesis are percentages of gross income from all sources.
Source: Field survey.

Improving Ecosystem

The regular protection and maintenance of the pastureland seem to have greatly contributed to the improvement of the grassland ecosystem of Chhota Saradhana. This is discernible in the changes that have taken place in the physico-chemical and biological characteristics of the soil.

One of the noticeable changes that have taken place in the pastureland is that the vegetative cover in it has created a friendly environment conducive to the growth of various species of plants.

This achievement is due to an increase in the soil moisture content and humic substances through litter fall and, of course, restricted cutting of grass approximately four inches above the ground. The very survival of vegetation in the same area and grass production despite no rain for the past three years explains the enhanced resilience that the grassland ecosystem has achieved due to institutional intervention (Hollings, 1983; Hollings and Meffe, 1999). This, however, is completely missing in the unprotected grazing land.

Along with the regulatory pattern of use of grassland, one may take note of the conservation steps taken to avoid run-off and soil erosion. In the unprotected land no such steps are taken which is why neither the soil is conserved nor is moisture retained. Soil is gravelly and stony while it is yellowish-red and sandy loam in the protected land. All this makes considerable difference in the nutritional content of the soil that has increased consequent to the presence of biomass content in the soil. The presence of millipedes, centipedes and insect species shows a favourable microenvironment in the protected land. The unprotected land, however, did not undergo such changes. A symbiotic relationship between soil quality and vegetation cover seems to have been established. For, grass provides an adequate canopy against the action of raindrops. It obstructs easy flow of water through adventitious roots and binds soil (Hazra, 1995). As a result, there is no indication of soil nutrients and humus declining nor is there any loss of soil due to wind and water runoff. Such a relationship assumes great importance in the management of dry land ecosystem (Dasgupta, 2001).

The second most important aspect of improvement in the ecosystem is the growth of the native plant and grass species. Some of the grass species such as *Cyanodon barbasi, C. dactylon, Cenchrus ciliaris, C. setigerus,* and *Lasirus sindicus* are grown in the pastureland and are observed in patches in association with the perennial tree species. The common plant species grown in the protected land are *Acacia senegal, A. nilotica, A. leucaphaloe, Prosopis cineraria, Commiphora wightii, Dalbergia sissoo, Salvadora persica, S.oleoides, Tecomella undulata, Ailanthus excelsa, Anogerissus pendula, Cordia gharaf, Euphorbia caducifolia, Calotropis procera, Zizyphus mauritiana* and *Z. nummularia*. Floral diversity to such an extent has enhanced the capacity of the ecosystem to expand its resilience.

In the unprotected land, plants such as *Aristida adscensionsis* are observed to be predominant. It is an indicator of overgrazing and erosion. As trees surround the protected pastureland, adverse effects of the particulate matter from mining are minimised. However, this is not so with the unprotected land due to the absence of any vegetative cover.

The improvement in the ecosystem can further be attributed to the silvi-pastoral development, which has been opted for as a means of grassland development. For, silvi-pastoral development improves the natural variation through combining good grass, legumes and a variety of tree species. This enhances the value of the protected vis-à-vis unprotected grassland (Hazra and Singh, 1992; Hazra *et al.,* 1994; Yadava and Rajora, 1995). Trees have supported growth of small plant species (herbs, grass, etc.) by way of providing shade to the latter that helped in reducing evapo-transpiration. Water saved is captured by small plants and naturally utilised for their growth. Although the ecosystem is revived in the protected land, it is not lush green, but it does exhibit accumulation of strength for survival even in the event of three consecutive drought years. It has happened due to the circulation of natural cycles in the protected land that seems to have witnessed microbial reactions (bio-geochemical cycles such as N, P and S cycles.) It is needless to mention that bio-geochemical cycles perform better owing to the presence of organic content and moisture in soil.

The improved status of the grassland ecosystem of Chhota Saradhana is maintained at a low level of regenerative capacity at present. However, the regenerative capacity of the same is sure to witness definite improvement under favourable climatic conditions due to the presence of bio-geochemical cycles. Rejuvenation of the regenerative capacity of the ecosystem of the unprotected land may be difficult to achieve as such cycles and vegetative covers are absent there.

CONCLUSION

Local institutions have a potential to offer development approach in the management of common property resources even in the heterogeneous social and economic conditions if they are renovated.

In such situations, the institutional outcomes are less likely to be concentrated in the hands of the rich. The present case study reveals that the poor and the disadvantaged such as women can have an equal access to the improved resource endowment and share the institutional outcome equally. This happens if the disadvantaged sections of the people across all the social groups polarise even when all including the rich and the poor are not equally vulnerable to natural calamity such as a drought. Of course, one has to recognise the role of external intervention which must not perpetuate. The village community must not develop the dependency syndrome. Chhota Saradhana is no longer in such a syndrome. Furthermore, the built-in flexibility of the institutions which has given space for combining both traditional and modern scientific knowledge for the revival of the regenerative capacity of the grassland ecosystem should be considered as an institutional achievement. The division of the pastureland into different plots allocated to different groups of households who are inclined to follow different norms of management of the land may not eventually reduce the significance of institutional approach. While asserting against the possible backlash on the collective ideology of the community due to such a division, a woman from the scheduled caste community said, "*We are all benefiting from our protected pastureland for the last 10 years. This land has given incredible strength to the growing unity of the village community. We will never allow it to disintegrate.*" This strongly reflects the overriding importance given to the institutional choice.

REFERENCES

Ballabh, Vishwa, and Balooni, Kulbhusan (2002): "Why Local Resources Management Institution Decline? A Comparative Analysis of *Van* (forest) Panchayats and Forest Protection Committees in India", *World Development* 30(12).

Baland, J.M., and Platteau, J.P. (1996): *Halting Degradation of Natural Resources: Is there a Role for Rural Community?* Oxford: Clarendon Press and FAO.

Bardhan, P. (1999): "Rational Fools and Cooperation in a Poor Hydraulic Economy". In Basu, K.; Patnaik, P.; and Suzumum, K. (eds.) *Choice, Welfare and Development: A Festsch rift in Honour of A. K. Sen,* Oxford.

Chopra, K. (2002): "Social Capital and Development Process: Role of Formal and Informal Institutions". *Economic and Political Weekly* (July 13).

Chopra, K., and Kadekodi, G.K. (1999): *Operationalising Sustainable Development, Economic-Ecological Modelling for Developing Countries.* New Delhi: Sage Publications.

Dasgupta, Partha (2001): "Poverty and Environmental Resource Base". In Ulganathan, Sankar. (ed.) *Environmental Economics.* New Delhi: Oxford University Press.

Espeland, W.N. (2001): "Value Matters". *Economic and Political Weekly* (May 26).

Government of Rajasthan (2000): "Statistical Abstract". Directorate of Economics and Statistics, Jaipur.

Harris, John (2001): *Depoliticizing Development: The World Bank and Social Capital.* New Delhi: Leftward Books.

Hazra, C.R. (1995): "Soil and Water Conservation Aspects of Range Grasses and Legumes". All India Coordinated Research Project on Forage Crops, Indian Grassland and Fodder Research Institute, Jhansi.

Hazra, C.R., and Singh, D.P. (1992): "A Silvi-pastoral Approach for Revegetation of Barren Hills and Wastelands: An Experience at Gaharawa Watershed in Bundelkhand. *Journal of Soil Water Conservation* 36(3&4): 105-44.

Hazra, C.R.; Singh, D.P.; and Kaul, R.N. (1994): *Greening of Common Lands in Jhansi through Village Resource Development: A Case study.* National Afforestation and Eco-Development Board, New Delhi.

Holling, C.S. (1983): "Resilience and Stability of Ecological Systems". *Annual Review of Ecological Systems* (4).

Holling and Meffe (1999): "Command and Control and the Pathology of Natural Resource Management". In Dodson, Stanley, I. *et al.* (eds.) *Reading in Ecology.* Oxford University Press.

Leach, Melissa; Robins, Merns; and Scoones, Ian (1997): "Community-based Sustainable Development: Consensus or Conflict? *IDS Bulletin* 28 (4): October.

Mohapatra, B.N. (2001): "Social Connectedness and Fragility of Social Capital: View from an Orissa Village" *Economics and Political Weekly* (February 24).

O' Neill, John (2001): "Market and the Environment: The Solution is the Problem". *Economic and Political Weekly* (May 26).

Veblen, T. (1919): "Why is Economics Not an Evolutionary Science". In T. Veblen, *The Place of Science in Modern Civilisation and Other Essays,* New York: Russel and Russel. [from Samuel, J.W. 1990. "Institutional Economics and the Theory of Cognition" *Cambridge Journal of Economics*].

Wade, R. (1988): *Village Republics: Economic Conditions for Collective Action in South India.* Cambridge: Cambridge University Press.

Warren, Mark, R.; Thompson, P.J.; and Saegert, Susan (2001): "The Role of Social Capital in Combating Poverty". In Saegert Susan; Thompson, J. P.; and Warren, Mark R. (eds.) *Social Capital and Poor Communities* New York: Russel Sage Foundation.

Yadava, M.S., and Rajora M.P. (1995): "Pasture Development Research in Western Arid Region". In Hazra, C.R., and Misri, Bimal. (eds.) *New Vistas in Forage Production,* Jhansi: Indian Grassland and Fodder Research Institute.

20

Role of Multiple Stakeholders for Sustainable Management of Water Resources

The Case of an Urban Wetland of Madhya Pradesh[1]

MADHU VERMA, NISHITA BAKSHI and RAMESH P.K. NAIR

Wetlands and Urban Ecosystems

Wetlands are ubiquitous and can be found in all the regions and climates. The term "Wetland" first came in use in the 1970s and was soon generally accepted. Wetlands may be defined as *habitats where the water table is situated at or near the ground surface, bearing vegetation adapted to more or less continuous waterlogging.* Wetlands form a buffer between waterways and commercial, residential and agricultural lands. They are complex natural processes and contribute to the overall order and stability of the ecosystem. The Ramsar Convention defines wetlands as *areas of marsh, fen, peatland, or water whether natural or artificial, permanent or temporary, with water that is static or flowing, fresh, brackish or salty, including areas of marine water, depth of which at low tide does not exceed six metres* and may include *riparian and coastal zones adjacent to the wetlands or islands or bodies of marine water deeper than six metres at low tide lying within* (IUCN 1971).

They are very important ecosystems performing essential and highly valuable life-supporting functions for human societies (Odum, 1989). Monetary valuation of wetlands has usually concentrated on specific environmental services such as water supply, flood prevention, and pollution reduction. In addition, their contribution towards fish and wildlife production, provision of recreation, and enhancing the aesthetics of the landscape is also considered (Hammack and Brown 1974; Lynn *et al.* 1981; Faber 1987). Less frequently, attempts have been made to estimate the life support value of entire wetland ecosystems which are generally required to sustain each environmental service (Odum 1984; Costanza *et al.* 1989).

Wetlands occupy an estimated 6 per cent of the world's land surface (Mitch and Gosselink 1993). Tropical wetlands, in particular, are on the whole poorly understood and yet collectively they represent some of the most important areas of the world's wetlands. In India Wetlands occupy about four million hectares of land. A survey by the Ministry of Environment and Forests in 1990 estimated that about 1.5 million ha. are natural wetlands like tanks, and reservoirs occupy 2.6 million hectares. According to the Forest Survey of India, mangroves now cover an additional 453,300 hectares (Sustainable Wetlands, EG-2, Cap 21). However, according to the *Directory of Asian Wetlands*, wetlands in India occupy roughly 58.2 million hectares. Whereas as many as 93 wetlands meet the criteria under the Ramsar Convention, only 8 wetlands are declared as Ramsar sites. Very recently (in December, 2002), 11 more sites have been declared as wetlands of international importance taking the number to 19 covering 648,507 hectares. Many of the sites qualify on hydrological grounds, many for their birds and some for their sea turtles, others for their support for fisheries, and a few are considered sacred in one way or the other (www.ramsar.org).

Urban wetlands are places within the city limits where water and soil mingle. They range from "remnants" of ponds or creeks that once existed on sites where buildings now stand, to drainage ditches resulting from inadequately planned or engineered development. Urban wetlands have been utilised as natural cleansing agents to mitigate the additional pollutant levels introduced within the urban landscape. Like many other common property resources, wetlands are up for grabs. Everyone claims a stake in their use, but only a few are willing to pay for their use. These urban wetlands have often been used as open access resources (as easily accessible source of various resources) and as "wastelands"—as most convenient and costless dumpsites. They absorb large amounts of point source pollutants like sewage, solid waste and industrial waste and also those "runaway" pollutants from their source like agricultural fields, hospitals and open garbage dumps in rainwater. The typical runoff from cities carries iron, lead, copper and other heavy metals as well as toxins, phosphorous, nitrogen, hydrocarbons and acids. Such wetlands are found all over the country, both natural and man-made, and have been the lifeline of most cities in India. They were preserved and looked after by the people as their main source of water supply for drinking and irrigation. Over the years, they have gradually depleted, leading to a number of problems in urban areas such as flooding, water scarcity and waterlogging (environvircle.com 2002). The very existence of wetlands, which are one of the best ways to provide open spaces and much-needed relief in the concrete jungles that our urban areas have become, is in danger. While we have been exploiting our wetlands, we have not been making any investment for their maintenance and restoration.

Surprisingly, many wetlands in India are in urban areas. In the old days the towns and villages away from the rivers and sea had lakes, ponds, or water streams without which survival was difficult. Even today several important cities are located on the lakes like Bhopal on the Bhoj Lake, Srinagar on the Dal Lake, Hyderabad on the Hussain Sagar Lake, and Thane on the Masunda Lake. Under the Indian Constitution municipalities are mandated to look after the lakes within their jurisdiction. But these wetlands are mostly neglected; they become the first target of any urban development plans. Our short-sightedness has allowed them to be filled up and encroached upon for the construction of housing colonies, bus stops, and even industries. The human intervention has played havoc with the natural rainwater drainages of these towns, which are often reduced to cesspools in monsoons (Sustainable Wetlands, EG-2, Cap 21).

Need for Sustainable Management of Wetlands in India

Wetlands are generally highly productive ecosystems providing many important benefits. These benefits have been variously described as "goods and services", "wetland functions" (for instance, groundwater recharge and flood control), "uses of wetland", as their "products" (for instance, a site for wood collection or a research site), or "attributes of the wetland" (an aesthetic component of the landscape or its religious significance). In order to successfully, utilise the benefits provided by wetlands, it is important to identify and assess the benefits that a particular wetland provides. These ecosystems through their numerous functions provide substantial benefits to society. However, despite their important role in maintaining the ecology and economy of the regions, almost all wetlands in India are endangered by the lack of appreciation of their role. A few of the country's wetlands, which have a great deal of biological wealth, are protected under the Wildlife Protection Act, 1972, whereas others, which may not be as biologically rich, do not have the same protection, and are an easy target of developers. Considered wastelands, wetlands are the obvious choice when land is needed for development. More often than not, the benefits wetlands offer are not recognised or are undervalued as they fall outside the ambit of the market economy (Sustainable Wetlands, EG-2, Cap 21). *People have well understood the uses of wetlands but not their use values.* There has not been much effort in the past to assign the use value or a price tag to the various extractive and non-extractive uses of wetlands so that they can be sustainably managed. People in the urban areas must learn to live in harmony with nature in their own habitat. The wetlands, the green belts and the flora and fauna of these areas have to be preserved for the urban areas to survive and remain healthy.

Bhoj Wetland: Location, Stakeholders, Uses, Threats

The Bhoj wetland, located in the heart of the Bhopal city, is an example of the degradation of wetlands ecosystem on account of excessive use by the fast-increasing urban population. The wetland has multiple stakeholders.

The Bhoj wetland, a lacustrine wetland, comprises two lakes, the Upper and the Lower. The Ministry of Environment and Forests (MoEF) of the Government of India declared the Bhoj Wetland as a Wetland of National Importance in 1988. It is one of the sixteen wetlands in the country that have so far been identified for conservation and management.

The Bhopal lakes are very famous and a number of verses have immortalised them. One of the most quoted ones is as follows:

Tal to Bhopal tal aur sab talaiya
Rani to Kamlapati aur sab ranaiya
Garh to Chittaurgarh aur sab garhaiya
Raja to Ramachandra aur sab rajaiya.

(If there is a lake, it is the Bhopal tal, and all others are but small ponds / If there is a queen she is Kamalapati and all others are minor queens / If there is a fort it is Chittaurgarh, all the rest are fortresses / If there is a king, he is Ramachandra, all others are petty chiefs.")

The Upper Lake is the much diminished remains of the large lake constructed by Raja Bhoj in the 11th century. The seasonal river Kolans, originating from Sehore (about 48 km. from Bhopal), and several small feeder streams on the western side of the lake form the source. It has a catchment area of 361 km^2 and the water spread area of 31 km^2. The Lower Lake, also known as Chotta Talab or Small Lake, is situated towards the east end of the Upper Lake and is almost fully surrounded by built-up areas. It has a small catchment area of 9.60 km^2 and the water spread area of 1.29 km^2. The Lower Lake receives its inflows in the form of seepage from the Upper Lake in addition to the drainage coming from eight *nallahs* or drains. A constant water level is maintained by a regular outflow through a waste weir at Pul-Pukhta into Patra Nallah.

The wetland (mainly the Upper Lake) originated as a man-made lake in the 11th century primarily to supply drinking water to the city's population. But over the years it has acquired the features of a wetland and has begun to perform other functions for a variety of users. Numerous benefits have been extracted from it, but little attention has been paid to its maintenance.

These multifarious benefits are either under-priced or not priced at all since various environmental values are not considered in the existing management strategy of the wetland. In the light of the above, the study, undertaken by the Indian Institute of Forest Management, has attempted to value various wetland benefits/resources for an appropriate allocation of wetland use so as to help the planners and policy makers to draw up a socially acceptable, environmentally sound and economically feasible strategy for wetland management.

Bhopal as a city has been growing rapidly especially in the past few decades. There has been heavy migration into the city from the other parts of the country; migrants came to work in the Bharat Heavy Electricals Limited, a large public sector unit in Bhopal. To provide for the needs of this workforce, several businesses moved in. Thus the city has been constantly growing in size. The population changes in the city in the last hundred years are given in Table 20.1.

Table 20.1: Changes in Population of Bhopal

Year	*Population*	*Change in population*	*Percent growth*
1901	77023	—	—
1911	56204	-22819	-27.04
1921	45094	-11110	-10.77
1931	61037	+15943	+35.35
1941	75228	+14191	+23.25
1951	102333	+27105	+36.04
1961	185374	+83041	+81.17
1971	298022	+112648	+60.77
1981	672329	+374307	+125.60
1991	1063662	+391333	+58.21
2001*	1500000	+436338	+41.02

* As projected
Source: Census Report 1991

As per the demands of an increasing population, there have also been significant changes in the landuse patterns of the city. The city has been growing as represented in the maps in Figure 20.1.

The salient features of the Upper and Lower Lakes of Bhopal are presented in Table 20.2.

The Catchment Area: A Socio-economic Profile

There are 8,259 huts and houses in the catchment area of the Upper Lake. Its total population is 44,166; 67 per cent of the population use the open land as lavatory. Everyday 2,000 persons use the lake waters for bathing, washing clothes and cleaning vehicles with soap and detergent which directly enter the lake waters. There are roughly 15,000 domestic animals such as buffaloes, cows, oxen, pigs and goats in the catchment area. Agriculture uses up 2,485 ha. of land and another

692 ha. are used as pastureland for grazing animals. The farmers usually grow two crops a year of wheat, rice, sorghum, maize, pulses, gram, vegetables, etc., using fertilisers such as urea, compost and Growmore. A few farmers also use herbicides and pesticides. Most of the agricultural residues find their way into the Upper Lake as run-off (Environmental Status Report of Upper Lake, Bhoj Wetland, Bhopal).

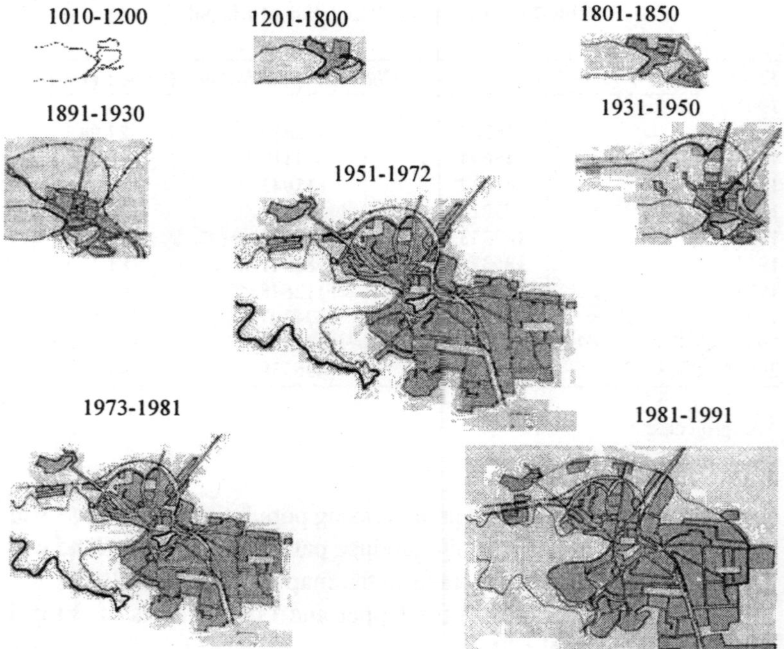

Habitation area in shown in gray
Partial boundary of the lake is shown in black in the west of the city.

Fig. 20.1: Maps of the Bhopal City Since the Formation of the Upper Lake

Uses of the Bhoj Wetland

Drinking Water

Nearly half of the city's drinking water supply comes from the Upper Lake, and this is the most important use of the wetland as far as the welfare of the citizens is concerned.

Employment

The Bhoj Wetland provides employment to various communities like the fishermen, washermen, boatmen and vendors. Approximately 300 families are engaged in fishing and *trapa* cultivation, while 100 washermen also make their living from the wetland. There are 50 boatmen whose livelihood depends on the Bhoj Wetland.

Table 20.2: Salient Features of the Upper and Lower Lakes of Bhopal

Sl. No.	*Item*	*Upper Lake*	*Lower Lake*
1	Constructed in	11th century	Late 18th century
2.	Type of Dam	Earthen dam	Earthen dam
3.	Location: Longitude Latitude	77°18' ~ 77°24' 23°13'~ 23°16'	77°24' ~ 77°26' 23°14'30" ~ 23°15'30"
4.	Catchments area: km² (sq. miles)	361 (141)	9.6 sq. miles
5.	Submergence area at FTL/water spread area km² (sq. miles)	30.72 (13.9)	1.29 sq. miles
6.	Maximum water level RL m (ft)	508.65 (1666.80)	
7.	Dead storage level RL m (ft)	503.53 (1652.00)	499.88 ft.
8.	Storage capacity 10^6 m³ (mft³)	101.6 (3588)	8 (282.5)
9.	Deepest bed level RL m (ft)	499.26 (1638.00)	
10.	Maximum depth m (ft)	11.7 (38.4)	9.4 ft.
11.	Mean depth m (ft)	6.0 (19.7)	
12.	Total length of weir m (ft)	102.1 (335)	
13.	Crest level of spillway RL m (ft)	504.38 (1654.80)	
14.	Designed flood discharge m3/sec	2208	
15.	Moderate flood discharge m3/sec	538.02	
16.	Sewage water inflow m3/day (MGD)	33080 (7.3)	
17.	Sources of water	Rain water	Seepage from Upper Lake, sewage
18.	Main use of water	Potable water	Washing clothes, recreation

Source: SAPROF Report 1994
FTL: Full Tank Level, MGD: Million Gallons per Day, ft: Feet, m³: Cubic Meter, km²: Square Kilometer

Micro-climate Stability

The micro-climate of Bhopal is quite moderate compared to that of the surrounding areas. The city should actually have an extreme type of climate according to its geographical location, but the proximity of the wetland has a moderating effect on the temperature. A cool land breeze blows in the evenings making even the summer evenings enjoyable. The moderating effects are also exerted by other factors such as the vegetative cover.

Recreation

The Bhoj Wetland provides ample recreational opportunities to the people of Bhopal. There are parks and fountains as well as boating facilities with paddle and row boats.

Stakeholders of Wetland Uses

The location of the wetland in the heart of the city makes it accessible to many users who are well aware of its various uses but not its use-values. A list of the stakeholders and their stake in the wetland are given in the following box.

List of Stakeholders in the Bhoj Wetland

City population: Drinking water and recreation
Lake front property owners: Aesthetic beauty
Washermen: Washing clothes in the lake
Fishermen: Fishing activities
Trapa cultivators: Cultivating trapa
Water supply agencies: Water purification and distribution
Bhopal Municipal Corporation: Management of Lake
DoHE*, Government of Madhya Pradesh: Decision making process
MPTDC: Tourism development in the lake
Vendors: Secondary benefits
Photographers, bird watchers, students, researchers
Funding agencies like JBIC, the state government
International and local organisations (Ramsar Bureau, Worldwide Fund for Nature): Database maintenance and research
*Department of Housing and Environment

Threats to the Wetland

The various benefits extracted by the multiple users of the Bhoj Wetland impose tremendous burden on the lake's ecosystem: the lake faces major threats from siltation, solid waste pollutants, sewerage from the adjoining housing colonies and catchments areas, release of detergents due to washing of clothes by the washermen community, and sedimentation by dead plants due to *trapa* cultivation, encroachment, increasing population, flow of medical waste and agricultural waste (resulting in eutrophication leading to excessive resulting weed growth), immersion of idols and *tajia* with chemical paints, and boating. All these damage the health of the wetland ecosystem; they have affected the wetland both quantitatively and qualitatively.

The quantity of water available for specific uses declines with the larger amounts of pollutants flowing into the water body. The quality of water also deteriorates and as a result its economic value goes down and water use may successively shift from drinking to bathing, for the livestock, for agriculture, and for industry. This is what has happened in the case of the Upper and Lower Lakes where the water quality levels have been reduced to Class C and E respectively. The ultimate goal of the restoration project is to bring the water quality of the Upper Lake to the designated Class A and that of the Lower Lake to the designated Class D according to the primary water quality criteria exhibited in Table 20.3.

Table 20.3: Primary Water Quality Criteria

Primary Water Quality Criteria					
Criterion	*Class A*	*Class B*	*Class C*	*Class D*	*Class E*
Dissolved oxygen (mg/l) minimum	6	5	4	4	
BOD (mg/l) maximum	2	3	3		
Total Coliform count (MPN/100 ml.) maximum	50	500	5,000		
PH	6.5-8.5	6.5-8.5	6-9	6.5-8.5	6.5-8.5
Free ammonia (mg/l) maximum				1.2	
Conductivity (micro mho/cm) maximum					2,250
Sodium absorption ratio maximum					26
Boron (mg/l) maximum					2

BOD: Biochemical oxygen demand; pH: a measure of the acidity of alkalinity of water, MPN: Most probable number, Mho: unit of conductivity.
Class A: Drinking water source without conventional treatment
Class B: Water for outdoor bathing
Class C: Drinking water with conventional treatment
Class D: Water for wildlife and fisheries
Class E: Water for recreation and aesthetics, irrigation, and industrial cooling

Source: Dying Wisdom (CSE Report) 1997

About 15 pollution control and environmental conservation measures have been taken up by the local organisations managing the Bhoj Wetland with the JBIC-supported project. The measures are: Desilting and Dredging of Lakes, Deepening and Widening of the Bhadbhada Spill Channel, Restoration of Takia Island, Afforestation and Creation of Buffer Zones, Construction Of Check Dams, Silt traps, Toe Walls and Cascading for Controlling Silt Entry, Construction of Garland Drains, Prevention of Sewage Pollution, Retghat–Lalghati Link Road, Solid Waste Management, Prevention of Pollution from Dhobi Ghat, De-weeding, Monitoring of Water, Installation of Floating Fountains, Biological Control through Aquaculture, Public Participation and Environmental Awareness Building.

Stakeholders' Perceptions for Conservation of Bhoj Wetland

Approach

The study first identified various stakeholders through a pilot survey following which a stakeholders' workshop was conducted. First the management issues of the Bhoj Wetland were identified which was followed by the development of an ecosystem model using the water quality parameters. The results of the modelling exercise were used to administer the valuation techniques. The workshop used the "Sticky Cloth and Paper" method to facilitate the discussion and list and prioritise the issues for management of the wetland. Numerous stakeholders were identified: population of Bhopal city, washermen, boatmen, water chestnut cultivators, fishermen, non-governmental organisations, various line departments, corporators of different municipal wards, etc. It was recommended that three major issues—sewage and waste disposal, fishing and washing activities, and recreational activities—should be addressed for sustainable management of the wetland (Annexure I). Having listed the stakeholders, various threats and management issues, it became imperative to generate quantitative information on the status of the ecological functions and the economic benefits of the wetland, which could serve as a powerful tool to influence decision-making.

For achieving the same, stakeholders' participation was sought at multiple levels. To further probe the issues, a detailed conceptual model with causes, impact and feedback control strategy (restoration

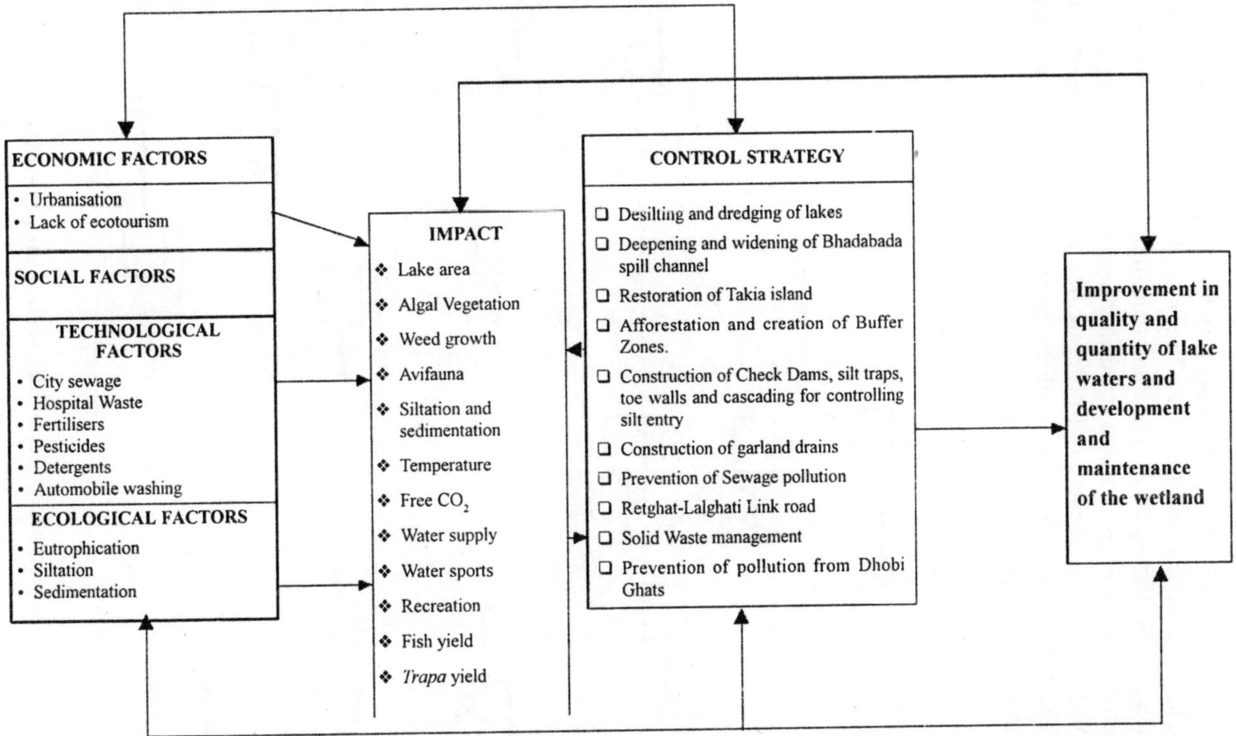

Fig. 20.2: Conceptual Model Deoicting Causes, Imapct and Feedback Control Strategy for Bhoj Wetland Developed for Bhoj Wetland using Oakerson's Basic Interaction Model for Common Property Resource Management

and pollution prevention activities) was developed using Oakerson's Basic Interaction Model for Common Property Resources Management (Figure 20.2). The model attempts to assess the impact of economic, ecological, social and technological factors on the lake's ecosystem and suggests control strategies through the feedback mechanism. Thus it follows a holistic approach for the sustainable management of the Bhoj Wetland.

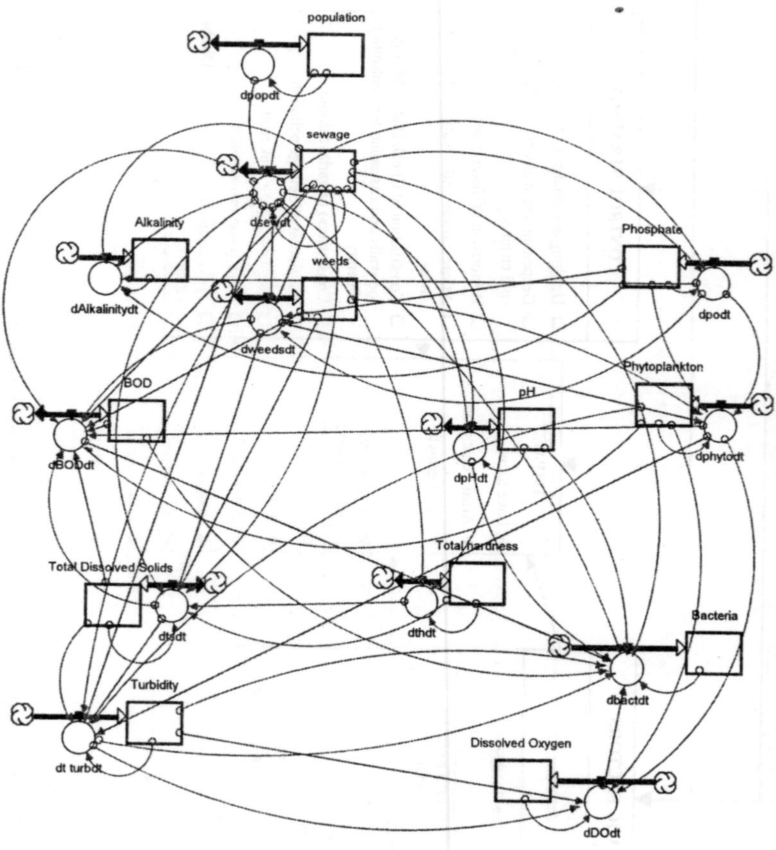

Fig. 20.3: Ecosystem Model for Bhoj Watland Using Water Quality

Due to the lack of other data, only an ecosystem model was developed for the wetland using water quality parameters, for instance, the sewage outflow and its subsequent impact on weeds was observed. The other water quality-related parameters were: Dissolved Oxygen (DO), Biochemical Oxygen Demand (BOD), pH, Total Hardness, Total Alkalinity, Phosphate, Turbidity, Total Dissolved Solids (TDS) and Bacterial Count. The linkages of the model were established using the STELLA software which provided an insight into the dynamics of the wetland ecosystem. The model was developed to understand the health of the ecosystem model and it was given various scenario runs for 25 years, with and without interventions in the form of control strategies so as to represent the future health of the ecosystem of the wetland.

Stakeholders' Perceptions as Captured through Multiple Valuation Techniques

The scenarios obtained through the ecosystem modelling exercise were represented through various complex graphs which were then converted into picture cards for an easier explanation of the status of the lake to the respondents in the survey. Having attempted the ecosystem modelling and knowing the extent of the degradation and threats, valuation was undertaken for the various stakeholders. Monetary gains and losses were taken into account when benefits were directly or indirectly marketed, and the people's perceptions for the conservation of the wetland resource were taken into account when there were no markets. Since it was difficult to encapsulate the various benefits and the different users in a single value, a spectrum of valuation techniques was used to capture the economic value of the various uses.

The valuation exercise included calculating the values of supplying drinking water to the city; benefits accruing to various people whose livelihoods depended upon the wetland; preventive measures that people used to avoid water-borne diseases; and the willingness of the people to pay for enjoying better recreational facilities from the Bhoj Wetland. In addition, the effect of the presence of the Upper Lake on the property prices was also estimated.

A number of very important observations were made during the course of the survey, for example, when people were asked to rank the various problems facing the country as perceived by them. The rankings are depicted in Table 20.4.

Table 20.4: Ranking of Problems Facing the Country

Problems	*Rank 1*		*Rank 2*		*Rank 3*		*Rank 4*		*Rank 5*		*Total*
	No.	*%*	*No.*	*%*	*No.*	*%*	*No.*	*%*	*No.*	*%*	
Corruption	592	74	121	15.13	61	7.63	15	1.88	11	1.38	800
Foreign infiltration	375	46.76	220	27.43	133	16.58	54	6.73	20	2.40	802
Pollution/Environmental degradation	412	51.31	245	30.51	105	13.08	31	3.86	10	1.25	803
Lack of a stable government	342	42.59	204	25.41	156	19.43	62	7.69	39	4.86	803
Economic Issues	400	49.14	213	26.53	136	16.94	34	4.23	20	2.49	803

Thus it can be seen that most of the people give maximum weightage to corruption as a national problem followed by environmental pollution, then economic issues, and so on. On the other hand a very small percentage of the people interviewed claimed pollution or environmental degradation as the least important problem.

Among the environmental problems, the specific problems were ranked as given in Table 20.5.

Table 20.5: Ranking of Various Environmental Problems

	Rank 1		*Rank 2*		*Rank 3*		*Rank 4*		*Rank 5*		*Total*
	No.	*%*	*No.*	*%*	*No.*	*%*	*No.*	*%*	*No.*	*%*	
Deforestation	501	62.4	186	23.2	80	10.0	28	3.5	8	1.0	803
Urban waste	421	52.4	231	28.8	118	14.7	23	2.9	9	1.1	802
Noise Pollution	167	20.8	220	27.4	298	37.1	87	10.8	31	3.9	803
Vehicular Pollution	289	36.0	246	30.6	196	24.4	54	6.7	18	2.2	803
Industrial Pollution	244	30.4	238	29.6	174	21.7	115	14.3	32	4.0	803

According to the people of the city who were interviewed, the biggest environmental threat in the country is deforestation followed by urban waste and vehicular pollution. Noise pollution is not considered an important problem by the majority.

The majority of the city population obtains its drinking water from the municipal supply. A break-up of the sources of supply of drinking water for the sample is given in Graph 20.1.

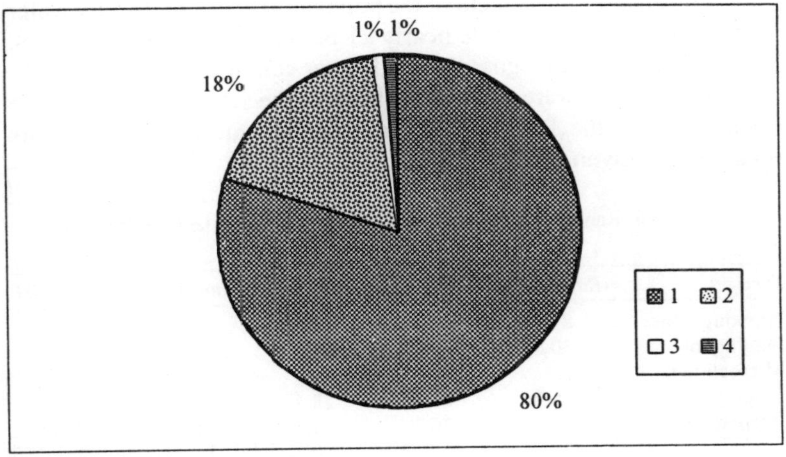

1. Municipal Supply, 2. Tube Wells, 3. Tankers, 4. Dug wells

Graph 20.1: Drinking Water Sources in Bhopal City

Thus 80 per cent of the sample interviewed obtained their drinking water from the municipal supply, 18 per cent from tube-wells and 1 per cent each from tankers and dug wells.

The water purification techniques used by the people were also studied and the findings are presented in Graph 20.2.

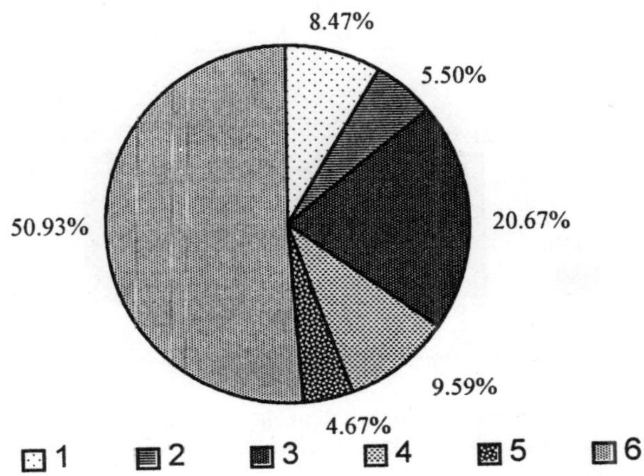

1. Aquaguard, 2. Zero B, 3. Ordinary Filter, 4. Chlorine/Alum, 5. Boiling, 6. None

Graph 20.2: Water Purification Techniques Followed in Bhopal City

Thus nearly 51 per cent of the population does not use any water purification measures, while nearly 21 per cent uses ordinary filters, 8.5 per cent use "Aquaguard", and 5.6 per cent use "Zero B".

The people were also asked to rank the few services that are obtained from the Bhoj wetland as per their attitude. The results obtained are given in Table 20.6.

Table 20.6: Ranking of Various Services Obtained from the Bhoj Wetland

Services	*Rank 1 (%)*	*Rank 2 (%)*	*Rank 3 (%)*	*Rank 4 (%)*	*Rank 5 (%)*
Drinking Water	82.0	8.6	5.3	2.5	1.6
Stability of Microclimate	30.8	35.0	23.5	6.8	3.9
Employment	25.7	21.8	28.4	16.8	7.3
Recreation	37.6	26.7	23.3	8.6	3.9

From Table 20.6 it is evident that the maximum number of people consider drinking water to be the most important service obtained from the Bhoj Wetland. The next highly rated service was recreation, followed by stability of micro-climate. Employment was rated last, showing that fewer people found it important as compared to the other services.

The percentage of people and the frequency with which they visit the lakes was also examined. The findings are shown in Graph 20.3.

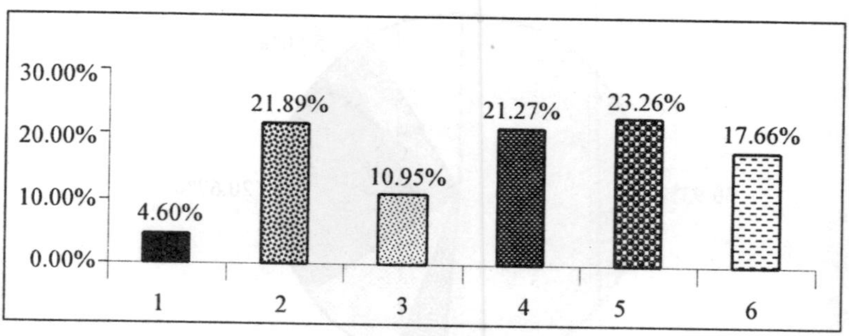

1. Not at all, 2. Every week, 3. Once in a fortnight, 4. Once in a month, 5. Once in six months, 6. Once in a year, **X Axis:** Frequency of Visits, **Y Axis:** Percentage of People Visiting the Lakes

Graph 20.3: Frequency of Visits to the Upper and Lower Lakes

From Graph 20.3 it is evident that nearly 41 per cent of the population visits the lakes infrequently, from once in six months to once in a year. Quite a significant number visit it every week, even though they might be living quite away from the lakes.

Many problems plague the lakes and threaten their very existence. The attitude of the people and their opinions about the effects of these threats were studied. These are presented in Table 20.7.

From Table 20.7, it can be seen that, according to the people, the most important threats to the lakes are from hospital waste, sewage and solid waste, while the least threat is perceived as coming from

Table 20.7: Ranking of Various Threats to the Bhoj Wetland

Threats	*Rank 1 (%)*	*Rank 2 (%)*	*Rank 3 (%)*	*Rank 4 (%)*	*Rank 5 (%)*
Siltation	40.8	24.6	20.4	7.8	6.3
Solid Waste	63.9	24.4	9.0	1.6	1.1
Sewage	77.9	14.4	5.2	1.9	0.6
Washermen	35.6	29.4	20.5	8.8	5.7
Trapa cultivation	15.2	19.9	23.8	16.9	24.1
Encroachment	43.7	23.1	19.0	8.2	6.0
Increasing population	47.4	19.8	13.4	9.8	9.6
Weeds and Eutrophication	44.2	25.9	17.7	6.5	5.8
Boating	6.0	9.0	14.8	13.3	57.0
Agricultural Waste	13.8	17.4	22.5	17.3	28.9
Idol Immersion	44.7	22.9	13.1	8.0	11.4
Hospital Waste	82.6	9.2	4.2	1.9	2.1

boating, cultivation of *trapa* and agricultural waste that flows into the Wetland. In another exercise, people were asked what importance they gave to the few selected factors while buying a piece of property. (The property prices in particular areas in the city were obtained and these areas were ranked against the parameters of neighbourhood, proximity to markets, ease of access, environment, housing density, and presence and absence of lake.) The rankings thus obtained are given in Table 20.8.

A Comparative Analysis of Various Values

Using various valuation techniques, the values which generate incomes for stakeholders from activities like fishing, boating, *trapa* cultivation,

Table 20.8: Ranking of Various Factors Considered While Buying Property

S. No:	*Factor*	*Scores*
1.	Drinking Water	0.99
2.	Safety	0.94
3.	School	0.88
	Quality of Construction	0.87
	Hospital	0.87
6.	Age of House	0.85
7.	Park	0.80
	Market	0.79
	Air Pollution	0.79
10.	Work Place	0.77
11.	Density	0.70
	Noise Pollution	0.70
13.	Lake	0.67
14.	Household Help	0.56
15.	Road	0.31

washing of clothes, and secondary selling activities were obtained. Then the values in terms of the costs incurred by the population for the treatment of water-borne diseases and getting good quality water as well as the costs borne by the various agencies to purify and distribute water were obtained. Finally, the recreational value for the entire population and property price differentials for the lake-front property owners were estimated. The results of these exercises are summarised in Table 20.9.

It is evident from the Table that drinking water, recreation and property attributes command high values from the lakes, whereas other income-based values are important to specific sections of the people. The estimated values have not been aggregated since some stakeholders use the Lake for multiple values and, therefore, overlapping cannot be avoided. Further, other important values such as biodiversity and micro-climatic effects have not been estimated because data are not available. But the exercise undertaken does give an insight into the multiple values which have not been considered to the possible extent in the current management activities.

Further, even if one is able to collect the revenue through what the people were willing to pay in the form of voluntary contributions to the society (Rs. 4,84,68,956 per annum) or in the form of tax to the government (Rs. 59,32,922 per annum), the amount so collected would be much more than the current estimated cost of maintenance of various sub-projects of the Bhoj Wetland (BWL) agency (Rs. 80,70,00 per annum) if the collected revenue is from voluntary payment and reasonably collects 74 per cent of the amount through taxes.

Table 20.9: Estimation of Economic Values of Bhoj Wetland

(Annual for 1999-2000)

Uses / Impacts	*Stakeholders*	*Valuation Techniques*	*Value (in Rs)*
A. Drinking Water	Water supplying agencies	Supply Cost	9,54,13,962
B. Fish Production	Fishermen	Market Price of Existing Production	80,00,000
C. Boating	Boatmen	Income Estimation	24,37,880
D. *Trapa* cultivation	*Trapa* (water chestnut) Cultivators	Market Price of Existing Production	50,000
E. Washing of clothes	Washermen	Income Estimation	36,00,000
F. Secondary Activities Maize cob selling Sugar cane juice selling Snacks and cold drink stalls Horse rides MPTDC (a) Cafeteria (b) Boating	Maize Cobb sellers Sugarcane juice sellers Individual owners Individual owners MPTDC	(i) Income Estimation (ii) Income Estimation (iii) Income Estimation (iv) Income Estimation (v) (a) Revenue Generation (b) Revenue Generation	(i) 1,44,000 (ii) 2,73,600 (iii) 2,06,400 (iv) 7,92,000 (v) (a) 18,00,000 (b) 6,74,635
G. Water borne Diseases	Population using lake's water	Cost of Illness	12,00,254
H. Quality water	Population using lake's water	Purification Costs	1,24,35,876
I. Recreation	Entire population of the city	CVM (i) As Voluntary Payment (ii) As Compulsory tax	 4,84,68,956 59,32,922
J. Increase in property prices	Lake front property owners	Hedonic pricing	50 per cent difference in property prices

Recommendation

The critical need today is to recognise the inter-linkages and benefits that could be obtained if the wetland is *managed in an integrated manner* and *used sustainably.* It is a challenging task and requires action at many levels. It needs delicate integration of diverse issues and management institutions. Such an approach must begin with involving all stakeholders in the wetland in the form of local area institutions that can elicit their views for use and future management of the Bhoj Wetland. The structure and functions of such an institution are depicted in Annexure II. It is hoped that if such an institution is set up for future management of the Bhoj Wetland, it will help in evolving economically wise, environmentally sound and socially acceptable processes for sustainable management of such an important urban wetland.

NOTE

1. This paper is an outcome of EERC, World Bank assisted project titled "Economic Valuation of Bhoj Wetland for Sustainable Use" accomplished in October, 2000.

REFERENCES

Agrawal, Anil, and Narain, Sunita (1997): "Dying Wisdom: Rise, Fall and Potential of India's Traditional Water Harvesting Systems". New Delhi: Centre for Science and Environment.

Allaby, M. (1994): *The Concise Oxford Dictionary of Ecology.* Oxford: Oxford University Press,

Barlow, S.M.; Bridges, J, W.; Calow, P.; Conning, D.M.; Curnow, R.N.; Dayan, A.D.; and Purchase, I.F.H. (1992): "Toxicity, Toxicology and Nutrition in Risk Analysis, Perception, Management". Report of Royal Society Study Group. London: The Royal Society. pp. 35-65.

Census of India (1991): Published from the office of Registrar General & Census Commissioner, India

Convention on Wetlands (1971): Articles 1.1 and 2.1. Ramsar, Iran, (1971)

Costanza, Robert, Stephen C. Farber and Judith Maxwell (1989): "Valuation and Management of Wetland Ecosystems", *Ecological Economics,* 1 pp. 335-361.

Farber, S., (1987): Value of coastal wetlands for protection of property against hurricane wind damage, *Journal of Environmental Economics and Management.* 14: 143-151.

Hammack, J. and G.M. Brown (1974): Water fowl and Wetlands Toward Bio economic Analysis, John Hopkins University Press, Baltimore.

Holling, C.S. (ed.), (1978): *Adaptive Environmental Assessment and Management.* London: John Wiley and Sons.

Kadekodi, Gopal K., and Gulati, S.C. (1999): "Root Causes of Biodiversity Losses in Chilika Lake: Reflections on Socio-Economic Magnitudes". Study report. Institute of Economic Growth and Centre for Multi-Disciplinary Development Research. New Delhi.

Krebs, C.J. (1978): *Ecology: The Experimental Analysis of Distribution and Abundance.*

Lynn, G.D., P.O. Conroy., and F.J. Prochaska (1981): Economic valuation of marsh areas for marine production process (Florida) *Journal of Environmental Economics and Management* 8: 175 186.

Mitch, J. and James Gosselink (1986): *Values and Valuation of wetlands,* 2nd Edition pp 393-414.

Odum, E.P. (1989): Ecology and our Endangered Life-support Systems, Sinauer, Stanford, C.T.

Robertson, David; Bundy, Alan; Muetzelfeldt, Robert; Huggith, Mundy; and Uschold, Michael (1991): "Eco-Logic". Cambridge: The MIT Press. pp. 9-13.

SAPROF (Special Assistance for Project Formation) (1993): Feasibility Report for Bhoj Wetland Restoration Project prepared for the OECF.

Sustainable Wetlands, Environmental Governance Series No. 2. Capacity 21.

Swartzman, G.L., and .Stephen, P.K. (1987): *Ecological Simulation Primer.* New York. Macmillan Publication Company. pp. 01-05

Treeweek, Jo (1999): *Ecological Impact Assessment.* Oxford and London: Blackwell Science Ltd, pp. 159-163.

Verma, Madhu; Bakshi, Nishita; and Nair, Ramesh P.K. (2000): "Total Economic Valuation of Bhoj Wetland for Sustainable Use". Paper prepared for presentation in the Beijer Research Seminar on Environmental Economics, organised by the Beijer Institute, Stockholm, September 18-20, 2000, at Dhulikhel, Nepal.

Walters, C.J. (1993): "Dynamic Models and Large Scale Field Experiments in Environmental Impact Assessment and Management". *Australian Journal of Ecology* 18: 53-61.

ANNEXURE I

Stakeholder Workshop for Identification of Various Management Issues of Bhoj Wetland

The participants were introduced with the objectives and methodology of the project and how different valuation techniques like the Contingent Valuation Method Hedonic Pricing, market analysis shall be used to arrive at the economic value of the wetland. It was also mentioned that the co-operation of all the stakeholders in the Wetland will be required for effective completion of the project. This was followed by division of the participants into three groups and taking up of one issue by each. The sticky cloth and paper technique was used to facilitate the discussions. The groups dealt with three important topics like sewage and waste disposal, fishing and washing activities and recreational activities. The outcome of the group discussions and the respose of the concerned departments who replied to the queries, problems and alternatives suggested are listed in the table given below:

Group 1: Sewage and Waste Disposal

Epco Action	*Problems Faced or Remaining*	*Alternatives and Additional Action Needed*	*Information Gap*	*Response of the Concerned Deptt.*
Deweeding	Unhealthy Environment	Removed weeds to be converted into compost/ manure		
Relocating sites of Idol immersions	Not practical	Small, metallic idols can be encouraged		
Sewerage system in all lake peripheral wards and its treatment	Waste disposal from slum areas where no sewage line exists	Treatment of sewage water and putting the water back into the lake to maintain water level		Non-traditional sesage plants, based upon the famous Calcutta system are being set up
		Use of sewage water in irrigation		No response to problem of waste disposal in slums

contd.

(contd. Group 1)

Epco Action	*Problems Faced or Remaining*	*Alternatives and Additional Action Needed*	*Infor-mation Gap*	*Response of the Concerned Deptt.*
Solid Waste Management, Waste Collection Bins and Municipal System for collection and disposal of waste in open land	Vegetable waste disposal from weekly market areas Cost & time required for collection of waste *vis-a-vis* creation of unhygienic conditions	Ask for advice from MJS, Lucknow, an NGO, which is successfully managing solid waste collection and treatment (organic compost throuth vermiculture) Dumping of solid waste to alternate site vis a vis alternate use of waste by processing		Such action is welcome/will be encouraged
Removal of slums from the fringe area and link road construction		No alternative		Policing systems are not enough to ensure total removal

Group 2: Fishing and Washing Activities

Epco Action	*Problems*	*Alternatives*	*Infor-mation Gap*	*Response of the Concerned Deptt.*
Plantation	Litter fall Organic Matter/Bird Droppings More Pollution Skin Problems	Plantations should be carried out away from the shore line		Plantatation near the shore line is no longer being carried out but in the buffer zone
Deweeding	Nets are damaged Other weeds come up	Navigation routes of motor boats used in deweeding operations should be damarcated		To be pointed out the BWL Project authorities
Fencing and Road	No place for fishing boats to land No access to lake for fishermen Water hyacinth	Gaps in the fencing should be provided to give space to the boats for landing		Van Vihar National Park is a notified area and so nothing can be done about it

contd.

(contd. Group 2)

Epco Action	*Problems*	*Alternatives*	*Infor-mation Gap*	*Response of the Concerned Deptt.*
Grass Carp	No information given to the fishermen about the stocking rate fingerlings are flushed out from the spill way when the Bhadbhada gates are opened	Land should be provided in the vicinity of the lake to stock seed during rains Make Bhadbhada sluice gates an overflow system (as existed previously)		Project is already done with and check with PWD about the previous type of dam at Bhadbhada
Desilting	No information No idea about its impacts	Fishermen should be informed before the operation		Pamphlets to be distributed about this. Desilting to be done only in areas where there are no fishing activities
Removal of Dhobi Ghats	Two ghats belonging to dhobis, the one with the larger community is consulted and not theirs Alternative space is insufficient for drying washed clothes	Adequate water for washing and drinking and sufficient space for drying clothes should be provided		Area has been chosen by BMC and has been found to be the least unsuitable. Community involvement is to be encouraged

Group 3: Recreational Activities

Epco Action	*Problems*	*Alternatives*	*Information Gap*	*Response of the Concerned Department*
Retghat Lalghati Road	Additional Lead and SPM going into the Lake Not acting as the proposed buffer between population and lake Solid waste likely to be thrown into lake from road side Building activities continue south of the road near Khanugaon	Chain Link fence to stop waste? Environmental Information Awareness Campaigns? Effective Policing? Close Road?	Scientific testing of impact needed	People look for aesthetic utility from the lake and not just its existence
Chain Link Fencing and Social Forestry	People in *jhuggi jhopris* breaking fence for access to lake for water, sanitation and livelihood needs	Rehabilitate (relocate) *those jhuggi jhopris* which haven't been shifted elsewhere Reforest the area with community participation	EPCO provisions for rehabilitation Who will look after the newly planted trees?	Policing not efficient and enough anyway
Deweeding— Water hyacinth	Complete removal upsets ecosystem How to harvest optimal amounts in future? Who? Problem with carp introduction?	Limnology Department and local fishermen to estimate optimal harvest High Powered multi-disciplinary expert group (including ITK) to look into issues Same for *Ipomoea* and other aquatic grasses Collaborate with other Ramsar Lake actors and conventions	How much of water hyacinth is useful? Has EPCO done any studies	

contd.

(contd. Group 3)

Epco Action	*Problems*	*Alternatives*	*Infor-mation Gap*	*Response of the Concerned Department*
Inaction against Ranjit Hotel Inaction against con-struction of residential complexes Jehanuma proposal—all 3 within 50 m buffer zone	Precedent for others Possible contamination despite cleaning systems	Since these are illegal constructions, the State Government can demolish these structures. A legal precedent is the demolitation of Kamal Nath's hotel in H.P. for violating environmental norms. This will help enforce existing laws.	Has EPCO made a formal represen-tation against Hotel Ranjit?	Pressure from the public needs to be put so that more such hotels cannot come up
Discouraging boating and moved to spill channel	Loss of revenue to M.P. Tourism	No alternative; but apply ban uniformly		Yes, plans to shift the boating are on. Sports cannot be banned since they do not contribute to the pollution as such
Floating fountains	Not effective with regard to sewage control and uneconomical Who will bear the operation and manage-ment costs after the BWL project is over? Dirty water being sprayed on people on road	Discontinue if not possible to maintain. Concentrate instead on sewage flowing into lake.		

ANNEXURE II

Functions and Activities of the Bhoj Wetland Maintenance Society

- **Maintain Water Quality and Improve Lake Management**
- **Build Parks and Maintain Them**
  - ❑ Better Boating Facilities with Introduction of Water and Adventure Sports
- **Encourage Sports Fishing Using Roads**
  - ❑ Hold Summer Camps For Children and Youth for Water Related Recreational Activities
  - ❑ Promote Ecotourism by Encouraging Visitors to Learn about Lake Ecosystem and Biodiversity and How to Decrease Water Pollution by Regulating Use of Polythenes, etc. and Water Consumption
- **Develop View Points with Sitting and Refreshment Arrangements**
- **Introduction of Dal Lake Type *Shikaras***
- **Generate Awareness for Clean Lakes by holding Annual Lake Festival, Distributing Souveniers, Declare Lakes as City's Heritage, etc.**

PART V

WATERSHED DEVELOPMENT
As If People Mattered?

21

Watershed Reforms in India

MIHIR SHAH and P.S. VIJAY SHANKAR

Reforms for the Poor

The programme of economic reforms dominates the policy-making discourse in India today. The period following the 1991 Budget presented by the then Finance Minister Manmohan Singh generated much excitement among the economists, policy-makers and within the corporate sector, in particular. Sadly, the discourse has paid less than sufficient attention to the precise mechanisms by which the reforms may impact the poor. There has merely been a carrying forward of the presumption of the "trickle-down" effect of higher rates of growth made possible by reforms, without exploring the processes that would ensure that reforms translate into concrete benefits for the poor. A unilinear movement in the direction of privatisation is widely accepted as an unquestioned, ubiquitous "good" without a detailed investigation into what the reform package should or should not include. This has had an unfortunate consequence: policy makers have not focussed on the need for and scope of reforms in programmes that more directly influence the livelihoods of the disadvantaged people. The present paper seeks to take a small step in this direction.

We turn the spotlight on to the watershed development programme that has major implications for the livelihoods of the poor. In our work *India's Drylands* (Shah *et al.*, 1998) we have shown that spending a mere one per cent of the national income on watershed development programmes can lead to both employment guarantee and food security in rural India. Not only that, we argue that these goals could be attained in a manner that is both non-inflationary and sustainable. For what watershed programmes yield is, to use the phrases made famous by Joan Robinson and K.N. Raj, not merely short-term and "revolving", but truly long-term, "sedimented" employment.[1] It is not very widely known that according to the National Sample Survey data, nearly 80 per cent of the agricultural labour households in India do own some land.[2] But the land they own has such a low productivity that it does not yield enough income to support their families. So they are compelled to work outside their farms as labourers. Watershed programmes aimed at increasing the productivity of such small and marginal farmers in the drylands hold the key to future agricultural development, employment generation and poverty alleviation in India.

The past four decades have seen an increasingly widening gap between the productivity of irrigated and dry land agriculture. This has, of course, been no accident. It is a direct and predictable consequence of the strategy adopted in the mid-1960s of "betting on the strong", whereby massive investment flowed to the already well-endowed regions and farmers of the country, in the hope that the benefits of their accelerated growth would eventually "trickle-down" to the vast majority. But this strategy has led to a situation which can only be described as absurd: in recent years we have been facing a succession of droughts even as the godowns of the Food Corporation of India overflow with stocks of foodgrains. This surely must be regarded as the final nail in the coffin. The dry lands of India have suffered massive neglect, in terms of both public investment and appropriate research and development. These are the regions where the poorest of our poor live. These, especially the tribal pockets within them, are often the flashpoints of violent protests, a reflection of intense disenchantment with the national mainstream. It is for these regions that we most urgently need a new watershed approach.

We must also remember that the distribution of water resources in India is highly uneven. The exploitable water per unit of land area is estimated to vary from over 119 cm. in the eastern parts of the country to merely 41 cm. in the west. This means that indiscriminate interventions, not fine-tuned to reflect these inter-regional differences, are bound to fail. According to the water balance projections of the Central Water Commission (Central Water Commission 1996), even after full realisation of India's water resource potential, gross utilisation of water for irrigation and other uses comes to only 25 per cent of the total water resources (105 million hectare metres), whereas evaporation from the soil moisture is about 33 per cent (140 million hectare metres). It is clear that much more water is lost through evaporation than what is utilised for irrigation development. Thus, we need to give the highest priority to technologies that reduce the rates of evaporation and make possible productive use of soil moisture. This is all the more so because the rate of growth of irrigation development in India, as also everywhere else across the globe, has been steadily decelerating, after peaking in the 1970s. And the life of our irrigation sources themselves, whether they are dams (big, medium or small), wells or tube-wells, depends crucially on the treatment of their catchments to reduce the rates of siltation and on the groundwater recharge works, both key ingredients of watershed development. So watershed programmes have an abiding relevance in a country where 60 per cent of the area is dry land, with a high concentration of poverty within it.

At the same time, since we have accumulated experience of watershed programmes in India, it is worthwhile to reflect carefully on the strategy being adopted for their implementation. Several aspects of the present strategy need urgent reforms for the programmes to succeed. Otherwise, there is a real danger that they will go the way many government development programmes have gone since independence.

Watershed Development: Departure from the Past

Watershed development, as an approach, is seen as marking a radical departure from the water policies that have dominated the landscape, right from the earliest days of planning in India. This departure is evident in many senses:

- *Decentralisation of Planning*: Here is a programme that breaks with many years of centralised plan making; its plans are necessarily made and executed at the micro-watershed level.
- *People's Participation*: The decentralised plan is to be made and executed under the leadership of village-level committees, ensuring central role for the village community at every stage—from plan conception, formulation, implementation—right up to maintenance of assets created. This constitutes a

major step in the direction of decentralised natural resource management.

- *Location-specificity*: Unlike the centralised plans of the past, made without reference to the great agro-hydro-geological diversity of India, watershed plans are supposed to be location-specific, reflecting not only the differences in conditions across watersheds, but also intra-watershed diversity in slope, soil and hydrogeology.
- *Sustainability*: Such a location-appropriate approach is also seen as a guarantor of sustainability of the growth path since it avoids pitfalls of indiscriminately applying technologies such as deep drilling of tube-wells that have, for example, led to dramatic declines in water tables in many hard-rock regions of India.[3]

Experience of Watershed Programmes in India

In many instances, this promise of the watershed approach has been realised. However, it is sad to observe that these instances remain exceptions to the general rule of failure of watershed programmes in India. Indeed, the experience of these programmes has not been significantly different from the long history of the failure of other government programmes over the past fifty years. The first fact to be recognised is that watershed remains overwhelmingly a bureaucratic programme. Despite the attempts of some state governments, most notably Madhya Pradesh, to adopt a *mission mode,* ostensibly to overcome the problems of bureaucratisation, and the very real commitment of some politicians (such as the Chief Minister of Madhya Pradesh) and officials (many District Collectors all over India), watershed development has suffered from the same weaknesses that have characterised most government programmes since independence. These are:

- Unmotivated and cynical project officers
- Target-orientation
- Poor technical quality of work
- Lack of people's participation
- Insufficient attention to people's empowerment

- Absence of institutionalized mechanisms for transparency and accountability leading to widespread corruption.[4]

Watershed programmes, when led by Non-governmental Organisations (NGOs) too, have had their own set of problems. While in each of the above respects NGOs may have fared better, their work also suffers from certain conceptual and strategic weaknesses that still afflict watershed thinking in India today. The aim of the present paper is to focus on these weaknesses and suggest ways of overcoming them, so that the full potential of watershed approach may be realised. The paper concludes with an outline of the significance of a reformed watershed programme for food security in India.

Watershed Reforms: Need and Scope Shedding Watershed Fundamentalism

Water resource development in India appears condemned to swing between the fundamentalism of the irrigation engineers on the one hand and the orthodoxy of soil and water conservation engineers, on the other. While the former refused for years to see the importance of treating the catchment areas of the dams they were building, the latter appear to suggest that once ridge area treatment is done, there is no need to treat the major drainage lines at all! It is even suggested that building any kind of dam, big or small, will—or rather should—become redundant, if the catchment area is treated with the necessary intensity and rigour.[5] This has given rise to an quite unnecessary opposition between those advocating watershed programmes and those in favour of irrigation. The important thing is to see the essential complementarity between the two programmes. No irrigation project can become sustainable in the long run, if catchment area treatment is not done either prior or at least simultaneously with its implementation. Indeed, advocates of the Green Revolution irrigation strategies of big dams or tube-wells must realise that it is only watershed development that can help revive fallen water tables and prevent dams from prematurely silting up. Likewise, watershed advocates must acknowledge that in many parts of the country (especially eastern and central India) there is a vast unutilised irrigation potential. Community-based micro-irrigation programmes can play a major role in drought-proofing these areas.

Within the watershed approach, problems are sometimes created by an excessive insistence on what is termed as "ridge-to-valley principle". Simply stated this means that watersheds are to be treated in a sequence beginning with the ridge area and moving gradually down the slope of the watershed. Interventions vary according to the slope and "order" of the stream in the watershed.[6] This, indeed, represents the strength of the watershed approach, reflecting its emphasis on location-specificity. It ensures that dams built in the lower reaches of the watershed are protected from excessive siltation, something that would tend to happen, if the upper catchments were not treated first.

The problems begin when this principle, rather than being considered a guiding rule, takes the form of rigid orthodoxy. For, it often happens that village communities inhabit the lower reaches of the selected micro-watershed. Success or failure in watershed programmes depends on how closely the community is involved in it right from the stage of action plan formulation. A rigid insistence on the ridge-to-valley sequence often alienates communities unwilling to understand the point of working so far from their fields and wells. From the very inception then, the implementing agency, in the consciousness of the villagers, is relegated to an interloper status, destroying all chances of success of the programme.[7]

Indeed, after years of experience of working in the field, we feel it would be best to completely restructure the way watershed programmes are conceived. The current practice is to demarcate the selected micro-watershed on a Survey of India toposheet and then plan various interventions within the watershed, from ridge to valley. It would probably be better to identify significant water harvesting sites within the selected watershed in a participatory fashion and then plan their construction, as also the treatment of their catchments, in a more or less coterminous manner. This would simultaneously address the need to involve the village community while ensuring that the catchments of the proposed structures are treated well in time, in anticipation of their storage. We would thereby achieve both, strong community participation and adherence to the ridge-to-valley principle.

De-romanticising Community

One must not make the mistake of romanticising the notion of the village community. Indian rural society today—*adivasi* pockets are no exception—is deeply divided socially and economically. Discrimination against women, *dalits, adivasis,* and the poor in resource-use and access is widespread. Any development programme based on local initiative needs to be necessarily accompanied by an effective social mobilisation in favour of these socially and economically disadvantaged groups. Detailed agreements on sharing of water and other benefits need to be worked out well before any construction activity is started. The interests of the landless have to be specially borne in mind. Otherwise the harvested water will be cornered by the dominant elite. And this is what has happened in most watershed programmes in India. That this has happened with the techno-managerial solutions imposed from above by the bureaucratic implementers has been no surprise. But the real tragedy is that social activists of various hues have made the same mistake by romanticising the notion of *samaj,* ignoring the very real deep fissures within it. Such activists also tend to overplay the role of "voluntary" contributions in watershed programmes, basing their experience on limited areas where the beneficiaries have been the richer farmers. They overlook the fact that poor *adivasi* and *dalit* farmers, facing years of drought in succession, can hardly be expected to make large "voluntary" contributions. Rather, for them the issue is really one of securing a reasonable livelihood by obtaining paid work that watershed programmes have the potential to provide. Thus, this fanciful notion of community ends up reinforcing the right-wing discourse of the state withdrawing from its critical responsibility in protecting livelihoods of the weakest in our country.

Integrating Dry-land Agriculture Packages with Water Harvesting

Watershed development in India has been one-sided; it has been preoccupied with supply augmentation. Little attention has been paid to the end-uses of the harvested rainwater. In this respect it has failed to break with the dominant development paradigms of the 20th century, all of which are characterised by supply-side solutions. These solutions are caught in the infinite regress of trying to catch up with an ever-expanding demand. They are a major reason for straining the delicate fabric of the eco-system, within which economic processes necessarily unfold.[8]

We need to recognise clearly that it is not merely enough to harvest rainwater. However, much water we may conserve and collect, it will prove inadequate unless we put it to sustainable uses. What is required is to find ways of not just increasing supply but reducing demand and regulating end-uses. So long as we do not question the emerging pattern of end-uses and pose the central question of efficiency of utilisation of our resources, we will be called upon to do the impossible: augment supply endlessly. The fundamental binding constraint is really provided by the demand side. An integral element of the conservationist approach has, therefore, to be a quantitative and qualitative regulation of end-uses and demand.

The first step in this direction has to be the integration into programmes of water conservation of a *sustainable dryland agriculture* strategy. Only then can we hope to avoid the tragic spectacle of the pioneering Ralegaon Siddhi (located in Maharashtra's drought-prone Ahmednagar district) experiment which faces man-made scarcity of water because now sugarcane is grown on vast tracts of land, making a mockery of the watershed approach. Unfortunately, watershed programmes in India's dryland areas have failed to break with the Green Revolution (GR) type agricultural package. The major flaw in this strategy was to apply indiscriminately the same package to all areas, irrespective of the agro-ecological specificities of each region, in a country with such an immense diversity. The drylands of India have a delicate ecosystem, extremely vulnerable to external stress, whether it is induced by the weather or the market. The GR package made farmers more vulnerable on two counts. It made them critically dependent on high quanta and precise timeliness of irrigation and increased their reliance on expensive market-procured inputs, such as hybrid seeds, chemical fertilizers and pesticides. The poorest were naturally the worst hit by a production plan that was unsustainable, both in economic and ecological terms. The unprecedented increase in suicides by farmers in recent times is the most dramatic and tragic expression of this vulnerability. It is necessary, therefore, to arrive at a package of agricultural practices finely tuned to the resource endowments of each watershed, which is both accessible to the poor (*low-cost*) and sustainable (*low-risk*). We need an approach that:

- focuses on crops that form the nucleus of the livelihood security of the poor and marginal dryland farmers,

- reduces dependence on the market,
- reduces the need for water,
- respects the specific matrix of resource-availability of the particular agro-climatic region,
- builds upon the germplasm local to drylands, rather than imposing exotic varieties, and
- respects the ecological balance while planning increases in productivity, building in strategies of resource rehabilitation, along with resource exploitation.

Often the critique of GR strategies tends to take on an excessively romantic "back-to-nature" kind of tone. We are not advocating such an approach. We believe that there is no going back, as we are faced with a continuously evolving environment, to whose specific challenges newer and more creative responses have to be evolved. There is also the increased pressure of population that demands a level of productivity, beyond the capabilities of traditional seeds. At the same time, however, great care must be taken to ensure that the improvements we attempt are based on the germplasm of the drylands, which has attuned itself to their environment, as it evolved over the centuries.

Added to this must be the attempt to minimise dependence on external inputs. This means that all efforts should be made to increase self-sufficiency in seed production. Also organic manuring should be intensified on each field and also spread to as many farmers as possible, so that dependence on inorganic fertilisers is reduced. Adoption of organic pesticides such as neem oil, which can be locally produced, would also help in reducing external market vulnerability, while contributing to environmental sustainability at the same time.

A great deal of promising work in this direction has already been done at centres belonging to the network of Agriculture Universities spread all over the hinterlands of India; also by the field research stations of the Indian Council for Agricultural Research and Indian Agricultural Research Institute. The problem is that these centres work in isolation from the farms for which their research is meant. The crucial bottleneck has been the absence of an agency to effectively transmit the benefits of their research to farmers and obtain a detailed feedback from them. The packages developed by these scientists are crying out for field-testing; they remain ideal-types without the cutting edge of real-world trials.[9]

Long-term Goal Has to be Appropriate Land-use Planning

Indeed, what we require are not just viable agriculture packages but meticulously worked out *location-specific land-use planning modules* which make careful use of the harvested water and are fine-tuned to match the matrix of widely varying natural resource endowments of each field in the watershed. Except in the extreme cases of severely handicapped soils, all land can support some form of biomass production. Land use planning proceeds from an assessment of the capability of land to support life without deterioration over a long period. Soils are grouped into eight categories on the basis of the degree of limitation on their ability to produce biomass such as the extent of erosion, wetness and soil hazards. Land belonging to capability Class 8 is regarded absolutely barren and unfit for any form of biotic production. The remaining seven Land Capability Classes (LCC) are broadly divided into two: LCC 1 to 4 are fit for cultivation, while LCC 5 to 7 are unsuited for cultivation but can support tree or grass cover. On the basis of this classification the best landuse system can be identified for each LCC type.

Sustainable Groundwater Harvesting: Integral Part of Watershed Programmes

A logical extension of the supply-side preoccupation of watershed programmes is the lack of attention to the challenge of sustainably utilising groundwater, the single most important source of water in India today.[10] This is yet another facet of the emerging brand of watershed fundamentalism. Somehow, groundwater harvesting through well construction, deepening and repair are not regarded as admissible watershed practices, even in areas with unutilised groundwater potential. At the same time, a blind eye is turned to the over-exploitation of groundwater through tube-wells, a widespread phenomenon in many areas. An integral part of any watershed programme should be systematic studies of the storage and transmission characteristics of aquifers so that rational protocols can be set up collectively for pumping of wells and sequencing their use. This will ensure that groundwater neither remains under-utilised nor is it subject to indiscriminate and unsustainable over-exploitation. Appropriate community regulation of groundwater could be the key emerging issue of rural governance in the 21st century.

What is required is to take a three-dimensional view of groundwater and see each aquifer as a common property resource. Wells and tube-wells are to be viewed as the means used by farmers to extract water from the aquifer. This extraction needs to be carefully and collectively regulated. To place this regulation on a scientific basis, each aquifer needs to be mapped and its storage (s) and transmission (t) characteristics carefully studied. A model for optimal use of groundwater in wells which minimises interference and maximises productivity is shown in Table 21.1.

Table 21.1: Model for Optimal Use of Groundwater in Wells across the Season

Well Characteristic		*Storativity (s)*	
Transmissivity (t)		Low	High
	Low	Drinking Water	Last Use (3)
	High	Early Use (1)	Interim Use (2)

Such studies are best done with the close involvement of the farmers of the area. They would help the community decide the intensity and sequencing of use of water from different wells in the aquifer. To give a rough indication of a possible scenario—wells with both low storage and low transmissivity would be preserved for drinking water. Wells with a low storage of water and high rates of transmission out of it would be used in the first part of the season, as water is not going to last for long in these wells. Where storage is high but so are the expected losses due to transmission, water would be used in the middle part of the season. The best wells, which have high storage of water and lose it slowly (low t), would be used only at the fag-end of the season.

Of course, a high order of organisational development is required for such decisions to be effectively implemented. What we need is a

Water Parliament of Co-Riparian Farmers that embraces both surface and groundwater. The watershed to be considered must also include the groundwater basin. And it has to be defined at a level much higher than the micro-watershed of typical watershed programmes. What is required is a complex organisational structure, with close co-ordination between the local and supra-local level bodies.

In the present era of market fundamentalism, there are those who suggest that the best way to regulate groundwater and prevent its over-extraction is to develop groundwater markets. For them, the solution always lies in "getting prices right". They forget that we are dealing with a common property resource with significant externalities—a classic market failure scenario. They fail to understand that as water becomes scarce, prices will tend to rise, gradually putting it beyond the means of the poorest farmers. And those users, such as large corporate bodies, who can afford to pay a very high price, will enjoy a virtual monopoly over water, and could indulge in its unbridled exploitation.

The unique aspect of the situation is that water below *my* land is not *mine*. Groundwater is a non-stationary, fugitive resource that merges into water under another's land in a fluid sort of way. By lowering the depth of his tube-well, my neighbour can squeeze all water out of my well. If there is no proper collective arrangement for groundwater use, it is likely that there will be an infinite regress of competitive extraction, with farmers outbidding one another in depths of drilling. Competitive extraction of groundwater leads to disastrous outcomes, the worst of which are observable in the coastal areas of Gujarat and Tamil Nadu, for example. Here, the saline ingress of sea water poses a virtually irreversible environmental hazard for farmers who have engaged in competitive pumping of groundwater.

Critical Role of Grassroots Agencies

Watershed development is, therefore, not merely a matter of harvesting rainwater. Its success entails:

- working out collective protocols of equitable and sustainable groundwater use,
- bringing together of scientists and farmers to evolve a dryland agriculture package,

- detailed land-use planning at the micro-watershed level, and
- mobilisation of rural communities in the direction of the disadvantaged.

All this can be done effectively only by the people's—grassroots—organisations. The bureaucracy clearly has neither the willingness nor the ability. Mainstream political parties do not even have this issue on their agenda. The village community does not take it up spontaneously either. Whether we like it or not, social mobilisation will have to come from an external agency with all its attendant dangers and limitations.

Of course, one has to be very careful. Currently, agencies are proliferating in the voluntary sector, many of which are of a dubious nature. It is not clear whether they have come into existence to serve the poor. Further, it appears that corruption which is rampant in the government and civil society has crept into the voluntary sector as well. Many NGOs are fly-by-night operators who obtain government grants and then disappear without a trace. There are others who play a contractor-type role, thriving on huge government grants and resultant commissions.

Therefore one has to be careful in dealing with grassroots agencies; only those with the following qualifications may be selected:

- Solid field presence and deep commitment, so that the benefits can be sustained in the long run,
- Requisite technical skills, with a capability of conducting meaningful interface with scientists, translating their inputs into specific field conditions, marrying the insights of scientists with those of the farmers and providing a detailed feedback to scientists,
- Capacity to carry out empowerment programmes for the representatives of village level institutions, and
- Capability of networking with other genuine grassroot agencies so that the benefits can be transmitted far and wide, with significant multiplier effects.

After all, we do not want to create oases of excellence—rather the attempt must be to develop "living laboratories of learning", from which more and more people benefit, far beyond the immediate location of the grassroots agency. The problem is the lack of an alternative implementation mechanism that can match the operational scale of the government. Most NGOs tend to be localised in their operation. And those who try to work on a large scale suffer the problems of non-governmental bureaucratisation. The trade-off between scale and quality appears irreconcilable.

Challenge of Up-scaling with Quality

How does one overcome this dilemma? The answer must come from within the voluntary sector itself. Both the problem of quality of agency and operational scale can be overcome through the concept of the Support Voluntary Organisation (SVO). It should be the role of SVOs to search out and link up the thousands of disparate, small but sincere groups, working in far-flung corners of the country, and provide them the necessary wherewithal to both implement watershed programmes in their areas and mobilise rural communities for this purpose. These agencies could include not just grassroot NGOs but also community-based organisations, watershed committees, forest protection committees, self-help group clusters, Gram Panchayats, and the committees of the Gram Sabha that look after natural resources.[11] The SVOs would provide them all logistical support from resource mobilisation to action plan implementation.

The Government of India has already made a small beginning in this direction. It has designated seven NGOs as SVOs[12] for the Council for Advancement of People's Action and Rural Technology (CAPART) watershed programme.[13] Each SVO can be visualised as a nucleus, giving rise to many nuclei of empowerment all over the country.[14] Through the SVO concept we can project how the watershed programme could be scaled-up over, say, the next 20 years, with carefully selected partners being in the forefront of implementation. Each SVO can conceivably support 200 partners over the 20 year period and each of which could in turn cover 25 micro-watersheds of 1,000 hectares each. If we have 20 SVOs, this could add up to 100 million hectares of land being covered over the next 20 years.[15] This would be no mean achievement. Apart from its direct impact, such work once it reaches a critical mass could have a major demonstration effect on government-run programmes.[16]

The programme must, of course, move much more slowly than the current target-oriented approach with its four-year period for the implementation of a typical watershed action plan. The basic unit of implementation in a typical watershed programme is the micro-watershed of between 1,000-2,500 hectares. Funds are allotted to these watersheds at the (recently revised) rate of a maximum of Rs.6 per hectare. In fact, usually every micro-watershed gets up to Rs.1.50 crore, to be spent in a specified short span of four years. This leads to a massive concentration of resources in a few villages, creating inequities between the selected and left-out villages. The inequities give rise to resentment, especially since there are no justifiable criteria for the selection of villages in the first place. It would be far better to move much more slowly, spending smaller amounts of money per year in each village across a larger number of villages, over a longer period of time (say, 10 years). This would allow the more critical processes of people's mobilisation for equity and empowerment to take a proper shape. This would also enable the kinds of qualitative research inputs described above to be integrated into the interventions planned in each watershed. Research studies would also benefit from the wider scale, making them both cost-effective and enriched by the variations in the range of conditions studied.

State Support—Indispensable

This potentially powerful thrust towards drought-proofing India presupposes that the requisite level of public investment would be forthcoming. Preoccupation with curtailing the fiscal deficit must not imply reductions in such a vitally important and highly productive expenditure. The trend in the public gross capital formation in Indian agriculture is alarming: it had peaked at Rs.18 billion around 1980 and has steadily fallen in real terms over the past two decades, to well below the levels of the 1970s. Reversing this trend is crucial, especially for the sustained growth of India's drought-prone areas. Such public investment would also have a very positive multiplier impact on private investment by the farmers in these regions.

We have worked out the financial implications of scaling up the watershed programme in India. About 200 million hectares of India's land area is in need of watershed treatment. At Rs.6 per hectare, the total expenditure required is Rs.120 crore. Since we visualise the effort to be completed over a 20-year period, the annual expenditure comes to Rs. 6 crore. The Tenth Five Year Plan projects an average annual expenditure of nearly Rs. 24 crore on rural development, land resources and drinking water. So we need to earmark around 25 per cent of this amount for watershed programmes. This is not too much to ask.[17]

Part of this finance could come from the 55 million tonnes of grain currently rotting in the godowns of the Food Corporation of India. The incomes generated by these programmes would generate demand for goods in the rural areas, providing a much-needed boost to the recession-hit Indian industry. In a period of unutilised industrial capacity, huge foodgrain stocks and exploding foreign exchange reserves, this state expenditure could open up a completely safe, non-inflationary growth path for the Indian economy.

The role of the state is critical in one more area as well—encouraging location-appropriate cropping patterns, critical for ensuring sustainable water use. The crops suited to the drylands of India have been discriminated against in state procurement and price-support operations. Farmers tend to grow water-intensive crops because they are favoured by state procurement and pricing policies. Today, the country is burdened with huge stocks of wheat and rice, while the per capita availability of pulses has fallen to less than half of what it was at the time of independence. The annual rate of growth of coarse cereal output declined to an all-time low of 0.12 per cent in the 1990s. Rice and wheat constitute almost all of the grain procured in India. And just the three states of Punjab, Haryana and Andhra Pradesh account for 80 per cent of this. Minimum support price and procurement operations need to be diversified to include regions and crops that have suffered historical neglect—regions inhabited by the poorest people and crops grown and eaten by the poorest people in India.

Significance of Watershed Programme for Food Security

Such a reformed watershed programme holds out an immense potential for the macro-economic growth in India. Apart from long-term drought-proofing, this could also provide food security in rural India. The urgency of the need to adopt this approach has never been greater. For the first time since independence, the 1990s witnessed a decline in the per capita output in Indian agriculture. As can be seen from Table 21.2, in the 1990s there was a sharp decline in the rate of growth of output and yield in across the board. This is reflected in the decline in the per capita availability of foodgrains as shown in Table 21.3. It is evident that the worst scenario over the entire period has been that of coarse cereals and pulses, the grains eaten by the poorest in the country, grown in the drylands, and nutritionally of the greatest significance. The major cause of this decline is the very strategy that has informed the Indian agriculture for the past 30 years or so. This strategy meant a concentration of investment in the resource-rich regions and farmers, to the complete neglect of India's dryland areas. Therefore, the impact of the Green Revolution has been restricted mainly to the alluvial pockets of the Indo-Gangetic Plains and the Kavery and Godavari deltas, and to crops such as rice and wheat. The period since the mid-1960s has seen an increasingly widening gulf between the Green Revolution pockets and the drylands of India (Table 21.4).

Table 21.2: Rate of Growth of Production and Yield of Foodgrains in India, 1962-1999

Crop	*1962/65 to 1970/73 (in %)*	*1970/73 to 1980/83 (in %)*	*1980/83 to 1990/93 (in %)*	*1990/93 to 1996/99 (in %)*
Rice (P)	1.52	2.23	3.56	2.03
Rice (Y)	1.05	1.60	3.01	1.46
Wheat (P)	10.85	4.51	3.81	3.49
Wheat (Y)	6.26	2.66	3.19	1.70
Coarse Cereals (P)	0.61	1.32	0.91	0.12
Coarse Cereals (Y)	0.69	1.88	2.70	2.10
Pulses (P)	-0.33	0.38	1.38	1.22
Pulses (Y)	0.89	-0.15	1.63	1.34
All Foodgrains (P)	2.28	2.26	2.92	2.12
All Foodgrains (Y)	1.82	1.86	3.22	2.12

Note: P: Production; Y: Yield
Source: Directorate of Economics and Statistics 2000.

Table 21.3: Per Capita Net Availability of Foodgrains in India, 1951-2001

Year	*Cereals (grams per day)*	*Pulses (grams per day)*	*Foodgrains (grams per day)*
1951	334	61	395
1956	360	70	430
1961	400	69	469
1966	360	48	408
1971	418	51	469
1976	374	50	424
1981	417	38	455
1986	434	44	478
1991	468	42	510
1996	443	33	476
2001(P)	391	26	417

Note: P: Provisional
Source: Government of India 2001

Table 21.4: Rate of Growth Productivity of Drylands and Irrigated Areas in India, 1962-1990

Period	*Drylands (in %)*	*Irrigated Areas (in %)*
1962-65 to 1970-73	1.06	1.97
1970-73 to 1980-83	1.70	1.56
1980-83 to 1988-90	0.66	4.20
1962-65 to 1988-90	1.18	2.49

Source: Shah *et al.* 1998, Table 4.13

Raising the productivity of the drylands is imperative if we are to meet the goal of national food security in the coming years. We have estimated that, *even in the most optimistic scenario of further irrigation development in India*, nearly 40 per cent of the national demand for food in 2020 will have to be met through increasing the productivity of dryland agriculture (Table 21.5).

Table 21.5: Projected Demand and Supply of Food Grains in India in the Year 2020

Projected Demand in 2020	338*
Production in 2000	199*
Gap to be met	139*
Maximum Possible Contribution of Irrigated Agriculture of which	84*
From Irrigated Area Expansion	47*
From Increases in Productivity of Irrigated Agriculture	37*
Minimum Balance required from the Drylands	55*
Share of Drylands	40%

*million tonnes

On the basis of the projected growth of population and income elasticities, the food demand is estimated to be around 338 million tonnes (MT) by the year 2020 (Praduman Kumar, 1998, and Government of India 2001). The gross foodgrain output in the year 2000 was 199 MT. To maintain food security even at the current nutritional levels, 139 MT of foodgrains have to be produced additionally by 2020. We know that the cropped area has plateaued in India since 1970. It has remained static at around the 140 million-hectare mark for the past three decades. This is no longer a source of increased output in Indian agriculture. As for irrigated agriculture, its contribution can increase from two sources—expansion in the area under irrigation and yield improvements in the areas already under irrigation.

The ultimate surface water irrigation potential has been estimated at 75 million hectares (CWC 1996). The latest estimate of the groundwater potential is 64 million hectares (CGWB 1998). India's ultimate irrigation potential is, therefore, now estimated to be 139 million hectares. As per land-use statistics, India's gross irrigated area (GIA) was 71 million hectares in 1995, which left a balance of 68 million hectares yet to be exploited. The critical fact of Indian agriculture is that it is marked by great inter-state diversity, in both agro-hydro-geological conditions and level of development. Each of these combines to determine the residual potential contribution that each state can make to the national food security in 2020. Certain states with a greater primary potential are nearing exhaustion in terms of growth possibilities. The real unutilised irrigation potential is in the eastern parts of the country, comprising the medium-to-high rainfall regions of West Bengal, Bihar, Chhatisgarh, Eastern Uttar Pradesh, Jharkhand, Northern Andhra Pradesh and Orissa. These areas together account for nearly 65 per cent of the unutilised irrigation potential in India today. We have made state-level projections of a possible rise in the GIA on the basis of past trends, incorporating a locational shift in the pattern of irrigation towards the hitherto unirrigated tracts (Table 21.6)[18]. As shown in Table 21.6, the GIA can be expected to reach a maximum of 101 million hectares by 2020. Thus, we are projecting a rise of around 30 million hectares between 1995 and 2020. This is an increase of 1.2 million hectares per annum. If the irrigated area grows at this rate between 2000 and 2020, we would have an additional 24 million hectares under irrigation by 2020.[19] Even if the share of foodgrains in the GIA does not fall (which it well might, with the growing crop diversification in the Indian agriculture), only an additional 15.6 million hectares of foodgrain would come under irrigation by 2020.

Now since much of this addition to the irrigated area would be in eastern India, and given the current low yields under irrigated conditions, even under a most hopeful scenario, irrigated yields here are unlikely to cross 3 tonnes per hectare by 2020. We can, therefore, the expect *expansion in the irrigated area to contribute an additional 47 MT to the total annual output of foodgrains by the year 2020.*

Table 21.6: Irrigation Potential and Projected Irrigated Area, 1991-2020

State	*Ultimate Irrigation Potential*			*GIA* 1991*	*Projected Rate of Growth of GIA*	*Projected GIA 2020*	*Potential Utilised in 2020*
	Surface Water	*Ground Water*	*Total*				
(1)	*(2)*	*(3)*	*(4)*	*(5)*	*(6)*	*(7)*	*(8)*
Andhra Pradesh	7.31	3.96	11.27	5.40	1.61	8.72	77%
Bihar	8.38	4.95	13.33	4.19	2.17	7.98	60%
Gujarat	3.34	2.76	6.10	2.91	1.15	4.10	67%
Haryana	3.03	1.46	4.49	4.24	0.19	4.49	100%
Karnataka	3.40	2.57	5.97	2.60	2.81	5.97	100%
Kerala	1.83	0.88	2.71	0.38	1.00	0.51	19%
Madhya Pradesh	8.20	9.73	17.93	4.43	2.98	10.69	60%
Maharashtra	5.31	3.65	8.96	3.17	2.60	6.85	76%
Orissa	4.61	4.20	8.81	2.31	1.89	4.05	46%
Punjab	3.02	2.92	5.94	5.06	0.54	5.94	100%
Rajasthan	3.39	1.78	5.17	4.65	0.35	5.17	100%
Tamil Nadu	2.67	2.83	5.50	2.89	1.40	4.39	80%
Uttar Pradesh	13.68	16.80	30.48	14.77	1.86	25.67	84%
West Bengal	3.62	3.32	6.94	3.91	1.90	6.88	99%
Total	*75.38*	*64.05*	*139.76*	*62.47*	*1.62*	*101.41*	*73%*

Notes: (1) Total includes states and UTs not listed. (2) GIA = Gross Irrigated Area. (3) Irrigation potential and GIA in million hectares. (4) Figures in Column (3) are the latest revised estimates of CGWB (1998).

Sources: 1. Planning Commission (1992) for Column (2). 2. CGWB (1998) for Column (3). 3. Directorate of Economics and Statistics (2000) for Columns (5) and (6)

Another part of the additional food output could come from yield improvements in the areas already under irrigation. Out of the 71 million hectares of the GIA, 46 million hectares were under irrigated food crops in 1995. Yields of irrigated agriculture in India began to plateau in the 1990s and have even declined in some areas.[20] The average annual increment in the foodgrain yield recorded by irrigated agriculture was 0.04 tonnes per hectare in the 1970s and 1980s (Dhawan, 1993, p.72). Even if we optimistically assume that this trend is sustained over the next 20 years, the rise in yield by 2020 will be only 0.8 tonnes per hectare. *Thus, areas already under irrigation could contribute an additional 37 MT of foodgrains in 2020.* The total contribution of irrigated agriculture to foodgrain production from both area expansion and yield improvements put together is, therefore, likely to be around 84 MT, still leaving a shortfall of 55 MT of foodgrains in 2020. In other words, even in the best possible scenario of irrigation development, around 40 per cent of the additional supply of foodgrains needed to match the future rise in demand will have to come from the unirrigated segment of Indian agriculture, most of which is located in the dryland areas. And this demands that the productivity of drylands be raised through an intensive watershed work in these regions.

NOTES

1. As Raj wrote in 1956, "the employment associated directly with the investment process may be called revolving employment. The other type of employment, which is connected with the sediment of productive capital left by the investments, may be referred to as sedimented employment" (Raj, 1990, p. 179)
2. Those who earn more than 50 per cent of their income from agricultural labour.
3. Nearly 70 per cent of India's land area is underlain by consolidated and semi-consolidated rock formations ("hard rocks") that are characterised by extremely low rates of groundwater recharge. In such situations, deep drilling of tubewells leads, in a very short period of time, to what can only be described as "mining" of groundwater.
4. Indeed, "rent-seeking" has probably been aided by the fact that this is a programme with an unprecedented concentration of investment in a small geographical area and predominantly "earthwork" programme which makes it easier to fudge records of work done.
5. Very senior technical advisors of the Rajiv Gandhi Watershed Mission in MP, for example, would argue that since rivers are nothing but enlarged gullies formed due to soil erosion, the aim of watershed projects should be essentially to treat the catchments of rivers, that no drainage line treatment remains to be done, as there would be little run-off left to harvest!

6. Streams or drainage lines in a watershed are classified, according to their catchment areas, into lower and higher "order" streams. Interventions vary according to the order of the drainage line.
7. In a rather naïve counter-reaction, even some fairly respected practitioners have started to speak of the need to adopt a "valley-to-ridge" approach. The real point is to apply the ridge-to-valley principle in a manner that gives primacy to social mobilisation, even while respecting the power of location-specificity and sequencing of works.
8. We need the perspective of Ecological Economics—the economy as a sub-system of the larger eco-system, comprising human beings as also natural resources and non-human species. Unlike the closed, isolated, self-contained circle of conventional economics, the economy is here an open system, engaged in a unidirectional flow of entropy—drawing low entropy from the environment and dumping high entropy waste into it. To use Schumpeter's term, the "pre-analytic vision" is of the economy in co-evolution with the larger eco-system. Unlike the static equilibrium of the neo-classicals, evolution implies a dynamic and adapting disequilibrium, without necessarily suggesting either endless progress or impending doom.
9. A case in point is Samaj Pragati Sahayog (SPS), a grass-roots people's organisation, headquartered in a remote, backward, drought-prone tribal area in the Bagli tehsil, Dewas district, Madhya Pradesh. SPS works on dryland agriculture and focuses on 31 varieties of 7 crops—jowar, maize, tuar, cotton, soyabean, gram and wheat—developed in the laboratories of agricultural scientists at Indore, Khandwa, Khargone and Chhindwara and ICRISAT, Hyderabad. These varieties are based on indigenous seeds, which give good yields even with low external inputs. Multiplication of these seed varieties is carried out on the farms of selected local farmers. Appropriate cultural practices for each variety have been generalised into a typology of farm modules to match different household types in each watershed. Seven farm modules for different categories of households (as per availability of water and soil types) have been developed. Each module has (i) a crop mix; (ii) a second crop, where double cropping is possible; (iii) a set of low-cost and sustainable agricultural practices; and (iv) support systems in terms of land and water management practices that interface with other livelihood opportunities (minor forest produce, forest-based subsidiary occupations, aquaculture, etc.).
10. Wells and tube-wells account for nearly 60 per cent of the irrigated area in Indian agriculture today.
11. The 73rd Constitution Amendment has opened up a space for social mobilisation that must be utilised. However, a major weakness of Panchayati Raj institutions (PRIs), revealed by their functioning so far, is that they have often tended to become pawns in the hands of entrenched local vested interests. Further, even when well-intentioned, they have lacked the technical capabilities to carry out development programmes effectively. This is where the role of the voluntary sector becomes crucial – genuine grassroots NGOs can play a vital role in making PRIs genuinely pro-women, pro-*adivasi* and pro-poor. The NGOs can also undertake the technical empowerment of the PRI representatives and build up a

cadre of local people, capable of providing leadership to *the* Panchayat Raj in the future.

12. The Seven SVOs identified by CAPART have been assigned the responsibility of different groups of States: Hind Swaraj Trust and AFARM (Maharashtra), Development Support Centre (Gujarat and Rajasthan), People's Science Institute (Uttar Pradesh, Himachal Pradesh, Jammu & Kashmir, Punjab, and Haryana), Agragamee (Orissa, West Bengal, North-East), Peermade Development Society (Kerala, Karnataka, Andhra Pradesh and Tamil Nadu), and Samaj Pragati Sahayog (Madhya Pradesh, Chhattisgarh, Jharkhand, and Bihar).
13. CAPART is a semi-autonomous body registered under the Societies Registration Act, working under the aegis of the Ministry of Rural Development, Government of India, to provide financial and resource support exclusively to voluntary organisations for rural development.
14. The responsibilities of SVOs are to promote the watershed programme among prospective partners with a good track record, by pro-actively seeking them out, informing them about the programme, assisting them in preparing proposals and getting funds from the government; to impart training on watershed development to agencies engaged in watershed development; to provide technical and other required support through field visits to the watershed area at regular intervals; to act as institutional monitors for the watershed programme, evaluating the performance of agencies engaged in the programme or those wishing to join it; to conduct research on various aspects of watershed development; to disseminate widespread awareness by acting as ambassadors of the watershed approach.
15. To give an indication of what has already been achieved, it may be mentioned that over the past five years, Samaj Pragati Sahayog, one of the seven national SVOs, has identified and empowered 50 partners who have begun work on 100,000 hectares in their watersheds. Further, an SVO will not have to hand-hold each of its 200 NGO partners at the same time. There will be a typical phasing out period of 5-7 years, after which the NGO will be on its own, and will, in turn, empower other agencies in its area of work.
16. This is how we must visualise the NGO effort—not as a substitute for government initiative but as a stimulus for improving its quality.
17. Let us not forget that the Government of India is currently seriously considering spending nearly Rs.40,000 crore per year over a 14-year period to complete the grandiose scheme of interlinking of rivers.
18. In case the state is already near its full irrigation potential, we have projected a rate of growth that takes it to the full potential in 2020. In other cases, we have projected the historical rate of growth (3-yearly moving averages) for the period 1981-92. This is the period when the irrigation rates picked up in the hitherto neglected regions such as Eastern India and Madhya Pradesh. Taking the rates of an earlier period would have understated the potential of these emerging states.
19. It should be noted that this projected rate of expansion is a touch optimistic as it is almost equal to what was achieved in India during the period 1970-95 (1.3 million hectares p.a.).
20. See, for example, ICAR 1998.

REFERENCES

CGWB (1998): "Groundwater in India". Website of Ministry of Water Resources, Government of India (http://wrmin.nic.in)

CWC (1996): "Water Related Statistics". New Delhi: Central Water Commission, Ministry of Water Resources, Government of India.

Dhawan, B.D. (1993): *Trends and New Tendencies in Indian Irrigated Agriculture*. New Delhi: Commonwealth Publishers.

Directorate of Economics and Statistics (2000): "Indian Agriculture in Brief". New Delhi: Directorate of Economics and Statistics, Ministry of Agriculture, Government of India.

Government of India (2001): "Report of the High Level Committee on Long Term Grain Policy". New Delhi: Department of Food and Public Distribution.

Government of India (2002): "Economic Survey 2001-02". New Delhi

ICAR (1998): "Decline in Crop Productivity in Haryana and Punjab: Myth or Reality?" New Delhi: Indian Council for Agricultural Research.

Planning Commission (1997): "Ninth Five Year Plan—Vol. I". New Delhi.

Planning Commission (2001): "Approach Paper to Tenth Five Year Plan (2002-07)". New Delhi.

Planning Commission (2002): "Report of the Special Group on Targeting Ten Million Employment Opportunities Per Year over 10th Plan Period". New Delhi.

Planning Commission (2002): "Tenth Five Year Plan (2002-07), Volume I". New Delhi.

Praduman Kumar (1998): "Food Demand and Supply Projections for India". Paper No. 98-01,

New Delhi: Indian Agricultural Research Institute.

Raj, K.N. (1956): "Idle Rural Labour and its Investment Potential: A Re-appraisal". Reprinted in K.N. Raj. 1990. *Organizational Issues in Indian Agriculture*. New Delhi: Oxford University Press.

Shah, M.; Banerji, D.; Vijay Shankar, P.S.; and Ambasta, P. (1998): *India's Drylands: Tribal Societies and Development through Environmental Regeneration*. New Delhi: Oxford University Press.

22

Participatory Approach in a Resource-Centred Programme

A View of the Socio-Economic Issues

R.S. DESPANDE and M.J. BHENDE

The concept of watershed management involves planning the development of a resource region. The focus of planning is on the optimal and sustainable use of the resources beginning with water, land, and people. The approach of watershed treatment is holistic and involves the entire bio-social system. Broadly one can identify eight sub-systems within it: silvicultural, horticultural, pastoral, livestock, agricultural, hydro-geological, administrative and social. These sub-systems have a dynamic setting and they interface at two levels. First, there are interactions within the bio-systems as functions of the geographical and climatic conditions. These interactions decide the combinations and the content of technology. At the second level, there is the interface with the stakeholders, and with the administrative and social systems. In this context, the programme implementation processes and people's participation in the programme become crucial determinants of success. "The World Development Report" (1992) stressed the importance of a participatory approach in creating viable resource management institutions. Since the watershed development programme is an area-based programme, it can be successful only if there is an active support from the communities in the region. People's participation in the implementation of the programme becomes crucial. Pure technocratic solutions do not help in a resource-centred programme. Results of the technological component are usually demonstrated under laboratory conditions, but testing and implementation are on the ground. Hence, institutional, operational, organisational and other social parameters assume importance. Since these parameters are the components of behavioural sub-systems, their direct quantification is not possible. Therefore, one has to rely on proxies represented by responses and opinions.

Concept and Need of Participation

The concept of participation is interdisciplinary, but it stems from the discipline of social psychology. In a social psychological domain, participation forms the basis of group behaviour in a small or large group. (Cartwright and Zander 1968). The questions about group behaviour have also bothered social scientists from the perspective of development initiatives but the fact that it involves basic social psychological parameters is always overlooked. For social scientists it is the question of success or failure of a group initiative which is at stake and thus the determinants of success or failure are confused with the factors influencing group behaviour. But for social psychologists explaining group behaviour has always posed a greater challenge. According to some social psychological theorists, people join together because of common needs, shared goals and imminent common threats (Shaw 1971). Another view is that the most important conditions for group formation are homogeneity, consistency and similarities in skills and abilities (Penner 1978). Social scientists have also analysed the essential conditions required for the formation of a cohesive group. For instance, Olson (1965) has made a very pertinent observation: unless the group is small and there is coercion from outside or some other event threatens individuals' common interests, they do not come together shedding their self interests. Ostrom (1992) prefers to call these essential conditions *design principles.* The following seven design principles are advocated to achieve a strong and lasting institution:

1. Clearly defined boundaries,
2. Congruence between appropriation and provision rules,
3. Choice of collective arrangements,
4. Graduated sanctions against violating appropriators,
5. A well-set conflict resolution mechanism,
6. Recognition of the right to organise,

7. Nesting of various activities like appropriation, enforcement, monitoring, conflict, resolution and governance.

However, it is the location or group specificity that decides the pattern of formation and consistency of a group. Two social variables, namely, *role* and *status,* play a significant part. These variables are further classified into *relative role* and *relative status* and *expected role* and *expected status*. The divergence between the existing situation and the perceived situation also plays a significant role in explaining group dynamics. The compatibility of these two components goes a long way in deciding the sustainability of the programme.

In the literature on watershed, participatory management is defined as a process which operates at various levels right from planning through execution and finally ensures sustainability for future. This conception, however, excludes the necessary and sufficient conditions for participation as well as different forms and layers of participation. Pimbert and Pretty (1997) have identified the following seven forms of participation.

1. *Passive Participation:* Where people are told to share a component of work.
2. *Information Participation:* The participants are involved by supplying answers to the questions asked.
3. *Consultation Participation:* In this situation the respondents participate when they are consulted on the issues. The issues are posed from above.
4. *Participation by Providing Hard Resources:* In this case the beneficiaries provide the material resources required. This can include land, labour, or money.
5. *Functional Participation:* This is an institutional form of participation where the participants share the different functions of a formal or informal institution.
6. *Interactive Participation Process:* This is a true social engineering function. The participants are involved in a close interaction on an issue of their concern and arrive at a solution by consensus. There is flexibility on the issue of having an external initiator.
7. *Self-generated Participation:* When a group of people are

confronted with an issue which puts at stake their welfare, automatic participation is generated among the stakeholders.

These forms are, however, not exhaustive and can change in priorities and intensity according to situation. Sharma (1997) viewed the process of participation from the traditional culture and mores of people. His observation was from the specific standpoint of an upper Himalayan watershed. In a similar setting, Ostiani and Warren (1995) documented the learning from the field experience of the project on Inter-regional Project for Participatory Upland Conservation and Development. They classified the levels of participation into five categories:

1. Participation based on the need for information,
2. Participatory planning approach,
3. Participatory monitoring and evaluation,
4. Participation provoked by capacity building,
5. Participation through contribution.

In a similar vein, Cohen and Uphoff (1980) identified four layers beginning with decision-making and going through implementation, distribution of the accrued benefits and, finally, evaluating to correct the shortfalls in the process of implementation. A common feature in the above classifications is that these authors have specifically concentrated upon the functional aspect, and the utility of this aspect is limited to testing of the extent of participation and the depth of involvement.

Participation in any natural resource-based programme is essential and at the same time quite difficult. The necessity of participation arises out of the inter-linkages between activities, the process of internalisation of externalities, and sustainability of the intervention. Difficulties arise because any external intervention is viewed by the group with scepticism and the group takes its own time to internalise it. There are various other factors that also influence making or breaking of groups.

Participation in a Resource-based Programme

Participation in a resource-based programme is different from participation in any other development initiative. Its pre-conditions as well as the process of participation itself are different. On the positive side, such participation comes through quickly if the very availability of the resource is threatened in a short run. Thus it is often a threat to the sources of livelihood that enforces participation. But on the negative side, visualising future benefits and repercussions is a difficult task and thus the sustainability of the project comes under threat. In addition to this, the arrangement for sharing of the accruable benefits as well as the type of institutions evolved matter. Above all the process assumes greater importance.

The process of participation can be crucial in three stages. First, the design of the project should involve village communities. The commonly followed approach is the Participatory Rural Appraisal (PRA) method, in which the participants of the programme sit together to plan a strategy for the treatment of arable and non-arable lands. Projects funded by MYRADA, PIDOW, GTZ, and DFID have generally followed this method. The success of the method varies across the projects (Deshpande and Reddy 1991). However, it is not an essential component of the watershed programmes undertaken by Non-Governmental Organisations (NGOs) in the country. Many NGOs take participation for granted and plan the watershed treatments in isolation. It is essential because the technology involved is likely to contest the area allocation decisions of the farmers. Secondly, involvement of people comes at the time of planning the implementation procedure of the new technologies. At this stage, it is essential to understand the farmers' awareness of the technology and its impact on the overall system of watershed planning. This was tried in the National Watershed Development Programme in its second and third phases (Deshpande and Narayanamoorthy 1999). It was found that in such experiments often the farmers knew only the name of the technology used, but they are unaware of its influence or the necessity of its components in the overall design. Thirdly, if farmers have a clear perception of the concepts involved, then the sustenance of the watershed structures is naturally ensured. Unfortunately, the conflict between private and social benefits begins at about the time when the treatments are half-way through or nearing completion. Therefore, after the implementation, community participation is necessary to sustain the structures created and continue with the technology adopted. But it is difficult to obtain it at this stage. Participation is largely determined by the type of institutions that have emerged in the process (Deshpande and Nikumbh 1993) Keeping these three stages in view, we have analysed below community involvement in watershed projects.

Farmers' perception about the internal coordination is different from the usual understanding of the concept. They attach a great deal of significance to the work carried out in their fields and in the village as well as to the discussions about various disciplines. Therefore, theirs is a wider and operational perspective rather than a narrow understanding of the concept. It is quite interesting to note that about 74 per cent of the farmers visualise a good internal coordination. The proportion reduces as one moves from the upper to the lower reach.

Another important aspect to analyse is the participation of different disciplines in the project region which can be viewed from two different angles. First, from the official or project point of view, the density of work carried out under each component is to be compared with the actual need of the component. This approach may not yield any spill-over as the project is planned systematically with the involvement of scientists as well as administrators. Hence, it is difficult to get any answer other than the one indicating perfect planning. Second from the farmers' point of view. The farmers assign different levels of importance to the disciplines like crop husbandry (represented by the application of new technology), horticultural plantations, forestry, silviculture and soil conservation.

Community's Actions Towards Watershed Approach

The community actions towards the watershed approach can best be judged from the functions of the respondents. Reactions of the respondents were sought for three important factors. Firstly, awareness, attitude and perception of the respondents are quite important. The watershed concept has to be clearly understood by those who participate in it. It is not enough for the community to understand the meaning of the concept; it is necessary that the community is fully aware of the importance as well as the impact of the treatment. In the project area, all respondents had only a cursory understanding of the concept of watershed and the treatments given in the watershed programme. But this was not enough to understand their involvement. Therefore, we enquired about their perception of the treatment. Secondly, the respondents' views about the impact of the treatments also indicated their involvement in the programme. Thirdly, an important aspect of the farmers' involvement in the programme relates to their views about the simplicity, affordability, viability and replicability of the watershed components. All three aspects together indicate the overall involvement of the farmers in watershed treatments.

Role of Institutions

Village-level and other rural institutions influence the programmes of agricultural development. Most of the rural development programmes are directed through these institutions. *Gram Panchayat, Taluka Panchayat Samiti* and *Zilla Parishad* are the components of the three-tier Panchayati Raj institutions. These are the formal institutions which take part in the developmental activities. Apart from these, the cooperatives, educational institutions and socio-cultural organisations take an active interest in the development activities.

The role of the institutions can be analysed from two different angles. First, the formal public institutions or informal people's institutions, at the village level or at a higher level, may be directly involved in the developmental projects. The institutions may plan, initiate and implement the projects. One such example can be the *Shetakari Sahayak Mandal* of Adgaon or the Ralegan Siddhi experiment of Shri Anna Hajare. In these cases the involvement of institutions has to be analysed from the angle of institution as well as that of the participants. Secondly, when the projects are initiated, planned and implemented through government departments, the role of the institutions has to be gauged indirectly. The Manoli watershed project falls in the latter category where the role of institutions is not that of an initiator but that of a participant through the cultivators.

Method of Farmers' Organisation and People's Participation

In any resource-based programme, participation involves the process of seeking the stakeholders' concern. It is the process that largely decides the success of the participation. The process of formation goes through four stages, namely, initial planning, monitoring and involvement in the implementation, clear perception about the accruable benefits, and an accepted arrangement of benefit sharing. The initial steps require developing norms for participation.

In a resource-based programme the stakeholders are spread in three concentric rings. The first circle or the core of the stakeholders consists of direct beneficiaries who receive income or employment immediately after the treatment is completed. In a watershed context this group includes the lower reach farmers where moisture enhancement is the first accrued benefit especially in a low rainfall region (Deshpande and Rajasekaran, 1995). In the *Terai* region the immediate benefit goes to the upper-reach landowners (Deshpande, 1999).

People's cooperation is achieved by providing appropriate incentives; the best incentive is financial support. Participation of the community in the watershed development project is ensured by inviting participation of NGOs as they are aware about the local social dynamics and play an important role in motivating the people to participate in the project. Moreover, the credibility of NGO, and the competence of the staff also affect community participation in the watershed projects. The formation of watershed committees at micro-watershed level provides representation not only to the farmers but also to the members of self-help groups, landless labourers, and women. Financial support for various land-based and non-land-based activities ensures active participation of the local communities. Technical support also plays an important role in watershed development. Presence of technical persons or group infuses confidence among the participants. In most watershed development programmes, the technical group has the responsibility to organise the people to undertake project activities. The technical group should have the capacity to convince them about the benefits accruing from the project and thus enlist their participation.

Most importantly, the participation in the watershed project depends on the characteristics of the group (Olson 1965). A cohesive and homogeneous group with an able leadership is likely to participate in the watershed development programme actively. Participation in the project and the success of the project are conditioned by the homogeneity of the group, its goals and the incentive structure provided in the project. If there are conflicting interests or even diverse interests within the group, they may create problems of participation in and sustenance of the project. Frequency as well as chances of a conflict are minimal when one deals with a cohesive group. Often, an apparently homogeneous group may hide the differences in social, political, and economic interests of its members. The group with common goals and interest sustains participation in the programme. Participation in watershed activities is thus influenced by the characteristics of the group. Hence, the choice of the group becomes crucial for a successful participation.

In addition to the above, social and economic behaviour at the village level is dictated by the wider democratic processes and are also influenced by the local or village-level issues. The wider democratic forces affect the flow of funds, technological assistance, and administrative bottlenecks in the implementation of the project. However, the local democratic forces are stronger because they generate immediate political and social interactions. Village-level politics, personal prejudices and the standing of the group leader are some of the important factors that influence not only the participation in the project but also determine its success.

Participation in the project is directly associated with the level of the stakes involved. The higher the stakes for the community, the higher is the probability of sustenance of the project. A low level of the aggregate stakes means that sustenance will also be low. As the stake rises, the probability of sustenance also rises; and it reaches a peak at some level, and then turns asymptotic thereafter. Within the group, those who expect large benefits may participate more actively than those who anticipate peripheral benefits.

The success of the project and the level of participation also depend on how the project is interfaced with the local or village institutions. In a typical village set-up, four types of traditional institutions are important: (1) political institutions like the village *panchayat;* (2) social institutions like community or caste (*jati*) panchayats and youth associations; (3) religious institutions like the temple trusts; and (4) economic institutions like the cooperative societies, traders' associations and farmers' associations. These institutions influence participation of the community under their command. Thus any participative process has to take into account the presence of these institutions. The involvement of these institutions determines the success and sustainability of the project.

Although participation of the community is essential during all the four stages, i.e. (i) initial planning, (ii) implementation and monitoring, (iii) perceptions about benefit sharing, and (iv) distribution of benefits, it is more crucial in the first, second, and the final stage for the sustenance of the project. The benefits accruing from the project need to be distributed among the participants, and this provides an incentive for sustaining the project and hence participation of the group is essential at this stage.

A group is a collection of persons, and individuals differ in their perceptions and attitudes. What binds them together are the common interests and goals. A group has four types of constituent members. The first constituent, is the core leader. (The leader should be from the majority community and should be able to exercise his authority over the group.) He could be either feudal or assimilative. The second constituent are the contributors. They participate actively in the decision-making process. The third constituent is the mute member who does not contribute to the decision-making process and stays aloof most of the time. The fourth constituent is the splinter component. This represents the persons who are dissatisfied with the leader and find faults with the content of the decisions, the style of decision-making, etc. The composition of the group influences the nature of participation in the project.

Nature of Participation

The experience of participation of the community in the watershed development programmes is varied. Participation often grows and sometimes declines as the programme matures. The major factors which make or break participation are holding of group meetings, leadership in the meetings, and management of funds. Holding of regular meetings facilitates interaction and discussions between group members. However, frequent meetings may lead to breaking up of the group if the splinter component within the group is influential. A person having better knowledge about the project objectives, goals and activities should ideally lead the meetings. The leader should have a large stake in the project. In other words, the leader should be one of the core beneficiaries—a person whose wealth-ranking is influenced by the success or failure of the project. Such a leader motivates fellow members which results in better participation.

Professional management of funds instills confidence among the members and induces active participation. Management of funds includes not only managing funds received from the sponsoring agency but also mobilisation of the funds from the community. The community has to mobilise funds to set up an institution governing watershed structures in anticipation of benefits. Contribution generates a feeling of belongingness in the minds of would-be beneficiaries and encourages active participation. Since the watershed project has a long gestation period, accrual of benefits takes a long time. Hence, mobilisation of funds is a difficult task. However, participation is positively associated with mobilisation of funds. Higher the mobilisation of the fund, the better would be the involvement of people as their stakes rise. Nevertheless, mobilisation alone does not ensure participation; there should also be no major lapses in the management of funds. Maintenance of funds not only requires professional management of funds, sincerity and commitment to the cause, but it also calls for a thorough understanding of the concepts of the watershed programme.

The management of funds can be streamlined by auditing of accounts. Auditing of accounts by internal auditors offers flexibility in programme implementation and management of funds. It also helps understanding any major inconsistencies in the expenditure pattern at the ground level. Identification and location of inconsistencies help straighten out the auditing framework and rationalise the expenditure pattern of the watershed programme. At this juncture, internal and external accountability comes into the picture. Accountability is desired with three partners namely, the stakeholders, the funding/ sponsoring agency and the institutions involved in implementation. Accountability also helps in a proper implementation of the watershed programme and, therefore, the nature of participation becomes a direct component of such accountability. Of course this requires some level of autonomy in utilising the funds which is crucial in the management of funds. However, autonomy should be accompanied with well-defined checks and balances in the programme design.

The second most important factor in the nature of participation is the plan and execution of the scheme. The various stages in the process of planning and execution are usually dictated by the funding agencies/authorities. The major steps/stages involved in the planning and execution of development schemes are (i) choice of components, (ii) liaison with donor agencies, (iii) technical and manpower assistance, and (iv) developing norms for various activities. These stages have overlapping areas. Their influence is aggregate in nature towards the promotion of participation. The choice of the component has to match the thinking of the group. The programme-oriented, stakeholder-oriented, and technology-oriented components work together. A proper combination of these will result in better execution of the programme with enhanced participation. Participation also depends on the liaison with the donor agencies as well as the type of relationship the executing agency/group has with the donor agency.

The benefactor-beneficiary relationship is usually fragile; even then the partnership with the donor agency can sustain participation of the beneficiaries. This, however, requires a proper manpower and technical assistance from both the donor agency and the participating group. Dynamic, trained and courteous technical manpower improves participation of the group. In many watershed programmes technical manpower is usually borrowed from the sister/line departments. This results in superimposition of the culture of the line department on the implementing agency as well as on the stakeholder group.

While seeking participation in development schemes like the watershed programme, it is essential to involve the group in the planning and execution of the programme. It becomes necessary to lay down certain norms or guiding principles in order to seek active participation. These norms have to be developed keeping in view the feasibility of technology, stakeholders' interest, and the elasticity of their participation with respect to their interests. Ambitious schemes, offering better long-term benefits and planned with over-enthusiasm, may affect participation if they fail to convince the group. The requirements of the donor agency have to be fulfilled, and an overall balance has to be maintained across the components in the programme. Among the norms pertaining to participation, the norms related to the monetary contribution and labour-sharing and benefit-sharing arrangements assume greater importance. These factors together decide the nature of participation. A programme with well-defined norms and a proper arrangement for sharing the inputs and outputs encourages participation.

The nature of participation is more important at the completion of the programme since the created assets have to be managed by the community once the funding/sponsoring agencies begin to withdraw from the project. If the assets created are directly linked to the benefits and if this can be demonstrated or if the assets have positive externalities for the group, there will be greater participation in the management of assets.

Monitoring and concurrent evaluation of any land-based programme provides for "on-line" or mid-term corrections. This serves to locate and identify the problems in the process of implementation. The task of monitoring and evaluating, however, should be assigned to an outside agency which is independent of the executing group. Such processes instill confidence and better liaison among the stakeholders as well as with the funding agency. The nature of participation finally depends on the existence of a proper and well-defined conflict resolution mechanism.

There are five major areas of conflicts that act as stumbling blocks in the process of participation. These are: (1) social politicisation, (2) illegal use of resources, (3) lack of positive discrimination, (4) conflict between the accrued benefits in the upper, and (5) lower reaches, and displacement to accommodate different watershed structures. The social politicisation is the process in which various social groups become strong interest groups. The conflict between them is often a reflection of an already existing or dormant social conflict. This may be based on caste, community, religion, etc. Even the allegiance of the members/groups to different political parties may result in social politicisation. Similarly, in many watershed development programmes, influential participants/group members tend to appropriate most of the benefits of the common pool resources. The best example of such a practice is the location of stormwater drains or run off channels for excess water. The lack of positive discrimination among the participants determines the nature of participation in the watershed development programmes. The distribution of anticipated gains from the developmental activity should be guided by the principle that *all are better off and nobody is worse off*. This way every participant gains something. There should be some built-in mechanism to compensate participants from the upper reaches of the watershed since most of the time participants from the lower reaches derive benefits at the cost of the former. In the process of watershed development, a number of structures are constructed in the field. It is advisable to locate these structures in such places that they would not affect any participant significantly. For example, the location of a farm pond on a plot owned by a marginal farmer may deprive him of his land. He then needs to be compensated appropriately so that his livelihood is not affected. Participation is greatly influenced by conflicts – and conflicts do occur—and hence a provision for well-defined mechanisms for conflict resolution should be included in the project to encourage active participation.

Constraints in Participatory Management

Watershed development approach is an area programme and thus involves the participation at three levels. First, it is the internal integration of the implementing agency and its vertical integration with the state bodies. This allows an operational ease to the project team which is an essential component. The second level of interaction is built while implementing the project and through the continuous involvement of the beneficiaries in the planning and implementation of the programme. This is achieved through meetings held in the village and while explaining the programme components to the villagers of the region. The third level of participation is when the beneficiaries themselves approach the project officer for the purpose of their work. This phase is important because the consultation is initiated by the farmers themselves. The real test of awareness comes when the farmers expresses opinions about the maintenance of the structures and the constraints.

The cultivators identified the following five areas of vital importance which should be examined:

1. Policy constraints
2. Institutional constraints
3. Attitudinal constraints
4. Information constraints
5. Inter-agency coordination

First, the farmers feel that they should have been involved from the stage of planning. Though there were no reservations expressed about the implementation of the present project, the planning was carried out only at the official level. Of course, there are operational difficulties in the process and hence its feasibility has to be worked out carefully. Secondly, the infrastructural support in terms of marketing and credit facilities was inadequate to prop up the incremental production generated. Thirdly, some of the respondents felt that the density of the *bunds* and the *khus* key lines were not adequate. The suggestion was that the seed material for *khus* grass should be provided to the farmers themselves. Fourthly, the nalla bunding and nalla training activities need to be sustained for a longer period of time and, therefore, the responsibility of its maintenance should be assigned to someone immediately after the completion. In the absence of such an arrangement, these structures are neglected and do not serve the purpose. Fifthly, there were respondents who were not satisfied with the financial allocations in the programme and felt that more work should have been planned.

To conclude, countrywide evaluations of the watershed programmes indicated that the state-managed watershed programmes fail to deliver the intended results (Deshpande and Narayanamoorthy 2000; Kerr *et al.* 1998). At the same time it was clearly demonstrated that the programmes undertaken in the non-governmental sectors were quite successful. The latter also had long-term sustainability and equitable distribution of benefits.

REFERENCES

Cartwright, D., and A. Zander (eds.), (1968): *Group Dynamics: Research and Theory.* New York: Harper.

Chopra, Kanchan (1998): "Watershed Management Programmes: An Evaluation of Alternative Institutional and Technological Options". Delhi: Institute of Economic Growth.

Chopra, Kanchan; Kadekodi, Gopal K.; and Murthy, M.N. (1988): "Sukhomajri and Dhamala Watersheds in Haryana: A Participatory Approach to Management". Delhi: Institute of Economic Growth.

Cohen, John M., and Uphoff, Norman T. (1980): "Participation's Place in Rural Development: Seeking Clarity through Specificity" *World Development* 8(2).

Deshpande, R.S. (1996): "Watershed Development Programme: A Strategy under ACRP Approach". In D. N. Basu and S. P. Kashyap (eds.), *Agro Climatic Regional Planning in India,* Vol. II. New Delhi: Concept Publishers.

Deshpande, R.S. (1999): "In Response to Nature's Challenges: An Assessment of the Soil Conservation Project of the North Bengal Terai Development Programme (NBTDP)". Research Report NBTDP.

Deshpande, R.S., and Narayanamoorthy, A. (1999): "An Appraisal of Watershed Development Programme across Regions in India". Pune: Gokhale Institute of Politics and Economics.

Deshpande, R.S., and Thimmaiah, G. (1999): "Watershed Development Approach and Experiences of National Watershed Development Programmes in the Country". *Journal of Rural Development* 18(3).

Deshpande, R.S., and Rajshekaran, N. (1995): "Impact Evaluation Study of World Bank Aided Pilot Project for Watershed Development in Rain-fed Areas". Research Report. Pune: Gokhale Institute of Politics and Economics.

Deshpande, R.S., and Nikumbh, S.R. (1993): "Treatment of Uncultivated Land under Watershed Development Approach: Institutional and Economic Issues". *Arthavijnana,* 35(1).

Deshpande, R.S., and Reddy, Ratna V. (1991a): "Differential Impact of Watershed Based Technology: Some Analytical Issues". *Indian Journal of Agricultural Economics* 46(3).

Deshpande, R.S., and Reddy, Ratna V. (1991b): "Watershed Development Approach in a Fragile Resource Region: An Analytical Study of Maharashtra". Mimeograph Series No. 33. Pune: Gokhale Institute of Politics and Economics.

Deshpande, R.S., and Reddy, Ratna V. (1992): "Participatory Process in Watershed Management: A Case Study of Maharashtra". *Asian Economic Review.*

Farrington, J., and Lobo, Crispino (1997): "Scaling up the Participatory Watershed Development in India: Lessons from the Indo-German Watershed Development Programme". Natural Resource Perspectives. London: Overseas Development Institute.

Joshi, P.C., and Bantilan, M.C.S. (1997): "Vertisol Watershed Research in Semi-Arid Tropics: Directions for Impact Assessment". *Arthavijnana* 39(3).

Kerr, John (2002): "Watershed Development, Environmental Services and Poverty Alleviation in India". *World Development* 30(8).

Kerr, John; Pangare, Ganesh; Lokur-Pangare, Vasudha; and George, P.L. (1998): "ICAR-World Bank Research Project". New Delhi: The World Bank.

Kolavalli, Shashi, and Kerr, John (2002): "Scaling up Participatory Watershed Development in India". *Development and Change* 33(2).

Mosse, D., Farrington, J., and Rew, A. (1998): *Development as a Process*. London: Routledge.

Olson, Mancur (1965): *The Logic of Collective Action*. Cambridge: Harvard University Press.

Ostiani L., and Patrizio, Warren (1995): "Initial Methodological Lessons Learned in Participatory Watershed Management, in Watershed Management in Tropical and Upper Himalayas". WWW.fao.org/DOCREP

Ostrom, E. (1992): *Crafting Institutions for Self Governing Irrigation System.* San Francisco: ICS Press.

Penner, Louis, A. (1978): *Social Psychology.* London: Oxford University Press.

Pimbert, M. and Pretty, J. (1997): "Diversity and Sustainability in Community Based Conservation". Paper Presented at the UNESCO–IIPA Regional Workshop on Community Based Conservation in February, at New Delhi.

Shah, Amita (2000): "Watershed Development Programme in India: Emerging Issues for Environmental Development Perspectives". *Economic and Political Weekly* 33(26).

Sharma, Prem N. (1997): "Participatory Process for Integrated Watershed Management". PWMTA – FARM Field Document No 7, Kathmandu.

Shaw, M.E. (1971): *Group Dynamics: The Psychology of Small Group Behaviour.* New York: McGraw Hill.

World Development Report, (1992): Development and the Environment. Oxford.

PART VI

PARTICIPATORY IRRIGATION MANAGEMENT: A Reform or a Programme?

23

Objects and Accomplishments of Participatory Irrigation Management Programme in India

An Open Pair of Scissors

R. PARTHASARATHY

The view that community management of water resources has a significant potential for addressing the problems of stagnating agricultural productivity in the command areas of major irrigation projects has gained ground in recent years. One frequently cited reason for the opinion is that the existing irrigation systems are mismanaged; they are also in a state of serious disrepair. The breakdown, it is argued, can be seen most vividly at the village level where the government administration of water delivery has become so ineffective that in most cases farmers do not receive adequate and timely supply. On the other hand, in many cases too much water has led to problems of waterlogging, salination, and soil degradation. There is ample evidence to support these contentions. As a result, there is a growing consensus that the solution to these problems lies in Irrigation Management Transfer (IMT), that is, turning over control of irrigation management to the end-users, the farmers. Not only in India, elsewhere too, the creation of a new institution at the village community level, called the Water Users Association (WUA)—and in some cases vertically integrating them at the project level—has become the central focus of governmental programmes variously called Participatory Irrigation Management (PIM) or Farmer Managed Irrigation Systems (FMIS). These programmes aim at decentralising irrigation management and revitalising rural development at grassroots. Similar steps have been taken for community management of the watershed resources where user participation is on a very different scale.

The PIM solution to the mismanagement problem, while ingenious, is not without its share of difficulties. First, many village communities are neither prepared for the new water management system nor have the necessary experience in the operation and maintenance of canals. Further, in most states, there are no concerted post-turnover capacity building exercises. The complexities of conjunctive use of water in a given basin are yet to be sorted out. In addition, there is conflicting evidence whether WUAs can deliver water effectively and collect water charges so that the system becomes self-financing and less burdensome for the government. Second, it is not always clear who actually controls the allocation of water and who receives the benefits when the WUAs manage the resource. The question of the right to water and equity in access irrespective of the gender, land tenure status, and location of the plot in the canal network remains to be resolved. Third, canal water has many uses and diverse claimants (both within and outside the WUA). Thus, conflicts over the right to the resource has the potential to proliferate which would call for mechanisms for resolving disputes. The fourth problem lies in the environmental impact of community-based management of increased supply: the question is whether the WUAs can manage issues like soil degradation caused by waterlogging and salination. Ultimately, the resolution of such problems will depend on whether village communities and their WUAs can be linked in a basin irrigation network and empowered to take and implement decisions that would bring about an efficient, equitable and sustainable use of the resource.

This paper aims to analyse these issues drawing on the numerous studies—some are completed and others are in progress (Parthasarathy, 1998, 2000; Parthasarathy *et al.*, 2001; van Koppen, Parthasarathy, Safiliou 2002). The paper is organised as follows: The following section, Section 2, presents a heuristic framework. Section 3 presents an overview of the PIM programme in India and analyses one of the important factors influencing its susceptibility. An analysis of the targets and accomplishments of the PIM programme so far and an outline of the financial implications in implementing the transfer programme are also included in this section. Section 4 briefly explores the challenges identified in the analysis and searches for possible solutions to sharpen the instrument – participatory irrigation management programme—and to narrow the distance of the open scissor blades. Section 5 presents the Summary.

A HEURISTIC FRAMEWORK

It is important to note that the justification for the IMT or PIM lies in seeking not only improved water management but also an effective implementation of India's rural development strategy in order to meet the increasing burden imposed by the rapidly growing population and consumption of resources. The turnover of irrigation management to the end-users is a significant step because it coincides with the wider reform measures initiated by the Government of India and several states that aim at reducing governmental controls and subsidies. In rural India, the reform and revitalisation of rural development are unlikely to succeed unless they reach and evoke a response from the millions of cultivators long dependent on government administration.

The present analysis of the irrigation management transfer programme is situated at the intersection of a number of literatures. The literature on the decentralisation of development initiatives includes the work by Dreze and Sen (1995), Bardhan (1996) and Korten (1990). These works focus on the challenge of moving the decision-making control out of the hands of government bureaucrats and placing it into those of the end-users. They highlight the importance of providing incentives and requiring contributions in order to stimulate participation and inculcate a sense of ownership at both individual and community levels.

The literature on the management of common property resources provides a wealth of ideas and also presents an array of problems that bear on the community-based irrigation management. Ostrom (1992), Vaidyanathan (1999), Jodha (1992), Sengupta (1991), Shah (1993) and others have approached the dilemma of the "tragedy of the commons" from a variety of perspectives and using different methodologies. The on-going debate on the issue of linking land ownership with water rights has not resolved the problem of multiple claims on water for uses other than crop cultivation, such as for domestic consumption, for animals, for urban and industrial use, and for power generation. Little has been written about the fact that village communities inevitably find themselves nested in a wider context of powerful stakeholders for all of whom the state must find accommodation, and how the community-based institutions would deal with the competing claims.

Under the irrigation management transfer policies new rights are conferred on stakeholders. But in most cases clarity on what constitutes a "right" is absent. Legitimising the "rights" of hitherto marginalised users as well as those who have traditionally enjoyed water rights brings to the fore conflicts of interest and also managerial problems (Bruns and Meinzen-Dick, 2000). In addition to the existing irrigators' *rights,* there is a new focus on the rights of users such as municipalities, industries, etc. Thus how the different uses are to be prioritised must be decided.

What does a "community" mean in large-scale canal irrigation systems? Even within a WUA, in many cases its jurisdiction varies from just one village to as many as 10. In Andhra Pradesh, roughly, 6 to 10 WUAs make up a Distributary Committee, and about 8 to 10 Distributary Committees make up a Project Committee, when formed. Thus, the "community of water users" in a particular village is an integral part of the larger communities defined by different hydraulic levels within the same basin. When reference to a "community of water users" is made under the PIM, one should recognise that the members of this community may have a common interest in the use of the resource, or they may be in conflict over it. The proponents of decentralisation must confront the issue of how a community of heterogeneous groups would treat marginalised groups within its own fold such as women, disadvantaged castes and tribes, tenants, the land-poor, and the landless. The vast literature on India's rural sociology has developed several new foci: gender and equity analysis (Agarwal 1994; Meinzen-Dick *et al.* 1997; Shiva 1988; Mosse 1994; Moench 1998; van Koppen 1998, 2002; Zwarteveen 1997), the political-economy of caste relationships and mobilisation (Kohli 1987, 1990; Mendelsohn and Vicziany 1998) as well as changes in land and labour use patterns in the post-liberalisation era (Agarwal 1994; Bhalla 1976; Parthasarathy 1992). Within the field of irrigation management there is a substantial literature focused on community participation and conflict resolution (Chambers 1988; Chambers, Saxena, and Shah 1989; Mosse 1994; Brewer *et al.* 1999; Maloney and Raju 1994; Sengupta 1991; Parthasarathy 1998, 2000, 2002).

Common property resource mangement is intimately linked with environmental analysis and there is a burgeoning literature that provides warnings regarding the overuse or misuse of water. The developmentalist school points to consumption imperatives and argues that environmental problems are amenable to innovative solutions. The protectionist school, including Gadgil and Guha (1992, 1995) and Agarwal and Narain (1997), argues that it is the local citizens, as heirs to a conservationist tradition, who are most likely to utilise their resources rationally and sustainably. The concern is about the impact of the PIM on resource sustainability amidst increasing demands and usage. The irrigation literature provides ample evidence regarding the dangers of waterlogging and salination (Dhawan 1995; Merrey 1987; Joshi and Dinkar 1996). The impact of the IMT also requires an understanding of the engineering problems that arise when there is a dramatic change in the use of water and land. For example, in the new system, water is to be sold (ostensibly on a volumetric basis) to the village communities, which will require a complex measurement technology as well as administration of water rates that will make the system self-sustaining. Moreover, it is expected that the new irrigation will involve conjunctive use of both surface and groundwater that will require careful management if soil damage is to be mitigated. In general, a significant change in water and landuse invariably produces significant environmental consequences. As mentioned earlier, not only waterlogging and salination but also the overuse of fertiliser and pesticides, usually associated with the new "green revolution" technology, may affect the long-range sustainability of the resource. The experience, however, is that the WUAs so far have not shown an ability to cope with this class of issues.

Water distribution and management are is no way a new phenomenon in India. The users are accustomed to the traditional practices for allocating and utilising the resource and for resolving conflicts over its use. Sengupta (1991), Agarwal and Narain (1997) and Vaidyanathan (1999) have shown how these practices decayed over time and why they deserve a fresh attention even while the modern technology and management methods are being used. The IMT or PIM itself represents an attempt to adapt a tradition of community participation to a modern need, one that fits with the larger pattern of India's economic reforms. The policy documents, however, show no signs as to how the water-user communities can use the Water Users Associations as a bridge between the old and the new management techniques.

PIM IN INDIA: A HISTORICAL ACCOUNT

From the beginning of the 20th century, efforts have been made to encourage farmers to participate in irrigation management to improve the performance of the system. As early as 1938, the Irrigation Inquiry Committee, referring to the underutilisation of irrigation in the erstwhile Bombay state, had recommended farmers' participation in management. The subsequent Irrigation Commissions (1947, 1960 and 1972); the National Water Policy of 1987; and the Committee on Pricing of Irrigation Water (1992) had also stressed the need for farmers' participation in irrigation management.

The National Water Policy formulated in 1987 highlighted the need to make efforts to involve farmers progressively in the various aspects of management of irrigation systems. Later, all the state Governments were requested to take up the farmers' participation at least in one minor system comprising an area of 100—2000 ha. in each project to make a start. However, very few state governments responded to this proposal. The India Irrigation Sector Review by the World Bank in 1991 observed that while the Central Government policy statements supported the farmers' involvement in irrigation management little was actually done at the field level and much of what was done was promoted by non-governmental organisations (NGOs).

In 1992, the Committee on Pricing of Irrigation Water reviewed the PIM progress and observed that the area covered under the PIM was less than one per cent, while the outlet and canal committees were non-existent and their functions vague. There was also no cooperation from and coordination with the Irrigation Department. As a first step, the committee suggested a substantial reduction in the sphere of responsibility of the government and encouragement of user groups to take over maintenance, management of water allocation, and collection of water rates for a group of outlets serving at least one village[1].

The recent efforts to promote the PIM had actually begun in most states in 1970s. By then, it had become clear that there was a large gap between the irrigation potential created and the potential realised. Agricultural specialists had suggested that there was a need to pay more attention to the portions below the outlet to improve wateruse efficiency. In response, a Command Area Development Programme (CADP) was launched in 1974. Under the CADP, attempts were made to form organisations of farmers at the outlet level. These organisations or committees were confined to the outlet command and were made responsible for the distribution of water within the outlet command. In most states, however, these committees were not effective because the rights and responsibilities of these committees and of the irrigation department were not clearly defined. The programme also witnessed resistance from the irrigation department functionaries. Lack of institutional framework, legal back-up, and motivation among the irrigation officials have been reported as the major constraints. After the adoption of the National Water Policy in 1987, several states enacted, or are in the process of enacting, irrigation laws with an emphasis on irrigation management transfer. However, as discussed above there are many constraints in the course of implementation of the PIM programme.

Progress of PIM and Performance of WUAs

The analytical focus of the IMT or PIM, therefore, has come to rest on the capacity of the new community-based institutions, that is, the Water Users Associations located in a specific basin, to manage the allocation of a key resource—water—effectively, equitably and sustainably. The central process involved is irrigation management transfer whereby water users in the community assume a responsibility that has hitherto been exercised by the government. An analysis of this process requires a synthesis of several theoretical ideas highlighted in the literature as discussed above. These include decentralisation, community, participation, equity, rights, common property resource management, work and productivity, environmental impact, community and individual empowerment and institutionalisation. Clearly, the common thread that runs through all of these concepts is institutionalisation in the new sense of the word that embraces the development of a new capacity, new norms of behaviour and a new consciousness about shared responsibility, in this case with reference to communities and their role in the management of a vital resource.

However, the initial conditions that led to a thinking of transferring the management from government departments to users were not only difficulties in water retailing but also the upkeep of the canal system at various levels—from reservoir to field channels. How can then the key variable be only institutions and the related process of institution building? Further, institutions may be regarded as a dependent variable insofar as they (in this case the WUAs) are moulded by forces that are external (e.g., government decentralisation policy, capacity-building measures by NGOs) as well as internal (participation, leadership and community needs). But the WUAs, once launched, themselves become independent variables shaping the effectiveness of the PIM programme and its implementation, provided they are linked together. The key elements, such as productivity, rights, equity and conflict resolution depend on the successful operation of the WUAs.

It would be useful to have an overview of the progress of the PIM programme in the different states of India to understand the performance of WUAs. Overall, the irrigated area transferred to WUAs in India is about 14 per cent as against 45 per cent in Indonesia, 51 per cent in Mexico, 66 per cent in the Philippines, 22 per cent in Thailand, 35 per cent in Turkey and 19 per cent in Sri Lanka. There are considerable variations between the states (Table 23.1) and within a state between the irrigation systems. It is known that the progress of the PIM in almost all the states has been tardy. While some states like Andhra Pradesh, Madhya Pradesh and Chhattisgarh have adopted an Act and made participatory management compulsory, others for instance, Gujarat and Tamil Nadu, tried to build grassroot consciousness toward water users' associations through incentives and NGO support (for details on the PIM in Gujarat, see Parthasarathy 2000). However, states in the latter category like Gujarat are also in the process of enacting legislations that would make the PIM the only way to manage irrigation water. Gujarat has the tradition of user cooperatives and offers interesting lessons from the pilot phase of its PIM programme that commenced in 1996.[2]

Table 23.1: Target and Progress of PIM in Different States, India

State	*Number of WUAs*	*Area Covered ('000. ha)*	*Net Irrigated Area ('000 ha)*	*Area Covered as % to Total Net Area*
Andhra Pradesh	10292	4800.00	4395	91.6
Assam	2	1.00	572	0.17
Bihar	1	12.20	3624	0.34
Goa	39	4.59	23	19.96
Gujarat	476	19.00	3042	0.62
Haryana	554	110.80	2755	4.02
Himachal Pradesh	875	35.00	105	33.33
Jammu & Kashmir	1	1.00	313	0.32
Karnataka	193	138.38	2325	5.95
Kerala	3712	148.48	357	41.59
Madhya Pradesh (*)	1470	1495.00	6399	23.36
Chhattisgarh (*)	946	1135.00	—	—
Maharashtra	142	55.80	2567	2.17
Manipur	62	49.27	65	75.80
Orissa	88	34.31	2090	1.64
Rajasthan	35	15.93	5588	0.29
Tamil Nadu	328	426.40	2892	14.74
Uttar Pradesh	1	0.25	11999	Negligible
West Bengal	10000	37.00	1911	1.94
Total (*)	*29217*	*8519.41*	*Not available*	*14.93*

Note: (*) Revised figures for Madhya Pradesh, Chhattisgarh and total.

Source: 1. Mid-Term Appraisal of Ninth Five Year Plan (1997-2002), GOI, Planning Commission, New Delhi, October 2000, p. 103

2. Statistical Abstract India 2000, Central Statistical Organization, Government of India, New Delhi.

Targets and Achievements

Irrespective of the policy frame for the implementation of participatory management—building irrigation management transfer from the grassroots or through a legislative Act; targets, stated or otherwise, are an inevitable part of the programme.[3] As mentioned earlier, most systems whether large or small have serious problems relating to water distribution and use-efficiency. Therefore, just a shift in the responsibility of the day-to-day management could be a necessary but certainly not a sufficient condition to improve the performance of the system. Further, the evolution of water distribution protocols that are temporally or spatially sensitive cannot be achieved in the short run, unless enabling environment is created (see discussion under water rights). These constraints explain the slow physical achievement of management transfer programme (Table 23.1).

In the case of Gujarat for example, the target set for the PIM programme in 1997 was to "turn over" 50 per cent of the 1.5 million hectares of the command area of its extant irrigation schemes to WUAs by the year 2003.[4]

The area under the PIM and the area transferred to the WUAs in two contrasting schemes are shown in Table 23.2. The first is the case of Dharoi, which is water-scarce and the second is of Ukai-Kakrapar, a relatively water-abundant project. It is obvious that in the water-scarce system, the proportion of the area transferred to the WUAs to the total command area is higher than that in the water-abundant system. The scissor shaped curves of target and achievement show a sharp divergence in the area covered in the Ukai-Kakrapar command (Figure 23.1). From 1996-97 onwards the physical achievements of the PIM in transferring management to the users through forming WUAs have been declining steadily, while the targets have been rising sharply. As expected, the rate of anticipated growth in the transfer of areas to the WUAs by the department and the growth rate of actual transfer are interesting too (Figure 23.2).

As is the case with the Dharoi project, in the Ukai-Kakrapar command too, the bulk of the WUAs formed are in the tail reaches. The reasons for this skewed distribution are apparent. First, as mentioned earlier, the transfer programme has been one of managing day-to-day administration of water with little influence on supply. Secondly, the distribution rules are tradition-based and invariably fixed by the department, and the WUAs have little scope to innovate and redesign the water rotation schedules. There are some notable exceptions, of course. The Thalota WUA in the Dharoi command area in north Gujarat was formed with the help of the Development Support Centre (DSC), an NGO based in Ahmedabad. Thalota used its water rights to introduce a new rotation during the first dry year when there was a severe water scarcity. Under the new schedule, each farmer got water for one acre of land, irrespective of the total cultivated area. This ensured that a minimum quantity of water was supplied to all. While this method might be appealing from

Table 23.2: Distribution of Area under PIM by Location Dharoi and Ukai-Kakrapar Project

(Area in Hectares)

Details	*Head*	*Middle*	*Tail*	*Total*
	Distribution of Area under PIM: Dharoi Project			
No. of WUAs	*9*	*11*	*20*	*40**
Total command area of WUAs	2683 (25.5)	2819 (26.8)	5005 (47.6)	10507 100.0
IMT over	770 (14.1)	1543 (28.3)	3131 (57.5)	5444 (100.0)
Motivation and Registration	466 (14.2)	1138 (34.7)	1674 (51.1)	3278 (100.0)
Proposed	1447 (81.1)	138 (7.7)	200 (11.2)	1785 (100.0)
Total command area of the system				61,085
RBCCA to total command area of system (%)				78.7
IMT over to total command area of WUAs (%)	28.7	54.7	62.6	51.8
WUA command to RBCCA** (%)				21.8
IMT over to RBCCA (%)				11.3
Total command area of WUAs to total command area of system				17.2
	Distribution of Area under PIM: Ukai-Kakrapar Project			
No. of WUAs	*29*	*41*	*54*	*124*
CCA of WUAs (n=124)	8082 (17.7)	19408 (42.4)	18260 (39.9)	45750 (100.0)
Area under PIM (86)***	5906 (20.1)	11088 (37.8)	12349 (42.1)	29343 (100.0)
Area turned over (n=86)*	4114 (18.0)	8980 (39.2)	9803 (42.8)	22897 (100.0)
Area under PIM / total command area of WUAs	73.1	57.1	67.6	64.1
Area turned over / area under PIM	69.7	81.0	79.4	78.0
Total command area of the system	—	—	—	*3,31,557*
CCA / total command area of the system	—	—	—	13.8
PIM area / total command area of the system	—	—	—	8.9
Area turned over / total command area of the system	—	—	—	6.9

Note: Figures in parentheses indicate percentage to total.

Source: 1. Data on Dharoi Irrigation Project were obtained from Dharoi Division Office, Visnagar and Development Support Centre, Ahmedabad.

2. Data on Ukai-Kakrapar Project were obtained from Surat Irrigation Circle, Surat.

* Includes WUA on Right Bank Canal Command Area (RBCCA) only. There are a few proposed WUAs in the LBMCC like Lihoda, Pinchod, Unjha but the area covered under them is not known.

** RBCCA: Right Bank Canal Command Area.

*** There are 38 proposed WUAs in Ukai-Kakrapar Project. Details about the area under PIM and turned over are not available.

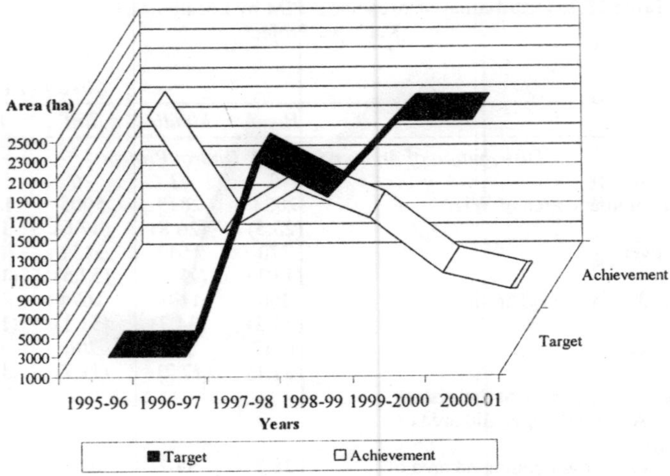

Fig. 23.1: Distribution of Area Covered Under P.I.P.: Ukai Kakrapar Project

Source: Surat Irrigation Circle, Surat.

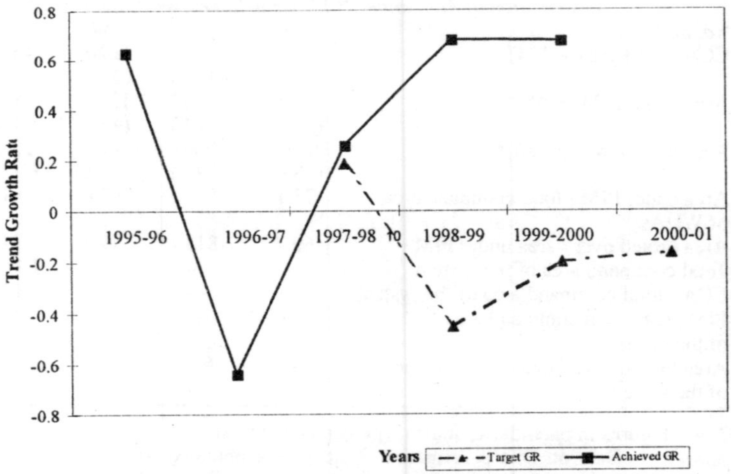

Fig. 23.2: Trend Growth Rate of Targets and Achievements in Ukai Kakrapar Project: 1995-96 to 2000-01

Source: Surat Irrigation Circle, Surat

distribution-based-equity point of view, its trade-off is with the objective of maximising productivity and production. Third, it is relatively easier for a WUA to distribute limited, fixed quantity of water in a few numbers of watering (as is the case with Thalota) than arranging distribution of variable quantities of water in a large number of watering. Last but not least, the PIM programme commenced with an objective of "improving the scarce resource" and hence its training programmes and capacity-building exercises have been geared toward water distribution and not water management. As a result, the WUAs in the head-reaches or in areas endowed with relatively more water do not have the capacity to handle problems of drainage, waterlogging and other environmental effects. Nor are policy measures in place to address these issues. There is thus a huge divergence between the grassroot needs and the policy provisions. Bridging this gap is one of the challenges faced by the transfer programme presently.

Obviously, the conception, adoption, and implementation of the programme have two components. First, the administrative aspect: here the commitment of the departmental staff and their perceived loss of power in the event of management transfer are often given as reasons for the slow rate of adoption and implementation of the PIM programme.[5] The second aspect is about the participants who take over the management. Though there are many evaluation studies on the performance of the users in the management (WUAs) or their readiness/reluctance in taking over irrigation management,[6] there are very few attempts to explain the apathy among the governments[7] to transfer the management and control to the people. While it appears that the governmental indifference in implementation of the irrigation management transfer is due to the participatory approach, but the obligations the government has to discharge before transferring the system slows down the process. In many cases, extensive repairs or renovation and in some cases modernisation is required on the canal networks. For the whole of India, it is estimated that 21 million hectares of irrigated area from major and medium projects require renovation/up-gradation/restoration. The total investment required is estimated at Rs. 20,000 to Rs. 30,000 crore over a period of 20 years (Planning Commission 2000). Indeed, repairs and rehabilitation is a prerequisite to improve the water-use efficiency, which at present is estimated to be only 38 to 40 per cent for canal irrigation and about 60 per cent for groundwater irrigation schemes (Planning Commission 2000).

The question then is whether and how much the states can spend additionally on the repair and rehabilitation of the irrigation schemes to make them attractive for users to take over and manage subsequently. Obviously, this is a major constraint in the PIM programme in almost all the states of India. The outlays and expenditures for major and medium irrigation schemes by the centre and states during the recent Plan period are given in Tables 23.3 and 23.4. It is interesting to contrast these expenditures against the performance. The ultimate irrigation potential through these projects has been assessed at 58.46 million

Table 23.3: Financial Outlays on Irrigation Sector (First Three Years) of Ninth Five-Year Plan: Central Sector

(Rs. Crore)

Details	*9th Plan Outlay*	*Actual Expenditure 1997-98*	*Actual Ependiture 1998-99*	*Outlay 1999-2000*	*Total 1997-2000 (3 years)*	*%outlay in first three years w.r.t. 9th Plan outlay*
Major and Medium irrigation	330.12	36.72	49.03	55.80	141.55	43
Minor irrigation	385.00	42.84	48.29	55.41	146.54	38
Command Area Development	860.00	129.26	174.90	177.00	481.16	56
Flood Control	716.13	67.17	74.57	81.79	223.53	31
Total	2291.25	275.99	346.79	370.00	992.78	43

Financial Outlays on Irrigation Sector (First Three Years) of Ninth Five-Year Plan: State Sector

(Rs. Crore)

Details	*9th Plan Outlay*	*Actual Expenditure 1997-98*	*1998-99 Revised Outlay*	*Approved Outlay 1999-2000*
Major and Medium irrigation	42629.22	7523.16	9273.12	12228.81
Minor irrigation	8977.03	1456.59	1746.81	2117.79
Command Area Development	2032.11	303.43	303.60	315.39
Flood Control	2212.12	351.87	573.21	662.36
Total	55850.48	9635.05	11896.74	15324.36

Source: Mid-Term Appraisal of Ninth Five Year Plan (1997-2000).

Table 23.4: Plan Outlays and Expenditure for Major and Medium Irrigation Projects during the Ninth Plan

(Rs. Crore)

Year	*Central Sector*		*State Sector*	
	Approved Outlay	*Actual Expenditure*	*Approved Outlay*	*Actual/ Anticipated Expenditure*
9th Plan	330.12	—	42629.22	—
1997-98	44.69	36.72	8362.91	7523.16
1998-99	50.25	49.03	10024.03	9273.12
1999-2000	55.80	48.12	12228.31	11002.42

Source: Mid-Term Appraisal of Ninth Five Year Plan (1997-2000).

hectares. However, only an area measuring 32.95 million hectares could be created. The details of the physical achievement of the major and medium irrigation schemes during 1992-97 (Eighth Plan) and anticipated achievement up to 2000 (Ninth Plan) are provided in Table 23.5. Evidently, most of the states could not actualise the potential created during the Plan periods. To a certain extent, the low level of performance could act as a dampener for the states; they may not try to avail of the institutional finance. The National Bank for Reconstruction and Development (NABARD) provides financial assistance to the states for irrigation development under the Rural Infrastructural Development Fund (RIDF) (Table 23.6). Clearly, the funds made available by NABARD for the irrigation sector in different installments show a decline.[8]

The budget expenditure on irrigation of the states has steadily grown over the period from 1985-86 to1999-2000, though there are significant variations between the different regions of India (Figure 23.3). It is interesting to see that in some of the states where the PIM is in progress (Andhra Pradesh, Maharashtra, Karnataka, Tamil Nadu and Gujarat) the budgetary expenditure has been either rising or the level is maintained in constant terms over the period 1988-89—1999-2000 (Figures 23.4 and 23.5). This implies that unless fresh avenues are found, the scope for increasing the government allocation to meet the new demands for funds due to the PIM is limited.

Table 23.5: Major and Medium Irrigation Schemes: Physical Achievement During Plan Periods (000' ha.)

States and UT	*Ultimate Irrigation Potential*	*Achievement up to end of March 1992*		*Achievement during 1992-97*		*Achievement up-to Marh 1997*		*1997-98 Achievement Major and Medium*		*1998-99 Anticipated Achievement Major and Medium*	
		Potential	*Utilised*	*Potential*	*Utilised*	*Potential*	*Utilised*	*Potential*	*Utilised*	*Potential*	*Utilised*
Andhra Pradesh	5000	2999.0	2847.0	46.10	36.80	3045.10	2883.80	76.52	12.10	116.17	158.79
Arunachal Pradesh	0	0.0	0.0	0.00	0.00	0.00	0.00	0.00	0.00	0.00	0.00
Assam	970	176.0	111.0	20.67	27.17	196.67	138.17	4.20	2.00	1.30	1.00
Bihar	6500	2766.0	2295.0	36.50	29.20	2802.50	2324.20	4.33	4.33	27.10	22.10
Goa	62	13.0	12.0	0.02	0.07	13.02	12.07	3.50	1.00	0.02	0.02
Gujarat	3000	1246.0	989.0	104.00	214.00	1350.00	1200.00	17.14	20.62	16.08	20.00
Haryana	3000	2035.0	1791.0	43.79	42.62	2078.79	1833.62	1.66	1.66	3.49	3.49
Himachal Pradesh	50	8.0	4.0	2.55	1.59	10.55	5.59	0.30	0.15	0.15	0.34
Jammu & Kashmir	250	138.0	136.0	15.70	11.57	173.70	147.57	2.07	2.62	0.22	2.86
Karnataka	2500	1377.0	1192.0	289.02	279.70	1666.02	1471.70	45.44	36.35	35.17	35.17
Kerala	1000	416.0	367.0	97.31	97.31	513.31	464.31	32.23	30.61	14.00	14.00
Madhya Pradesh	6000	1962.0	1395.0	355.60	225.95	2317.60	1620.95	32.00	23.30	20.70	10.30
Maharashtra	4100	2030.0	1036.0	307.00	251.17	2337.00	1287.70	151.00	150.00	187.00	187.00
Manipur	135	59.0	50.0	4.00	2.00	63.00	52.00	1.00	1.00	12.00	10.00
Meghalaya	20	0.0	0.0	0.00	0.00	0.00	0.00	0.00	0.00	0.00	0.97
Mizoram	0	0.0	0.0	0.00	0.00	0.00	0.00	0.00	0.00	0.00	0.00
Nagaland	10	0.0	0.0	0.00	0.00	0.00	0.00	0.00	0.00	0.00	0.00
Orissa	3600	1409.0	1326.0	148.75	116.66	1557.75	1442.66	34.57	54.14	40.39	191.30
Punjab	3000	2367.0	2309.0	145.86	142.25	2512.86	2451.25	12.62	22.85	5.01	5.01
Rajasthan	2750	1999.0	1887.0	274.88	201.39	2273.88	2088.39	58.90	46.46	11.50	98.70

(contd.)

Table 23.5 (contd.)

States and UT	*Ultimate Irrigation Potential*	*Achievement up to end of March 1992*		*Achievement during 1992-97*		*Achievement up to Marh 1997*		*1997-98 Achievement Major and Medium*		*1998-99 Anticipated Achievement Major and Medium*	
		Potential	*Utilised*	*Potential*	*UtiLised*	*Potential*	*Utilised*	*Potential*	*UtiLised*	*Potential*	*Utilised*
Sikkim	20	0.0	0.0	0.00	0.00	0.00	0.00	0.00	0.00	0.00	0.00
Tamil Nadu	1500	1545.0	1541.0	0.51	4.49	1545.51	1545.49	2.18	2.18	0.00	0.00
Tripura	100	2.0	2.0	0.30	0.30	2.30	2.30	0.85	0.85	0.20	0.80
Uttar Pradesh	12500	6789.0	5751.0	254.00	363.00	7043.00	6114.00	129.00	33.00	112.00	75.00
West Bengal	2300	1353.0	1258.0	79.68	57.28	1432.68	1315.28	53.41	43.22	50.00	40.00
Total States	58367	30709.0	26296.0	2226.24	2105.05	32935.24	28401.05	662.92	488.44	652.50	876.85
Total States & UTs.	58465	30724.0	26303.0	2229.75	2107.34	32953.75	28410.34	663.02	488.84	652.50	877.40

Note: The physical achievements during the Eighth Plan as above are anticipated and are likely to change.

Source: Mid-Term Appraisal of Ninth Five Year Plan (1997-2000)

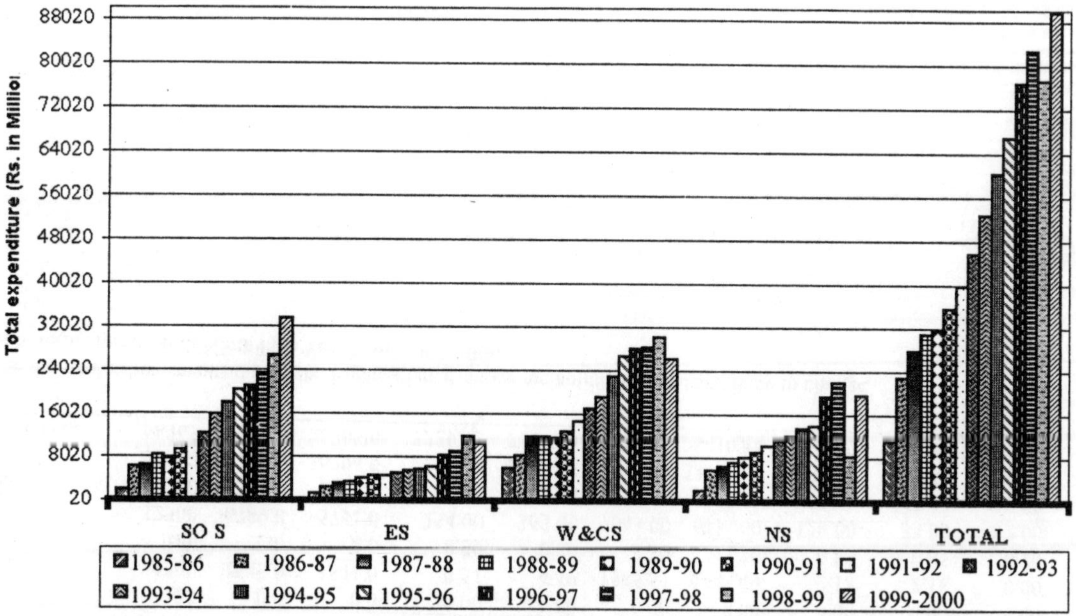

Fig. 23.3: Total Expenditure on Irrigation and Flood Control by Major States of India, 1985-86 to 1999-2000

Note: For the year 1985-86 to 1998-99, revised estimate figures on Irrigation and Flood Control have been used. For the year 1999-2000, budget estimate figures were used.

SOS = South states; ES = Eastern states; W&CS: Western and Central States; NS: Northern states

Source: Different volumes of states and Government of India budget.

Table 23.6: Rural Infrastructure Development Fund: Purpose-wise Disbursements (as on 25.02.99)

(Rs. Crores)

Details	*RIDF-IV*	*RIDF-III*	*RIDF II*	*RIDF I*
Corpus	3000.00	2500.00	2500.00	2000.00
Sanctions issued	3118.28	2671.28	2597.76	1797.63
Type of projects				
Major irrigation	317.37	223.88	412.51	227.73
Medium irrigation	170.96	203.99	237.28	838.88
Minor irrigation	436.67	512.68	581.15	616.36
Total	*925.00*	*940.15*	*1230.94*	*1682.97*

Source: Mid-Term Appraisal of Ninth Five Year Plan (1997-2000)

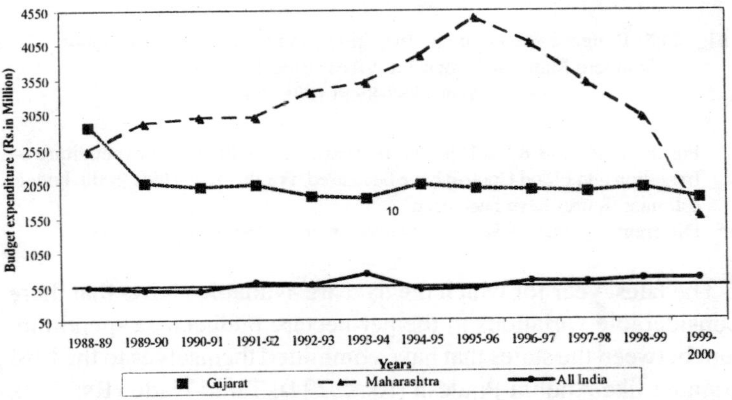

Fig. 23.4: Budget Expenditure on Irrigation and Flood Control for Major Western and Central States at Constant Prices (Base 1988-89 = 100) from the Year 1988-89 to 1999-2000

Note: For the year 1988-89 to 1998-99, revised estimate figures of expenditure on Irrigation and Flood Control have been used. For the Year 1999-2000, budget estimate figures have been used.

Source: Different volumes of States and Government of India budget.

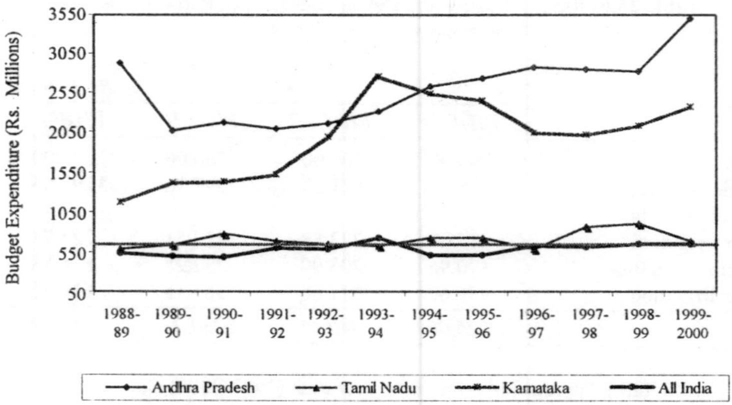

Fig. 23.5: Budget Expenditure on Irrigation and Flood Control for Major Southern States and Constant Prices (Base 1988-89 = 10) from the Year 1988-89 to 1999-2000

Note: For the year 1988-89 to 1998-99, revised estimate figures of expenditure on Irrigation and Flood Control have been used. For the Year 1999-2000, budget estimate figures have been used.

Source: Different volumes of States and Government of India budget.

The latest year for which the data are available shows that there are considerable variations in the per-hectare budgetary expenditure amount between the states that have committed themselves to the PIM programme like Andhra Pradesh (Rs. 2,294), Tamil Nadu (Rs. 729), Karnataka (Rs. 3,268), Gujarat (Rs. 2,255) and Maharashtra (Rs. 5,471) (Figures 23.6 and 23.7). Given the high commitment of funds already, it is not surprising that for new programmes like the PIM, adequate funds could not be earmarked, nor was it feasible for the existing programmes, like the CADP or Accelerated Irrigation Benefit Programme (AIBP) to absorb the costs.

Financial Implications of PIM

The additional demands for the PIM programme essentially stem from the repair and rehabilitation costs, plus the software costs of training and capacity building for the departmental staff and for the office-bearers of the WUAs. With the help of World Bank assistance,

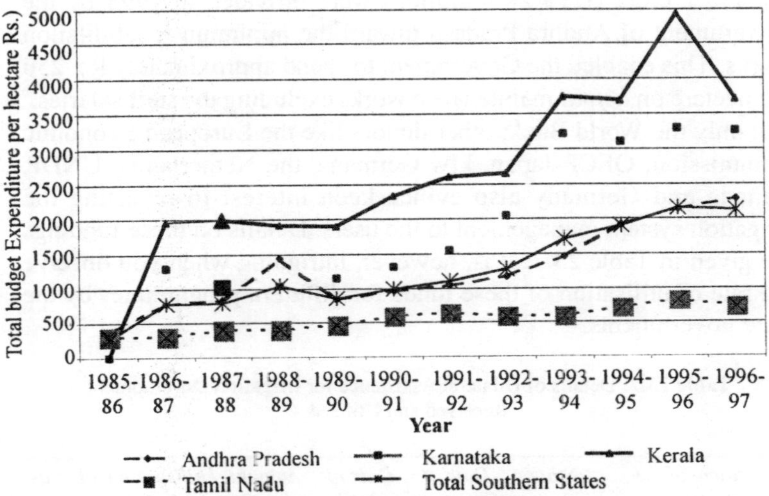

Fig. 23.6: Budget Expenditure on Irrigation and Flood Control per Hectare of Irrigated Area 1985-86 to 1996-97: Souther States

Note: For the year 1988-99 to 1998-89, revised estimate figures of expenditure on Irrigation and Flood Control have been used. For the year 1999-2000, budget estimate figures were used.

Source: Different volumes of states and Government of India budget.

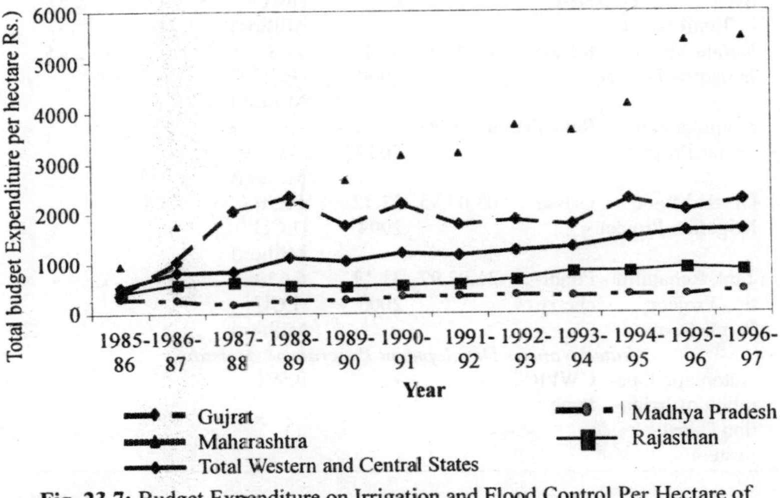

Fig. 23.7: Budget Expenditure on Irrigation and Flood Control Per Hectare of Irrigated Area, 1985-86 to 1996-97: Major Western and Central States

Source: Budget expenditure figures were obtained from different volumes of budget. Figures of net irrigated area were obtained from Weligamage et al (2002).

Rs. 118.1 crore (US$ 28.1 million) were provided in 1998 by the Government of Andhra Pradesh toward the minimum rehabilitation works. This enabled the Government to spend approximately Rs. 250 per hectare on *actual* maintenance works excluding the staff salaries.[9] Not only the World Bank, other donors like the European Economic Commission, OECF-Japan, kfw Germany, the Netherlands, UNDP, Canada and Germany also evince keen interest in reverting the irrigation system management to the users. Details on these fundings are given in Table 23.7. It is, however, intriguing when you observe the rate of utilisation of these funds for different programmes by the state governments.

Table 23.7: Details of Bilateral Assistance for Irrigation Development Received and Utilised

Sl. No.	*Name of the Project*	*State*	*Date of Commen-cement*	*Date of Comple-tion*	*Amount of Assis-tance*	*Utilisation of Assis-tance up to 31.12.98*	*Col. 8 as per cent to Col 7*
1	*2*	*3*	*4*	*5*	*6*	*7*	*8*
		Assistance from the European Economic Community					
1	Tank Irrigation System (Ph II) in Tamil Nadu	Tamil Nadu	24.07.89	31.12.99	24.5 (ECU Million)	19.787	80.7
2	Kerala Minor Irrigation Project	Kerala	21.05.92	31.12. 2000	11.8 (ECU Million)		23.5
3	Siamukh and Nohar Project	Rajasthan	0.706.93	31.12. 2000	45.072.8 (ECU Million)		
4	Orissa Minor Irrigation Project	Orissa	03.07.95	31.12. 2004	10.70 (ECU Million)	0.04	
5	Tank Rehabilitation Project Pondicherry	Pondicherry	21.02.97	31.12. 2003	6.650 (ECU Million)		—
		United Nations Development Programme Assistance					
1	Automatic Operation of Irrigation Canal System	CWPRS, Pune	—	—	0.691		—

(contd.)

Table 23.7 (contd.)

Sl. No.	*Name of the Project*	*State*	*Date of Commencement*	*Date of Completion*	*Amount of Assistance*	*Utilisation of Assistance up to 31.12.98*	*Col. 8 as per cent to Col 7*
1	*2*	*3*	*4*	*5*	*6*	*7*	*8*
			Japan				
1	Modernisation of Kurnool Cuddapah Canal	Andhra Pradesh	11.01.96	26.03. 2003	16049 (Million Yen US$M)	90.01	0.6
2	Rajghat Canal Major Irrigation Project	Madhya Pradesh	25.02.97	31.03. 2003	13222 (Million Yen US$M)	438.700	3.3
3	Rengali Irrigation Project	Orissa	12.12.97	05.02. 2003	7760 (Million Yen US$M)	644.322	8.3
			France				
1	Hydroplus Fusegates on 8 Dams in Gujarat	Gujarat	10.12.98	10.12. 2000	FF 17.85 M	—	—
			Netherlands				
1	Community Irrigation Project	Kerala	15.12.93	30.06. 2000	DFL 11.02 M	DFL 1.39 M	12.6
2	Bundelkhand Integrated Water Resources Management Project	Uttar Pradesh	12.06.96	31.05.99	DFL 13.388M	DFL 1.352 M	10.1
			Canadian Assistance				
1	Rajasthan Agriculture and Drainage Research Project (RAJAD)	Rajasthan	13.03.90	31.12.99	C$ 60.76 M	C$ 7.887 M	13.0
			Germany				
1	Rajasthan Minor Irrigation Project	Rajasthan	29.04.87	31.12.98	2.70	DM 1.635 M	60.6

Source: Mid-Term Appraisal of Ninth Five Year Plan (1997-2000).

One of the obvious difficulties has been the change brought about by some of the states in the traditional methods of implementation of irrigation programmes, for instance, construction of field channels and lining of the canal networks in WUA areas. For a long time it has been assumed that the farmers in large systems would take up the responsibility of construction of field channels and management below the outlet level (Stone 1984, Chambers 1988). However, the experience across systems and states in India disputes this. As a result, almost all governments experience shortage of funds when they have to carry out the necessary repair and maintenance works of the systems prior to turnover. In some WUA areas in Gujarat,

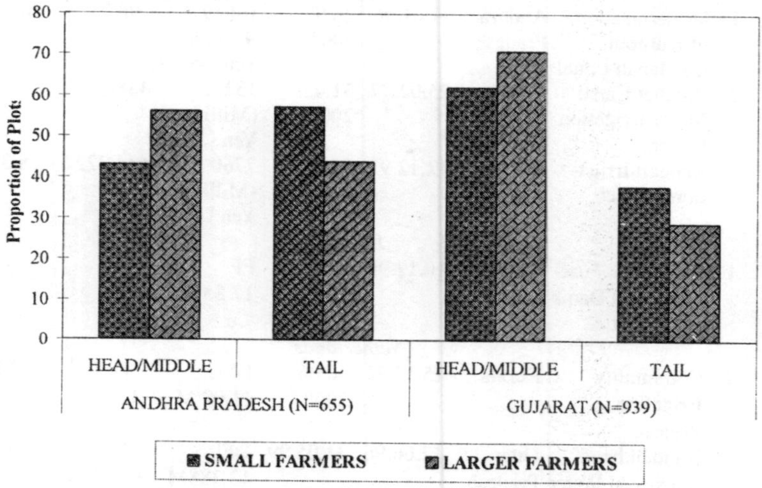

Fig. 23.8: Proportion of Plots by Location and Farm size: Andhra Pradesh and Gujarat

Note: Significance X2, Andhra Pradesh: Significant at 0.005 level and Gujarat significant at 0.005 level.
Source: van Koppen *et al.* (2002).

the actual cost of repair and rehabilitation work under the PIM was Rs. 1,485 in Thalota and Rs. 3,265 in Digas (Table 23.8). A major part of these expenses was incurred on lining the canals and constructing field channels. Assuming an average rehabilitation expenditure of Rs. 1,797 per hectare on canals prior to turnover under the PIM, a sum of Rs. 2695.4 million would be required for the existing 1.5 million hectares of the command area in Gujarat (for details, see Parthasarathy 2000). It is obvious that the budgetary provisions are already high in Gujarat and it is not clear how the PIM programme would be implemented at the state level.

Table 23.8: Estimated Cost and Expenditure on R&R Work by Projects and Systems in Gujarat

Details	*Thalota*	*Tranol*	*Kunjrav*	*Laxmipura*	*Digas*	*Chandra-wadi*
Name of the irrigation system	Dharoi	Mahi	Mahi	Danti-wada	Ukai-Kakrapar	Chandra-wadi
Total command area of the system	61,085	212,000	212,000	45,755	331,557	—
Total command area of the project	224	356	296	246	921	463
Total no. of bene-fiting households in the project area	216	334	425	151	432	222
Initial cost estimate for R&R (1995-96)	1,24,050 (dept) 2,59,000 NGO)	10,01,817	398,240	9830	NA	22,53,839
Revised cost esti-mate for R&R (March 1999)	—	—	—	100,000	—	35,33,532
Actual expenditure up to March '99	332,546	7,48,475	343,100	10 000	30,07,379	14,88,134
Cost per ha. (as per estimate)	1156	2814	1345	407	—	7632
Cost per ha. (as per expenditure)	1485	2102	1159	41	3265	3214
Cost per household (estimate)	1199	2999	937	662	—	15917
Cost per household (Expd.)	1540	2241	807	66	6962	6703
% Difference bet-ween revised esti-mate and initial cost estimate	—	—	—	1017	—	157
% amount spent to initial cost estimate	128	75	86	102	—	66
Projected expendi-ture for R&R for 50 per cent of the command area (based on cost per ha) in Rs. '000.	3530	—	220480	9311	541268	NA

Source: Parthasarathy (2000).

The alternative to the demands on government funds is recovering the costs through user-charges. The experience so far has been that the government has neither been able to ensure timely payments from the farmers nor has it been able to charge an economic price for water. The necessity of dealing with individual farmers has made water charge collection a costly exercise resulting in a low recovery rate. In Gujarat, for example, the average annual recovery has been 65 per cent of the total assessment and the total assessment for the year 1994 has been Rs. 12 crore. It is thus obvious that no matter how high the water charges are raised, they would cover only a fraction of the total cost of repair and rehabilitaiton R and R and operation and maintenance (O and M) expenses of the IMT programme. In fact, recovery of water charges constitutes only one-third of the total O and M expenditure in the current rates (for a detailed discussion, see Parthasarathy 2000). Though water charges might constitute a small proportion of the total operation and maintenance of the canal network for the government, water charges is an important source of finance for managing the WUA. Obviously, the adequacy of this source of income depends on the WUA's ability to charge a rate that leaves enough balance after paying the charges to the irrigation department. Most of the WUAs in areas where athe Irrigation Department levies and collects the water charges have recognised the importance of charging a higher water rate than the government rate. However, where the irrigation water fees are levied and collected by the Revenue Department as part of the land tax (as in Andhra Pradesh), there is hardly any inclination for the WUAs to even consider collection of water charges, let alone charging a higher rate to generate surplus. Strangely, though the PIM policy gives freedom to the WUA to fix the water rates, there is little incentive (other than getting back 50 per cent of water rates) for the WUA to actually embark upon what could be a potentially conflict-ridden decision.

Some of the WUAs formed in Gujarat have fixed a new water rate that is higher than the department's rate (for a detailed discussion see, Parthasarathy 1999, 2000). What is of concern is that the analytic of pricing of water appears to be complex. Partly the complexity is due to the presence of other sources of irrigation in the command area and partly due to the conventional view that water is not only a free good but also it is the government's responsibility to supply water to the fields. As mentioned earlier, the PIM policy and the programme have focused on the water scarce areas/system. However, in many cases, like north Gujarat, the systems have rarely provided more than three waterings even in the winter season. It is, therefore, pertinent to analyse the relative importance of different sources of water. When analysed in a comparative framework, it is evident that the charges for canal water are based on area and crops, while the groundwater source charges on the per-watering basis. Thus, it is possible that when the number of waterings from the canal increases, the utility value also increases and since groundwater is costlier than canal water, the net gain in the profit is also possible. However, farmers do not always view this in the strict profit or utility framework. This is because when the timeliness criterion is not met, the marginal utility of additional watering is not always positive. Therefore, an increase in the water availability is only a necessary condition to test the WUAs efficiency, the sufficient condition being efficiency in water distribution. This, however, appears a distant possibility since the individual WUAs, formed in the isolated portions of the command, could do very little about the supply of water. It is here that the discourse on common property resources is relevant and also the question whether large-scale canal water management is amenable to management by the user community.

Susceptibility of WUAs to Variable Water Availability

The susceptibility of the WUAs to the water availability is partly due to a lack of emphasis on federating laterally. In most states, presently, no two WUAs in a given system are linked (except in cases like Andhra Pradesh where the WUAs have been formed in all areas). Obviously, the WUAs' management of water supply is a function of the rate of utilisation of water in other parts of a given system, especially in the head-reaches. For water management to be effective, the PIM programme has to address the issue of federations and their roles. Even in cases where WUAs have been formed in all areas of a system as in Andhra Pradesh, the upper-tier body of the federation, namely, the Project Committee has not been formed. This is largely because of the political compulsions and not economic compulsions of having to address numerous demands from various stakeholders.

Given the fact that the canal irrigation accounts only for a part of the irrigated area, it is around 20 per cent of the irrigated area in Gujarat, most of the farmers depend upon other sources of irrigation (Parthasarathy and Joshi 2001). Unreliability of canal water even in the water-abundant areas has made farmers shift to more reliable sources of irrigation like tube-wells, which ensures higher production. Several studies have shown that the output is higher with the use of groundwater rather than canal water (Dhawan 1990). In the context of the availability or the potential of other sources of irrigation in a canal command, particularly groundwater, the issue of multiple or conjunctive sources of irrigation becomes important. Yet, little planning and provision are made even in the Andhra Pradesh Act under which the irrigation management transfer is carried out at the local level by forming WUAs. In order to be efficient and sustainable, therefore, the WUAs need to address this issue and the PIM policy and the programme should also offer an enabling environment by providing both information and technological support and a framework for the use of conjunctive sources. Obviously then, the PIM policy and the WUA formation should be positioned in a basin (or, in some cases, at the irrigation project level) framework besides addressing issues below the outlet level like water distribution. This, however, requires redefinition of some of the earlier thoughts and objectives of farmers' participation in the system management.

HOW THE SCISSOR BLADES WILL CLOSE? RATIONALISING WATER SUPPLY

As has been mentioned, most systems, whether large or small, have serious problems relating to water distribution and use-efficiency. Therefore, just a shift in the responsibility of the day-to-day management could be a necessary but not sufficient condition to improve the performance of the system. Further, there is a need to evolve water distribution protocols that are temporally or spatially sensitive.

It is clear that the single most important factor that influences the performance of the WUAs – the crucial institution on which the PIM or IMT is built – is their susceptibility to the variable water supply and distribution rules. It is also well known that in order to obtain a favourable cost-benefit ratio at the project proposal stage almost all irrigation systems have an overestimated command area. To achieve a modicum of equity in water distribution it is, therefore, essential that the basic anomaly of distributing water equitably over an imaginary command area be corrected. In various systems, this is being tried out in a number of ways. One interesting method adopted, without limiting the command area, is the rotational water supplies to different canal branches in different seasons/years. For example, the initial experiment in the Cauvery system on the command areas below the Metur reservoir in Tamil Nadu and the recent one (2001-2002) in Dharoi in north Gujarat where the Left Bank canal network was provided with running supplies throughout the winter season while the Right Bank network had a rotation period of 15 days. There could be other methods too but all of them would necessarily take the form of rationalising the supply of water, after taking into account the growing demands for multiple uses.

Water Rights

The issue of equity has not been adequately addressed in the PIM programmes so far. Almost always the issue of equity is construed as equivalent to addressing the problems of tail-reaches in the command for which engineering solutions are worked out, like R and R works. Perhaps recognising this inherent weakness, in some areas the WUAs change the water distribution mechanism to appear effective. (The example of Thalota discussed above is a case in point.) Some of the corrective methods being advocated, however, appear outlandish. For instance, supplying water first to the tail-end portions of the canal and gradually serving the head reaches later. It is common knowledge that no farmer would wait to watch water flowing down the canal without appropriating it. Even if the tail-to-head system is successfully adopted, it is doubtful that increments in the water-use efficiency will take place on a sustained basis. An equitable allocation of water among the cultivators in a command area is a question of more than addressing the tail–end problems. A systematic way of addressing this issue is by recognising the differences in the water rights among the different landowners. Unless water is allocated by the WUA, adequacy of water remains an elusive problem. A right if defined as a recognised claim for water cannot be guaranteed by the WUA presently because the association assumes responsibility only for the distribution of water while the supply and allocation of water are still in the domain of the department. If so, what having a right to water implies is a question that has to be answered first.

It is imperative that the sellers or distributors of water should formulate the rules of the game first. For example, shares in the association or cooperative could be allocated according to the size of the land owned in the command area. These shares could then be translated into the number of waterings depending upon the location of the plots, number of waterings feasible in a normal year in different seasons, and the crop pattern envisaged in the plan. Thus, in a hypothetical situation, a farmer in the command area of an irrigation scheme that supplies four waterings in a normal year for dry crops for one-hectare plot of land in normal topography could get four waterings. Thus, one share in this case is equal to four waterings. There are many possibilities for efficiency within this model. A farmer with a smaller number of shares could decide to grow a higher water requirement crop and purchase the deficit portion of water shares. There could emerge water share market controlled or regulated by the WUA.

Admittedly, such a system appears to favour large landowners. This is the case in the present system, whether managed by the department or the WUA. Currently, a share in the WUA is only a membership in the association, which entails a vote and a right to take part in the association's activities. It should be remembered that this membership does not provide a right to access water or to its timely and adequate provision. In fact, as suggested in Figure 23.8, in both Andhra Pradesh and Gujarat, the location of plots of farm households in the different reaches of the canal portions are not random. The distribution suggests that the large owners manage to have plots in the head and middle portions of the command and the small owners in the tail-end of the canal. This system is bound to have implications for equity, irrespective of who manages water distribution, and therefore, new institutions like the WUAs would have little interest to take over and manage the system.

Financing of Turnover Programme

It is evident that there are obligations that the government has to fulfil before transferring the system. In many cases, extensive repairs or renovation, and in some cases modernisation, are required on the canal networks. The budgetary expenditure on irrigation of the states has steadily grown over the past two decades leaving little scope for demanding additional government funds. This implies that fresh avenues have to be found to meet the new demands for funds for the PIM programme.

The additional demands for the PIM programme essentially stem from the RR (Repair and Rehabilitation) costs and software costs of training and capacity building of the members of the department and the office-bearers of the WUAs. One of the avenues for fresh funds has been the bilateral agency and this has already been sought for by some of the state governments. In so far as these are in the form of loans, the outcome of the PIM programme does not seem to justify the cost of these funds.

The alternative to the demands on government or borrowed funds is recovering the costs through user-charge. But it should be recognised that this would cover only a fraction of the total cost of the R and R and O and M under the IMT programme and yet, water charges is an important source of finance for managing the WUA. Strangely enough, though the PIM policy gives freedom to the WUA to fix the water rates, there is little incentive other than getting back 50 per cent of the water rates for the WUA to actually take what could be a potentially conflict-ridden decision.

Political Participation

In almost all states, the process of change towards the PIM could be viewed as a process that was shaped significantly by the actions of individuals in strategic positions of influence. Conversely, where such change agents are absent, even the policy process has been slow to evolve and the implementation is in a nascent stage. In both the situations however, policy makers and implementers on occasion face opposition from within and outside the government while adopting the change. The opposition from within the Irrigation Department was largely due to the perceived loss of power as a result of decentralisation of operations. In cases where there had been an enthusiastic response, there was a palpable sense of helplessness due to the lack of earmarked funds for the reform measures (PIM) in the states. Further, on the administrative side, the different responses between policy formulators and implementers continue. This is partly due to the separation between the decision-making and implementation that could be attributed to the decision-maker's own understanding of the influence of the factors like political influence, vested interests, and rent-seeking. Formulation of policy and decision-making, therefore, should encompass not only the executive branch of the state but also its political arm. Given the peculiarity of the irrigation system and the conventional view of its role and its impact on the society, it is indeed difficult to bring in reform without an explicit support of the political participation.

SUMMING UP

The preceding discussions show that the objects and accomplishments of the irrigation management transfer programme have been divergent with respect to many parameters. Briefly,

(a) Area turned over to WUAs.
(b) Awareness and capacity building measures of the department staff and WUA office-bearers.
(c) Extent of participation by the office-bearers and the level of awareness about the PIM among the WUA member-farmers.
(d) Supply of water.
(e) Conjunctive use of different sources of water.
(f) Repair and rehabilitation works on the canal networks.
(g) Budgetary provisions and finance allotted for the modernisation and upkeep of the irrigation system.
(h) Water rates collection.
(i) Evolving institutional mechanisms and legal provisions for an effective and efficient WUA management.
(j) Emphasis on water management rather than water distribution.

All these objects have fallen short of the targets or desired levels or expectations outlined in the policy and various documents and studies. In fact, all the components of the PIM programme and the irrigation sector resemble the graph presented in Figure 23.1, an open pair of scissors, i.e., objectives and outcomes moving in opposite directions.

The efficacy of the users' management of water resource is not in doubt; nor is an argument made out for continued retailing of water by the government agencies. There is, therefore, a need to assess critically the shortcomings of the programme. This paper has made an attempt in this direction. It is clear that there are critical areas the government, the policy makers and the various actors have to take note of. *Ceteris paribus*, this paper identifies four critical areas that appear to be the necessary conditions for a participatory approach in the irrigation management transfer programmes to succeed.

APPENDICES

Appendix Figure 1: Proportion of Households Participating in WUA Activities by Farm Size

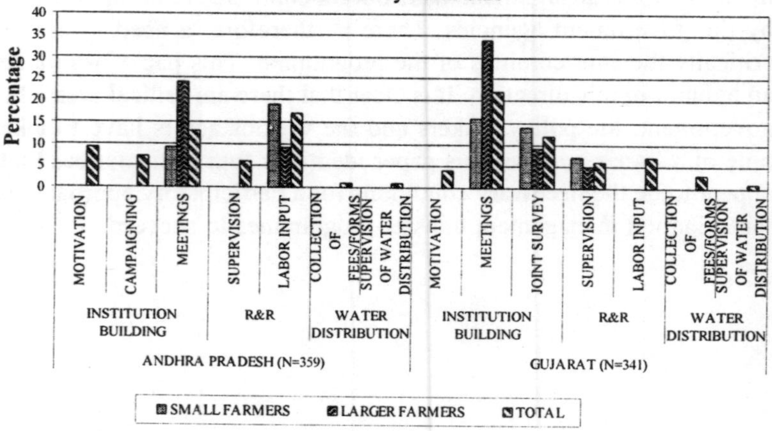

Notes: n.a.: not applicable. Significance X. Andhra Pradesh: Meetings: Significance at 0.005 level, labour input: significant at 0.025 level. Gujarat: Meetings: significant at 0.005 level. Joint survey, supervision of labour: not significant.

Source: van Koppan *et al.* (2002).

Appendix Figure 2: Proportion of Households Unaware of the WUA, by Farm size

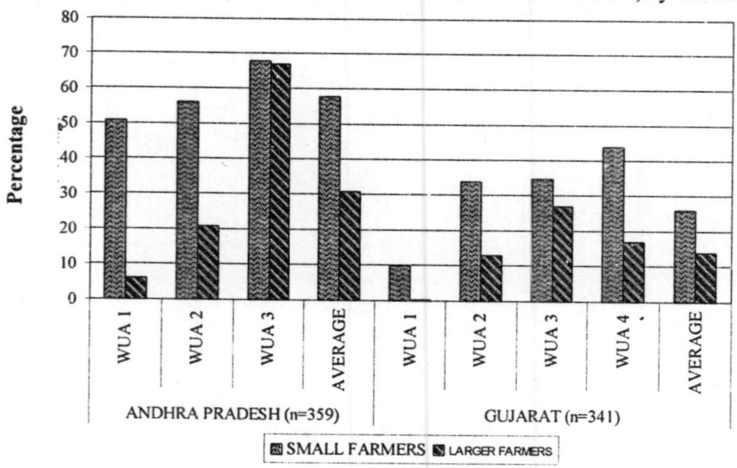

Notes: Significance X2. Andhra Pradesh: WUA(1), WUA(2), total: Significant at 0.005 level. WUA(3): not significant. Gujarat: WUA2: Significant at 0.05 level, WUA3, WUA(4): Not significant. Total: Significant at 0.025 level.

Source: van Koppan *et al.* (2002).

NOTES

1. In the January, 1997 National Conference, the Ministry of Water Resources officially recognised the imperative need of a paradigm shift in the irrigation management in the country. Following this, the Ministry once again urged all states to set-up a working group under the chief secretary; appoint a senior officer of a rank not less than the joint secretary to exclusively look after the PIM; set-up pilot projects; prepare an action plan for training; spread awareness about the PIM; give priority to rehabilitation in the PIM; etc. However, this time too, the states' response was lukewarm.
2. Following a seminar at the Water and Land Management Institute (WALMI), Anand, in 1994, in July, 1995 a Government Resolution was passed which authorised the setting up of 13 pilot projects in different major and minor irrigation projects. The implementing agency in six projects was an NGO; in the remainder, government officials undertook the transfer programme. The main feature was a gradual approach. The PIM in Gujarat envisaged a complete turnover of O&M to a WUA (called *Piyat Mandali*), even as the canals remained government property and major repairs continued to be the responsibility of the irrigation department. Thus, the day-to-day functioning of the system passed on to the users' associations.
3. Partly, this practice could be traced to the traditions of the government method of management (however, NGOs are also no exception as they too have internal or donor recommended targets to achieve) and partly to the fact that targets facilitate monitoring.
4. An additional 1.8 million hectares of land would be under the Narmada command which will also be brought under the PIM over a period of time
5. This is generally true for other people-centred programmes like watershed or joint forest management.
6. Many studies have tried to understand the level, extent, and impact of participation of member-farmers and executive committee members in WUA activities and the formation of WUAs itself (see, for instance, Brewer *et al.* 1999; Parthasarathy *et al.* 2001; van Koppen *et al.* 2002). As office-bearers as well as elected/selected representatives of the member-farmers, participation of the committee members in the WUA activities is expected to be higher than the participation of ordinary members. However, the extent of participation of committee members, though varied, is very low. Partly, the composition of a committee—generally it is dominated by large, affluent farmers—is given as a reason (Parthasarathy *et al.* 2001 and van Koppen *et al.* 2002). Interestingly, small and tenant farmers were found to be actively participating in the repair and rehabilitation (R and R) works under the PIM programme in Andhra Pradesh. Tenant participation is negligible in Gujarat though small farmers were found to be active in the R and R works. The strong stakes of tenants and small farmers in irrigated agriculture and their high dependency on canals are found to be the reasons (see, for details, van Koppen et al. 2002). Among the member-farmers, not only their participation in the works and in the decision-making process was low (Appendix Figure 1) but even their awareness about the WUA and its activities were a cause for concern (Appendix Figure 2).
7. A distinction should be made between the apathy of a government and that of the government staff. Generally the apathy among the staff is allegedly due to the fear

of losing power, less scope for rent-seeking and corruption, etc. These aspects are kept outside the purview of this analysis. However, apathy of a government could be due to the various factors discussed.

8. Over time NABARD has increased priority for roads and other sectors.
9. Prior to World Bank assistance, the government used to allocate Rs. 99 per hectare for repair and maintenance works each year out of which Rs. 86.73 were used for paying the Irrigation Department staff salaries and in meeting some fixed overhead costs.

REFERENCES

Agrawal, Anil, and Narain, Sunita (1997): "Dying Wisdom: Rise, Fall and Potential of India's Traditional Water Harvesting Systems". New Delhi: Centre for Science and Environment.

Agrawal, Bina (1994): *A Field of One's Own: Gender and Land Rights in South Asia*. London: Cambridge University Press.

Bardhan, Pranab (1996): "Decentralised Development". *Indian Economic Review* 31(2): 139-56.

Bhalla, S. (1976): "New Relations of Production in Haryana Agriculture". *Economic and Political Weekly* 11(13): A23-A30.

Brewer, J.; Kolavalli, S.; Kalro, A. H.; Naik, G.; Ramnarayan, S.; Raju, K.V.; and Sakthivadivel, R. (1999): *Irrigation Management Transfer in India: Policies, Processes, and Performance.* A collaborative study by the Indian Institute of Management, Ahmedabad, India and the International Irrigation Management Institute, Colombo, Sri Lanka. New Delhi: Oxford & IBH Publishing Co. Pvt. Ltd.

Bruns, Bryan, and Meinzen-Dick, Ruth (2000): *Negotiating Water Rights,* New Delhi: Vistar Publications.

Chambers, Robert (1988): *Managing Canal Irrigation: Practical Analysis from South Asia*. New Delhi: Oxford and IBH Publications.

Chambers, Robert; Saxena, N.C.; and Shah, Tushaar (1989): *To the Hands of the Poor: Water and Trees*. New Delhi: Oxford and IBH Publications.

Dhawan, B.D. (1990): *Big Dams: Claims, Counter Claims.* New Delhi: Commonwealth Publishers.

Dhawan, B.D. (1995): *Groundwater Depletion, Land Degradation and Irrigated Agriculture in India.* New Delhi: Commonwealth Publishers.

Dreze, Jean, and Sen, Amartya (1995): *India: Economic Development and Social Opportunity.* New Delhi: Oxford India Paperbacks.

Gadgil, Madhav, and Guha, Ramachandra (1992): *This Fissured Land: An Ecological History of India.* New Delhi: Oxford University Press.

Gadgil, Madhav, and Guha, Ramachandra (1995): *Ecology and Equity: The Use and Abuse of Nature in Contemporary India*. New Delhi: Penguin Press.

Government of Madhya Pradesh (2001): "Madhya Pradesh Sinchai Sandesh" July.

India Irrigation Sector Review. Supplementary Analysis. Report No. 9518-IN. Vol. 1: Main Report. Vol. 11: Agriculture Operations Division, India Country Department, Asia Region.

Jodha, N.S. (1992): "Common Property Resources: A Missing Dimension of Development Strategies". World Bank Discussion Paper No. 169, Washington, D.C.: The World Bank.

Joshi, L.K., and Dinkar, V.S., (1996): "Waterlogged, Saline and Alkali Lands: Prevention and Reclamation". New Delhi: Ministry of Water Resources.

Kohli, Atul (1987): *The State and Poverty in India: The Politics of Reform.* London: Cambridge University Press.

Kohli, Atul (1990): *Democracy and Discontent: India's Growing Crisis of Governability.* London: Cambridge University Press.

Korten, David C. (1990): *Getting to the 21st Century: Voluntary Action and the Global Agenda.* West Hartford, CT.: Kumarian Press.

Maloney, Clarence, and Raju, K.V. (1994): *Managing Irrigation Transfer: Practice and Policy in India* .New Delhi: Sage Publications.

Meinzen-Dick Ruth S.; Brown, L.; Feldstein, H.S.; and Quisumbing, A.R. (1997): "Gender, Property Rights and Natural Resources". *World Development* 25(8): 1303-15.

Mendelsohn, Oliver, and Vicziany, Marika (1998): *The Untouchables: Subordination, Poverty and the State in Modern India.* New Delhi: Cambridge University Press.

Merrey, Douglas J. (1987): "The Local Impact of Centralised Irrigation Control in Pakistan: A Sociocentric Perspective". In Little, P., and Horowitz, M. (eds.) *Lands at Risk in the Third World: Local Level Perspectives.* Boulder: Westview Press. pp. 352-72.

Moench, Marcus (1998): "Allocating the Common Heritage: Debates over Water Rights and Governance Structures in India". *Economic and Political Weekly* 33(26): A46-A53.

Mosse, D. (1994): "Authority, Gender and Knowledge: Theoretical Reflections on the Practice of Participatory Rural Appraisal". *Development and Change* 25(3): 497-526 (earlier draft as ODI Agricultural Administration (Research and Extension) Network Paper No. 44).

National Water Policy (1987): New Delhi: Government of India.

Ostrom, Elinor (1992): *Crafting Institutions for Self-Governing Irrigation Systems.* San Francisco: Institute for Contemporary Studies.

Parthasarathy, R. (1992): "Technological Differences and Labour Demand in Agriculture in Tamil Nadu". Mimeo. Gujarat Institute of Area Planning, Ahmedabad.

Parthasarathy, R. (1998): "Coordinating Participation to Transfer Irrigation Management: A Game Theoretic Paradigm". Working Paper 105. Ahmedabad: Gujarat Institute of Development Research.

Parthasarathy, R. (1999): "Political Economy of Irrigation Water Pricing". Working Paper 109. Ahmedabad: Gujarat Institute of Development Research.

Parthasarathy, R. (2000): "Participatory Irrigation Management Programme in Gujarat: Institutional and Financial Issues". *Economic and Political Weekly* 35(35 and 36): 3147-54.

Parthasarathy, R., and Joshi, Harish (2001): "Access to Water and Equity Dimensions of Irrigation Management Transfer: A Comparison of Gujarat and Andhra Pradesh, India". Report submitted to the International Water Management Institute, Colombo, Sri Lanka.

Parthasarathy, R. (2002): "Comparing Gujarat with Andhra Pradesh: Reforms in Irrigation Management and Peoples' Participation". In Hooja, Rakesh; Pangare, Ganesh; and Raju, K.V. (eds.) *Users in Water Management: The Andhra Model and its Replicability in India*. Jaipur and New Delhi: Rawat Publications. pp. 282-302.

Planning Commission (1992): "Report of the Committee on Pricing of Irrigation Water". New Delhi: Government of India.

Planning Commission (2000): "Mid Term Appraisal of Ninth Five Year Plan (1997-2002)". New Delhi: Government of India.

Sengupta, Nirmal (1991): *Managing Common Property: Irrigation in India and the Philippines.* Indo-Dutch Studies on Development Alternatives-6. New Delhi: Sage Publications.

Shah, Tushaar (1993): *Groundwater Markets and Irrigation Development: Political Economy and Practical Policy.* Mumbai: Oxford University Press.

Shiva, Vandana (1988): *Staying Alive: Women, Ecology and Development.* London and New Delhi: Zed Books Ltd.

Shiva, Vandana (1989): *The Violence of the Green Revolution: Ecological Degradation and Political Conflict in Punjab.* Dehra Dun: Natraj Publishers.

Stone, I. (1984): *Canal Irrigation in British India: Perspectives on Technological Change in a Peasant Economy.* London: Cambridge University Press.

Vaidyanathan, A. (1999): *Water Resource Management: Institutions and Irrigation Development in India.* New Delhi: Oxford University Press.

van Koppen, Barbara (1998): *More Jobs per Drop Targeting Irrigation to Poor Women and Men.* The Netherlands: Wageningen Agricultural University.

van Koppen, Barbara (2002): "A Gender Performance Indicator for Irrigation: Concepts, Tools and Applications". Research Report 59. International Water Management Institute, Colombo, Sri Lanka

van Koppen, Barbara; Parthasarathy, R.; and Safilou, Constantina (2002): "Poverty Dimensions of Irrigation Management Transfer in Large-Scale Canal Irrigation in Andhra Pradesh and Gujarat, India". Research Report 61. International Water Management Institute, Colombo. Sri Lanka.

Weligamage, P.; Barker, Randolph; Hussain, Intizar; Amarasinghe, Upali; and Samad, Madar (2002): "World Irrigation and Water Statistics 2002: With a Guide to Data Sources". International Water Management Institute, Colombo, Sri Lanka.

Zwarteveen, Margreet S. (1997): "Water: From Basic Need to Commodity: A Discussion on Gender and Water Rights in the Context of Irrigation". *World Development* 25(8): 1335-41.

24

Politics of Water Management

Missing Links in the Debate

VISHWA BALLABH

INTRODUCTION

A mammoth fresh water crisis seems to await the future generations of India. In 1951, the per capita availability of fresh water in India was 3450 m^3 per year. In 1999 it slided to approximately 1,250 m^3, and in 2050 it will further slide to 760 m^3 (Government of India 1999). The situation is already critical in six out of the 20 major river basins with the per capita fresh water availability going below 1000 m^3 (World Bank 1996). These national level statistics mask huge disparities between basins and regions. The utilisable water resources per capita per year vary between 3020 m^3 in the Narmada basin to about 180 m^3 or less in the Sabarmati basin and other basins of inland drainage. Out of the 20 major basins, 4 had more than 1700 m^3 per capita per year utilisable water resources, 9 had between 1000 and 1700 m^3, 5 had between 500 and 1,000 m^3, and 2 basins had less than 500 m^3 in the year 1991 (Government of India 1999). Similar variations exist within a basin and in different seasons of the year, which aggravate the problem of water scarcity.

The decline in the water availability, however, does not necessarily contribute to water scarcity in the absolute sense. There are a few but remarkable cases of community initiatives that have enabled people to survive the scarcity of water through collective action and prudent water management. On the other hand, an abundance of water does not necessarily mean that water is available to everyone. History is replete with examples of famines and droughts that have resulted from man-made situations rather than from the failure of nature. How else does one explain water scarcity in Cherrapunji—the area with the highest rainfall in the country—and no scarcity in the villages with less than 200 mm. of rainfall? These questions need to be explored in a water debate. Efforts that focus only on the augmentation of water supply *per se* and ignore the skewed social control over water resources by the privileged minorities are fraught with failure. This paper argues that the current hype and hysteria about water scarcity "as an absolutely natural phenomenon" is being created by the privileged minority which is dominant and influential in the water sector.

The paper is organised in four sections including this introductory section. Section 2 paper deals with the politics of water management: it broadly identifies interest groups in the water sector, discusses their objectives and resources, and assesses whether they have succeeded in achieving their goals or not. In Section 3, the level of political contestation in the water sector is discussed and the missing links in the discourse on water are identified. Section 4 presents a summary of the discussion.

POLITICS OF WATER MANAGEMENT

There are four key sectors for which water is allocated: (i) rural domestic, (ii) urban domestic, (iii) industry, and (iv) irrigation. The environmental and non-consumptive sector is emerging; it is still in a nascent stage in India. Often, the demand for water for environmental services is ignored in water resource planning, distribution and management. The above four categories of users are in fact, interest groups in the sense that each has a specific claim on the resources under contention and lobbies actively to promote its interests. In addition, there are water managers, pollution control boards, and social activists who influence water allocation and management; among the last three categories, water managers have a strong influence. The irrigation departments, water supply departments, and municipalities have a strong influence on the capture, storage and distribution of water resources. Their size and budgets have grown manifold as the past 150 years' history of water management in India shows. At present roughly one million persons are working in the irrigation departments alone.

Basic information about the seven players including the four key-use sectors—their nature and character, their claims, their strengths and their ability to influence water management and allocation—is given in the Table 24.1.

Table 24.1: Competition and Conflicts over Fresh Water: Who Wins and Who Loses

Who are they?	Rural domestic users	Urban domestic users	Landowners	Industrialists	Water managers/ municipalities	Pollution control boards	Social activists/ NGOs
How do they advance their claim?	Basic necessity	Basic necessity	Food security/ Productivity	Growth of economy and employment	Scientific experts, national and public good	Pollution control monitoring and enforcement	Collective consciousness, equitable distribution and conservation
Are they organised and homogeneous?	No, dispersed and highly stratified	Concentrated block although no formal association still exert pressure through/ on municipalities	Farmers' union, large vote banks, but segregated between large and small	Yes, have large clout over Central and State Governments.	Yes, cadre-based organisation	Cadre-based organisation	Unorganised and dispersed
What are their goals and interests?	Access to safe drinking water	Access to safe drinking water	Reliable and adequate supply of water for agriculture	Reliable, cheap and sufficient water for industrial production and facilities to drain out waste water	Retain control of decision making and resources; Manage water according to the rule book	Pollution control of water bodies	Conservation of water bodies, efficient and equitable allocation of water
Do their interests clash with other claimants' interests?	Yes, with land owners, urban water users and industrialists	Rural water users—both farmers and domestic users	Industrialists urban domestic water users	Rural people and urban domestic water users, pollution control boards	Farmers and users	Industrialists and urban municipalities	Large farmers, industrialists
Are they able to achieve their goals?	No	Only poor urban slum dwellers suffer	Small, tail-end farmers suffer	Yes, secured water supply and able to bypass pollution laws	Yes	No	Demonstrate alternative practices but unable to make impact on the sector as a whole

Source: Ballabh and Pradhan 2000.

It is common knowledge that the landowners use maximum part of the total fresh water. Their number is large, and they function as loosely organised groups under the banner of a farmer organisation. They constitute a large vote bank. However, landowners are not a homogeneous group; they are differentiated in terms of large, small, commercial and non-commercial farmers. Because of their size and organisations, they have a strong influence on the local legislatures and provincial governments. However, their clout varies widely in both time and space. A legislator said in a State Assembly, "We will not give a drop of water from sugarcane; instead a canal of blood will flow. Cane and sugar factory are the glory of Maharashtra" (cited from Singh 1997). This group becomes very active whenever the price of irrigation water or power tariff is raised.

The industrialists constitute the smallest group in terms of their number but have a disproportionate influence over the state and central Governments. They further their own interests by claiming to promote the national interest—by enhancing economic growth and raising employment—and by using their superior financial powers. As a result, they have often been able to secure rights over fresh water even during very adverse conditions and bypass the water pollution laws. Industry enjoys supremacy on account of its concentrated economic power and its ability to pay a high price for water. Lax pollution laws and weak enforcement allow industries to impose water pollution externalities and diseconomies on the rural people. People worst affected by these political contestations are the poorest in the villages, those in the far-flung areas, and urban slum dwellers (Ballabh *et al.* 1999; Vani, Prabhakar, and Ballabh 1999).

The urban domestic water users, who constitute the second largest group, have an advantage over their rural counterparts in terms of concentration. Their main objective is to have secure and safe drinking water. They exert pressure through and on municipalities which, in turn, helps them secure fresh water. When water is transported from distant rural areas, their interests clash with those of the landowners and rural domestic users. The urban domestic water users are not a homogeneous group; their access to fresh water varies based on their economic strength and location within the municipal areas.

The rural domestic water users by far are the largest in number, but they are the weakest among all the claimants of fresh water resources as they are dispersed and stratified. Although the quantity of water required for domestic purposes is small, often collecting it requires travelling for a few miles. In several areas agriculture receives plentiful water for irrigation, but no water is available for domestic purposes. The stated national water policy, which gives primacy to drinking water, has not been enforced. Due to the high level of extraction of groundwater for irrigation, the proportion of water utilised for household purposes has declined even in arid and semi-arid areas (UNICEF and WWF 1997). In these competing claims and political contestation, the scarce fresh water is allocated to the influential sectors, such as urban domestic users and industrial units. The urban domestic users are more articulate and politically powerful at the state and national levels and have to deal with an organised urban administration. Thus they are better placed to demand and appropriate fresh water resources for their own needs, while the rural domestic users get the last priority over scarce fresh water resources (Ballabh and Singh 1997).

The remaining three groups, namely, water managers and municipalities, pollution control boards and social activists and NGOs, are responsible for managing fresh water resources. The state irrigation departments are the most important players in this group. They are not only responsible for planning, constructing and managing irrigation projects, but are also responsible for monitoring and regulating water of the notified rivers and water bodies. Faced with water scarcity, the preferred approach of the water managers has been the identification of new sources, followed by capture, storage and transportation of water through a centralised system of administration. In the allocation of water, power relations play an important role in different sectors, regions and social groups. Water is allocated by default, rather than by design and there is a complete institutional failure in tackling the issues related to efficiency, equity and sustainability of water resources (Ballabh *et al.* 1999).

In addition to higher resource utilisation efficiency, the involvement of farmers' organisations in irrigation management can lead to decentralised management and local capacity building. So far, 13 states have formulated irrigation management policies that encourage an effective involvement of farmers in irrigation management. Under the Participatory Irrigation Management (PIM) programme, irrigation management functions are being turned over to the tertiary level farmers' organisations. However, the PIM programme is being implemented at a very slow place in many states for several reasons (Brewer *et al.* 1999). There is a lack of commitment on the part of irrigation managers to delegate power and authority to farmers' organisations. Thus, conditions for an effective decentralised management of irrigation have not yet been created.

In spite of known efficacy and proclaimed policies, the irrigation bureaucracy could not involve water users on a scale that would make a significant impact on the sector. One explanation of this failure is that the incentives offered to the irrigation officials are so designed that they have no interest in managing irrigation systems in the interest of farmers (for a detailed review, see Ostrom 1995). Others have argued that there is systematic corruption within the irrigation bureaucracy involving both lower and higher officials (Wade 1985). Rent seeking and corrupt practices have become very common. As a result, constructive responses from the community at present are sporadic and patchy; they are unlikely to provide a systematic and sustained strategy to solve the emerging problems. The involvement of the communities needs to be enhanced, and conditions have to be created for their meaningful participation.

The Government of India announced its new water policy on April 1, 2002 (Government of India 2002). The policy document has 27 sections dealing with various aspects of wateruse and management covering issues like growing scarcity of water and resultant conflicts; need for a good data base; necessity of a paradigm shift in water sector; implementation of basin-wise planning and management; and an emphasis on drought proofing. These are laudable goals, but strategies for achieving them have not been worked out.

The policy paper does not elaborate on the much needed institutional reforms to create space for democratic and sustainable participation of water users' organisations; it merely states that "the local bodies such as municipalities and Gram Panchayats (village councils) should particularly be involved in the operation, maintenance and management of water infrastructures/facilities at appropriate levels progressively with a view to eventually transfering management of such facilities to the user groups/local bodies" (Government of India 2002, Section 12.0).

However, the paper discusses the need for reorientation and even creation of new institutions, such as basin- and sub-basin-level organisations (Section 4.3), rotational water distribution systems and volumetric water allocation (Section 9.3), and emphasises the need to increase water charges to cover at least the operation and maintenance of the canal systems. Thus, the new water policy differs from the old one only in terms of the degree of emphasis on the need for user participation in the management of water services; it does not address the crucial issue of maintaining a balance of power between the water users' associations and the government departments of water resources.

The Government of India has also suggested to the state governments that they formulate their own water policies and several state governments have been following up the matter. The Government of Gujarat has drafted a water policy which will replace its old water policy. A critical review of the Gujarat policy suggests that even here the issue of balancing power and authority between the water resources department and the water users' associations has not been addressed. The Gujarat policy repeats most of the provisions mentioned in the national water policy and its focus continues to be on (i) technological and physical management of water and (ii) the supply side management. Although the document does deal with the demand side of water management, it fails to evolve an appropriate strategy for demand management.

So far, attempts to reform the management by the irrigation bureaucracy have largely focused on upgrading and broadening the skills of personnel through training, etc. However, the issues of improving the accountability, internal and external communication and structural reform have remained untouched by and large. The system is a near anarchy; it is dominated by rent-seeking and political lobbying. Reforming such a system without restructuring the relationship between the farmers and the irrigation bureaucracy, providing the former space in decision-making and control, and redefining the role of the civil society is an impossible task.

LEVELS OF POLITICAL CONTESTATIONS IN THE WATER SECTOR

In previous section, we presented various interest groups, their claims and counter-claims. The final outcome, however, depends largely on the compromises reached by the contestants.

Politics may be defined as a complex set of relationships between men, especially those relationships involving power and authority. In the light of this definition, several features of the claims and counter-claims in the various contests can be discerned: first, contestation over water is not at one level, it is being articulated and played out at different levels; second, at each level of these contestations, there are dominant groups which are interested in maintaining the status quo; and third, there seems to be coalitions of dominant groups between different levels, although not by design. Hence, there is little demand for change; the status quo is maintained.

Conceptualisation of Water Problem and Politics of Policy

First of all, the politics of water discourse is dominated by perceived and projected water scarcity. Once this paradigm is accepted, what follows is a discussion of a series of issues that pertain to practical solutions along the familiar lines, for instance, how to increase the supply, by how much and using which type of technology (Jairath 2003). Connected with this is the political nature of policy formulation and implementation process: the different interest groups contest and try to influence the policy process at all the stages from its formulation to implementation (Mollinga and Bolding, forthcoming). In the current discourse of politics of policy-making, the dominant paradigm is highly technocratic in nature; the emphasis is on infrastructure building and the prescriptive style of policy making and management. The emphasis on big projects and grand plans to connect the river systems, including the prescription of how and in what manner the people's participation should be solicited in water management, are the manifestations of technocratic dominance. The discussion about how the policy has evolved is generally missing. The need for the stakeholders' participation in policy formulation is recognised and it is enlisted, but their representation is questionable. Discourses on water politics among the civil society organisations are narrowly constructed whose formulation is largely concerned with commoditification of water and its consequences. A larger debate about the reorientation of the departments of water resources and irrigation seldom takes place.

Hydro-Politics

The allocation of water between states and different riparian groups is being negotiated through the Water Disputers Tribunal, an institution created under the Inter-state Water Dispute Act, 1956. Under the Act, the Central Government appoints a tribunal for adjudication of inter-state water disputes. The capability and credibility of this tribunal is obvious: not only are there delays in the resolution of disputes, often implementation of the award is not enforced. In fact, in the case of the Cauvery River the prescribed procedure has given way to direct negotiations between the state governments mediated by the Government of India. This shows that tribunals are not able to resolve disputes. As water scarcity increases in central and western India such disputes are likely to increase in the region. Overall, this hydro-politics is constructed around the scarcity of water, and the issues of management and devolution of power to the people's institutions are often ignored. In the overall macro-hydro-politics, the capture and creation of water resources become part of a grand strategy to mitigate the water scarcity. The state not only designs mega-projects, but also promotes those policies and programmes which help the dominant class of users to capture scarce water and control it.

Everyday Politics at the Grassroots Level

The growing scarcity and ineffective institutional arrangements for capture, allocation and distribution compounds the growing water crisis which is unlikely to be resolved by increasing water supply. When the requirement exceeds supply, the additional supply is diverted to people who are already well-off. To reiterate, in the struggle for capture of and control over water those who are left out are among the weakest—the small and marginal farmers and urban and rural domestic water users. Equitable distribution of scarce water among the multiple users poses a major challenge. Mismanagement of water in the deficient areas is also quite common. The natural scarcity of water is thus aggravated by its use by a few. Confining the use of existing resources for higher consumptive practices thus artificially generates part of the water shortages. The current state policies promote water-intensive crops and chemical-based industries; the latter not only consume large quantities of water but also create pollution. One of the major externalities of the above is the reduced availability of clean, drinking water.

The three levels of contestation over water, although not designed, reinforce each other. At the grassroots level, it is the well-off people who benefit from the current design and prevail in contestation. These groups subscribe to the strategies and policies which promise increased supply of water, preferably free of cost. This, in turn, suits the dominant group at the level of hydro-politics and at the state level discourses on water about short supply and crisis. Thus, the rationality and legitimacy of the current focus on increasing the water supply is reinforced. Since the problem is projected as large, the solutions also have to be large. The alternative which focuses on decentralised management of limited water and devolution of power to the local level is often ignored. The resilience of water resources departments should be seen from these perspectives. The issues related to devolution of power and authority and reorientation of water resources departments are largely absent even from the academic debates, and even from the academic circles.

SUMMARY

The paper has argued that the politics in the water sector could be understood at different levels. However, the interest groups dominant at one level strengthen the current thinking at another level. Overall, the interests of these groups coincide which helps maintain the *status quo* in the water sector. This also helps the water resources departments to maintain their power and authority in the water sector. Any real reform in the water sector, therefore, could be brought only through reorienting the water resources departments in such a way that the required space is created for a meaningful participation of the local bodies. Not reorienting them would only compound the existing problems. Thus, the strategy of only creating a new infrastructure in the water sector is not an answer to the current problems.

REFERENCES

Ballabh, V., and Singh, Katar (1997): "Competing Demands for Water in Sabarmati Basin: Potential and Future Conflicts". Paper presented at the IDPAD Seminar, Amersfoort, The Netherlands, October 11-17, 1997.

Ballabh, V; Prabhakar, R.; Dinesh Kumar, M.; Vani, Vina; Mudgerikar, Arun; and Joshi, Viswas (1999): "Western Regional Consultation on Fresh Water Issues". Workshop Report prepared by the Institute of Rural Management, Anand for UNICEF, Gandhinagar.

Ballabh, V., and Pradhan, Ujwal (2000): "India's Water Crises and Institutional Challenges". Paper presented at the Eighth Biennial Conference of International Association of Studies in Common Property, Bloomington: Indiana University.

Brewer, J.; Kolavalli, Shashi; Kalro, A.H.; Naik, G.; Ramnarayan, S.; Raju, K.V.; and Shakthivadivel R. (1999): *Irrigation Management Transfer in India: Policies, Processes and Performance*. New Delhi: Oxford & IBH Publishing.

Government of India (1999): "Water Resources Development Plan of India: Policy & Issues". New Delhi: Ministry of Water Resources, Government of India.

Government of India (2002): "Draft National Water Policy". New Delhi: Ministry of Water Resources, Government of India.

Jairath, Jasveen (2003): "Drought of Sanity and Flood of the Absurd: Politics of Water Discourse", Discussion Note, SaciWATERs, Hyderabad.

Mollinga, Peter, P., and Bolding, Alex (eds.) (forthcoming): *The Politics of Irrigation Reform: Contested Policy Formulation and Implementation in Asia, Africa and Latin America*.

Ostrom, Elinor (1995): "Incentives, Rules of the Game and Development". Annual World Bank Conference on Development Economics, Washington, D.C.: The World Bank.

Singh, Satyajit (1997): *Taming the Waters: The Political Economy of Large Dams in India*. Delhi: Oxford University Press.

United Nations International Children's Emergency Fund and World Wildlife Fund (1997): *Fresh Water for India's Children & Nature*. New Delhi: UNICEF.

Vani, Vina; Prabhakar, R; and Ballabh, V. (1999): "Water Scarcity in Western India: Agenda for Future Action?" Anand: Institute of Rural Management.

Wade, Robert (1985): "The Market for Public Office: Why the Indian State is Not Better at Development", *World Development*, 13(4):467-97.

World Bank (1996): "India's Environment Taking Stock of Plans, Programmes and Priorities: An Assessment of the Environmental Action Programme—India". South Asia Regional office: The World Bank.

25

Fading Shine of the Golden Decade

The Establishment Strikes Back

ANIL C. SHAH

The 1990s may be called the Golden Decade of Participatory Management Programmes (PMP) in natural resources. It was during this decade that three major programmes in forestry, land management and water were launched. These programmes were based on the Guidelines issued by the Ministry of Environment and Forests (MoEF).

In June, 1990, the Joint Forest Management (JFM) programme opened up forest management to local communities, hitherto an exclusive preserve of the State Forest Departments. Twenty-seven states passed orders operationalising the Guidelines. By 2002, 14 million hectares, 19 per cent of the total forest cover, were brought under the JFM through 63,000 JFM Committees.

In October, 1994, the Watershed Development Programme (WDP), implemented mainly in the drought prone areas, ushered in a *silent revolution.* It empowered local communities to make plans and execute them and to manage the local land, water, vegetative and animal resources. In 1997, the Andhra Pradesh Government transferred its canals to Farmers' Organisations (FOs) placing 32 lakh hectares of irrigated land under them. Madhya Pradesh followed suit; Tamil Nadu and Rajasthan have also passed similar laws.

Later an exercise on the Tenth Plan began and provided an opportunity for pushing the unfinished agenda of incorporating the design principles of participatory management. But, the Establishment instead of extending a helping hand was obviously waiting in the wings to sabotage the Golden Decade and usurp what truly blongs to the stake-holders. This paper calls for vigilance and action. Overt and covert moves by the Central and State Governments to distort and discredit the participatory approach that accords primacy to the stakeholders in the management of their resources should be thwarted.

The Genesis

June 1, 1990: JFM Launched

The MoEF issued an order on June 1, 1990 to involve forest communities in the protection and development of forests. This programme, known as Joint Forest Management (JFM) later, has been regarded as a watershed in the forest policy of India. After the order was issued, more than 20 state governments gave orders to operationalise the JFM: they laid down the principles of organising forest communities, delineated their roles and responsibilities and defined entitlement of the communities in terms of their share of minor forest produce and of timber value when trees mature and are harvested. The following box gives a glimpse of the changing scene.

Progress in JFM

The forest area under the JFM, which provides for sharing of the benefits of the forest conservation with the local communities, has increased from 7 million hectares in 1998 to 14 million hectares in 2002. The number of the Village Forest Protection Committees has also risen from 33,000 to 63,622; these committees conserve and manage 19 per cent of the country's forest cover. Twenty-nine lakh families are involved in the JFM of which 49 per cent are scheduled tribes and 29 per cent are scheduled castes. There are 1,70,000 villages in and around 32 million hectares of degraded forests in the country that are proposed to be brought under the Joint Forest Management by 2007.
(The Minister, Environment and Forests, at the meeting of the Ministry's Parliamentary Consultative Committee, February 10, 2003.)

A study carried out by the author on the costs and benefits of the JFM found that against the average investment of Rs.8,000 per hectare, the average benefit over the ten-year period was about Rs.25,000 (ranging from Rs.11,000 to Rs.50,000), per hectare. Interestingly over a period, the Forest Department gained more out of forestland protected by the village communities than from the forestland managed by its own staff.

October 1994: Silent Revolution of Watershed Development

Based on the report of the Hanumantha Rao Committee, the Ministry of Rural Development (MoRD) issued a set of guidelines on the Watershed Development Programme (WDP). The Committee had reviewed the working of drought combating schemes including the watershed development schemes. Inspired by the examples of participatory approach to the land and water resources development, particularly promoted by the NGOs, the Committee made a key recommendation to empower the local community to plan, implement and manage its natural resources on a watershed basis. The recommendation was incorporated in the MoRD scheme. The WDP, which had merged several area development schemes of the MoRD, was intended to create a major impact in the drought-prone areas of the country. By March, 2002, the programme had invested about Rs. 8, 677 crore and had covered 161 lakh hectares, giving an average of Rs.500 crore a year during the Ninth Plan. Watershed programmes have an abiding relevance in a country where 60 per cent of the area is dry with a high concentration of poverty in it.

A study carried out by the author found that the watershed villages were better off in terms of drinking water, fodder availability, crop areas and crop yields, employment, etc., than the neighbouring non-watershed villages that the study earned the title "Eloquent 'Silent' Revolution".

The Ministry of Agriculture (MoA) was running its own scheme of watershed development in the traditional top-down fashion. The MoRD programme influenced the MoA and the latter adopted the "Common Principles" which it jointly evolved with the MoRD. Further, the MoA also launched its own scheme in 2000 in which the place of participation is so central that the MoA has called it *sahbhagita*.

Massive Investment fails to Produce Results

Even though irrigation projects were intended to provide support in raising productivity in agriculture, the farmers were not involved in them; they were not considered relevant in the design, implementation, or management of projects. Irrigation project planning and management was assumed to be too technical for the farmers to understand, let alone take it up. After an investment of Rs.1,00,000 crore in the public irrigation system, it was realised that despite the massive investment, public irrigation projects did not produce the expected results in terms of efficiency, equity and sustainability. The National Water Policy of 1987 had recommended that farmers be involved in the management of irrigation projects at the minor level, i.e. "below the outlet". Without proper backing and empowerment, the FOs promoted, as a formality by the Irrigation Departments, were lifeless entities and began to wither away as soon as the department turned to new challenges and priorities.

But Andhra Pradesh embarked on a new path. Inspired by the successful examples in countries like the Philippines and the Mexico, Andhra Pradesh Government, under the leadership of a dynamic Chief Minister, transferred public irrigation systems to the FOs by passing a law in 1997. The Governments of Madhya Pradesh, Tamil Nadu, Rajasthan and Orissa followed suit. Some impressive gains of the Participatory Irrigation Management (PIM) are presented in the following box.

Some Impressive Gains of PIM

- Transparency in handling funds and executing works—contractors are out—result 30 per cent savings.
- In some parts of the upper Manor dam, canals were desilted after 14 years.
- Water reaches the tail-enders across the state.
- In Tungbhandra High Level Canal during the Rabi season, 1,30,000 acres of land was irrigated (without additional supplies) from the saving of water during the Kharif season—first time in the project history.
- Due to massive drainage works done by Farmers' Organisations, after several years the delta region was not submerged during the rainy season.
- Collection of water charges increased from 54 per cent in 1997-98 to 65 per cent in 1998-99.
- Government investment in the PIM has resulted in five-to ten-fold increase in the agricultural production according to the perception of some farmers and officials
- Many officials are happy that they have to deal with the farmers' problems not individually but in aggregation at the distributary level. Some are unhappy that the PIM has cut into their additional earnings, which may further decline.

"It is hard to dispute visible benefits."

Based on the findings of a study by K. V. Raju, Faculty Member, Institute for Social and Economic Change, Bangalore, which covered 38 irrigation systems (14 major, 5 medium, 19 minor) in Andhra Pradesh, spread over Telengana, coastal Andhra, and Rayalaseema.

The Nineties: A Golden Decade

Thus the decade of 1990s saw sweeping—almost revolutionary—changes in the management of the natural resources which are crucial for the well-being of the people living in the rural areas. No longer was the management run on the basis of dictates from the national or state capitals and implemented by the district bureaucracy; now the rural communities themselves would decide their requirements and prepare micro-plans appropriate for the local conditions and needs and implement them. Individuals and institutions working for rural development and committed to participatory approach regarded these developments as a major achievement and an important gain for the rural communities. In the initial phase this indeed was the case.

The Next Decade: Undoing Creeps in

When the Ninth Five Year Plan was coming to an end and the Tenth Plan was being formulated, those working for participatory management of the natural resources saw an opportunity for further strengthening the participatory approach adopted during the 1990s. They suggested:

- Community-Based Organisations (CBOs) to be the focal point of the schemes empowering them to plan, implement, and manage their resources with the necessary financial, technical and administrative support.
- Adequate funding arrangement: the central government was to provide a major share, the state government a smaller share, and the people were to contribute 10 per cent or more that should go into the Village Maintenance and Development Fund.
- Decision-making to be decentralised at the district level and in a consultative mode.
- Emphasis on, and provision for, software support to the programme by appointing experienced agencies that would be responsible for community organising and training.
- Flexibility in the technical and financial norms that could be adapted to suit the varying local conditions at state, district and village levels.

- Independent and reliable monitoring and evaluation that would help the policy-makers to take corrective action in time.
- Forums for consultation with stakeholders at district, state and national levels that will help control and curtail dominance of the bureaucracy and politicians.

Watershed Development

Even though it was far ahead of similar schemes sponsored till then by the Government of India, the watershed development programme of the MoRD had its own weaknesses. While there were some inherent flaws in the design, others were an outcome of the distortions in the implementation of the scheme. The MoRD and those who had a stake in the success of the programme had to constantly watch out for the distortions and flaws that would erode its value, though the outer shell may hold.

Weaknesses

1. Though sufficient financial provision is made for training, no strategy has been developed for capacity building of the key functionaries. As a result, provisions remain largely unutilised.
2. It is crucial to maintain the flow of funds as planned in the scheme. Interruptions caused by procedural wrangles or engineered by ulterior motives need to be monitored, censured and checked.
3. The Guidelines provide for the development of public lands, not only as a technical requirement of watershed development, but also as a measure for helping the resource-poor. However, public lands are seldom developed because they are increasingly threatened by encroachment. The MoRD, which is also in charge of revenue lands, has not initiated any action to remove the encroachments that should help the poor, although the MoRD has to address the issue of poverty reduction also. In fact, recent studies suggest diminishing dependence of the poor on public lands, possibly because there is nothing much left to depend because the resources have been severely depleted.

4. Only a few states have set up state-level advisory committees providing an interface between government agencies and other stakeholders. The district-level advisory committees have not worked as forums for mutual learning. The district-level bureaucracy dominates these committees demanding compliance from the partners implementing the programme.
5. A programme with new characteristics and expectations requires that it be placed in the hands of those who have the requisite understanding and sensitivity to appreciate and support new initiatives. This has not happened. If there are the right people in the right place in these programmes, it is not by design, but by accident. A study on the natural resources management, jointly carried out by the Overseas Development Institute (ODI), London, and other research organisations in October, 2002, has noted that there was a strong resistance to decentralisation from the established officials resulting in only a cursory fulfilment of the Guidelines: village selection criteria are subverted, PIA selection is not transparent, and implementation is done in such a manner as to favour the politically powerful, and in some cases even leading to rent-seeking by officials.
6. The built-in flexibility of the scheme is increasingly being overshadowed by rigidity and sometimes by fiats of whimsical officers.

Flaws

A serious flaw is the inadequate response to and corrective mechanism for the distortions in the implementation, though the MoRD (which has formulated, launched and largely funded the scheme) has enough resources to obtain the feedback on what is happening in the field and what needs corrective action. Somehow—may be for valid administrative reasons—it is rather slow in appreciating the gravity of the problems and in taking corrective actions.

The Revised Guidelines issued in 2001 have taken care of some of the quality parameters of the programmes, but they have yet to attend to the core issues of the right personnel manning the district bureaucracy and the right agency working as a Project Implementing Agency (PIA). The Revised Guidelines have, in fact, reversed some worthy initiatives of the original Guidelines. For instance, the schedules of rates for preparing cost estimates were to be prepared at the district level, now they have been centralized and have to be prepared at the state level. Earlier, the district agency used to release funds directly to the village institutions; according to the Revised Guidelines, they are to be routed through an intermediary—the project implementing agency—a sure recipe for institutionalising corruption!

An important design flaw is that the Guidelines mention nothing about productivity enhancement and value addition during the implementation which requires evolving agricultural practices fine-tuned to the resource endowments of each watershed that is accessible to the poor (low-cost) and sustainable (low-risk). Though the matter was brought to the notice of the Ministry, the Revised Guidelines are silent about the management of the post-investment phase. This is strange because the same ministry, when it was in charge of the community development programme in the 1950s, had extended the life of the Community Development Project from three years to nine years by preceding it with three years of National Extension Service and following it by calling it as Post-Stage II. In the watershed programme no thought has been given to maintaining the momentum. Neither does it consider how the newly promoted Watershed Associations, User Groups and Extension Volunteers will continue to function nor how the assets created will lead to the expected increases and continuously contribute to value addition and raising of productivity. In response the MoRD has come out with the concept of "Watershed Plus" in the Revised Guidelines, but without any elaboration.

Ominous Developments

Two more developments are taking place at the national level that would undermine the gains of the Golden Decade. First, the Revised Guidelines of the MoRD on watershed development had already signalled the rising importance of the Panchayati Raj institutions (PRIs) when it stipulated that the "PIAs should be preferably selected from PRI institutions". Though reliable information is not available, it appears that the MoRD is determined to hand over the watershed programme to the PRIs. Anticipating a move in this direction, the

ODI study reports that it is premature to test the policy tenet, namely, the PRIs are the most legitimate and sustainable institutions of local governance and implementation of development schemes. It is a contentious issue whether the PRIs assist in promoting equity in general and hence there will be apprehension whether they would promote equity in the watershed programme.

A study carried out by the Development Support Centre in consultation with PRI representatives, stakeholder groups and NGO workers unanimously recommended that the PRIs were ill-equipped to take over the management of development programmes like the watershed scheme from the stakeholder groups such as watershed associations; indeed they had yet to attend satisfactorily to their mandatory duties of governance.

Secondly, rather than consolidating its path-breaking initiatives in the participatory approach and spreading them to the various departments of its own ministry and to the other ministries, the Department of Drinking Water Supply under the MoRD launched a scheme, *Swajaldhara,* which would enable the local community to provide water for itself for domestic use in 2003. Though it aimed at self-reliance of the rural community in the most vital requirement of domestic water supply, the scheme flagrantly violates the admirable principles that were incorporated in the watershed scheme. For instance, the local community has to prepare plans and estimates, but there is no provision for a facilitating agency; the approvals are to be accorded by the Department of Drinking Water Supply for each and every proposal that would come from lakhs of villages across the country. There is no provision or arrangement for community organising and for capacity building. The NGOs that have spearheaded the demonstration of the participatory principles in the country have no role to play in the scheme. Keeping these in view the *Swajaldhara* scheme can't go together and is *doomed* to failure unless its essential features are kept intact.

These ominous developments that erode and even subvert the objectives and goals of the MoRD programmes emanate from the paramount desire of the Establishment to control the funds and operations which would oblige the community organisations and facilitating agencies to seek its patronage, obviously at a price and at the cost of distortions in the programme.

Ministry of Environment and Forest (MoEF) Turns Its Back on Participatory Basics

To further streamline the JFM approach and provide support to it, the Ministry appointed a committee to prepare a Central Scheme for the JFM for the Tenth Five Year Plan. Drawing lessons from the watershed scheme of the MoRD, the committee recommended a scaled-up scheme that would be truly participatory and productive. The JFM was sought to be strengthened during the Tenth Five Year Plan with the addition of the missing features worked out in the "design principles" such as:

1. Adequate funding to be shared by the Central Government, the State Governments, and the local communities.
2. Promoting JFM facilitating agencies, preferably NGOs active in the field, to organise and support local communities.
3. Adequate provision for software support—capacity building, community organising, monitoring and evaluation, consultative forums at district, state and national levels, incentives for good performance, etc.

Rather than streamlining the well-performing JFM programme, the MoEF launched the National Afforestation Programme by merging several centrally sponsored afforestation schemes for the Tenth Five Year Plan. The umbrella schemes aimed very high with the following objectives:

1. Institutionalisation of the people's participation in project formulation and implementation.
2. Augmentation of the availability of fuel-wood, fodder and grass from the regenerated areas.
3. Very liberal provision—of more than Rs. 25,000 per hectare—for afforestation of degraded forestlands.

For implementing the scheme, a two-tier set-up—Forest Development Agencies and Joint Forest Management Committees (FDAs and JFMCs)—is being established. There is no separate provision or role for the NGOs as facilitating agencies, no earmarked provision for capacity building and community organising or for monitoring and evaluation. The FDAs are expected to take care of everything. The character of the FDAs also needs to be looked into. Unlike the District Rural Development Agencies (DRDA) of the rural development programmes, the FDA is registered as a society under the appropriate Act and passed off as a people's organisation. The presidents of the JFMCs are being made members of the general body with special seats for women. However, the Chairperson is the Conservator of Forests and the Member Secretary and Chief Executive officer is the Divisional Forest Officer. JFMC Presidents are to be nominated by the chairperson on a rotational basis. One non-official representative is to be nominated by the apex PRI. No need is felt to include NGO representatives that had pioneered the Joint Forest Management in the country.

The FDA is not a supportive organisation; its functions are not only regulatory but also executive. It has to—

- *approve* plans for afforestation related activities.
- *implement* water harvesting and soil conservation measures.
- *prioritise* for schemes and activity-wise financial outlets.
- *decide* entry point activities.
- *formulate* guiding principles for the utilisation and sharing of the usufruct.
- *evolve* rules for the funds created.
- *improvise* technological improvements.
- *establish* and maintain decentralised nurseries.

But more damaging provisions are about the JFMCs. In the original JFM scheme, the JFMCs were CBOs, i.e. people's organisations with elected office-bearers run by the local communities. The functions and structure and composition of the new *avatar* of the JFMC are very different under the new scheme:

Functions

To assist in—

- preparing a micro-plan,
- the choice of species to be planted,

- suggesting physical and financial targets, and
- proposing entry point activities.

Structure and Composition

The following elements are to be part of the proposed structure and composition of the JFMC. Clearly, they are at odds with the basic principles of participation:

- Chairperson is elected by majority/consensus of members.
- Member-secretary is a *forester*.
- Treasurer is *to be appointed by the member secretary* in consultation with the President.
- Other members of the executive committee, including one member representing the panchayat, are to *be nominated by the member-secretary.*
- Six members are to be *nominated by the member-secretary* in consultation with the President.

Completely disregarding the JFM scheme prepared by the committee, the MoEF has produced a scheme for the Tenth Five Year Plan with provisions incompatible with the basic principles of participation. The CBO, i.e. the JFMC itself, is not a people's organisation but a creature that works under the thumb of a forester. It is shocking as well as depressing to find that the Ministry that was the first to launch the participatory approach in the natural resources management in the country with its historical circular of June 1, 1990, should get into a reverse gear. Now it has the entire programme not only regulated but controlled and managed by the forest bureaucracy. Contrary to the Minister's claim of the success of JFM as an endeavour being managed by people's organisations, it was found that establishment had taken it over decisively and forcefully.

PIM: The Establishment Must be Checkmated

Unlike in the JFM and watershed development, in the PIM the transfer of canals to Farmers' Organisations is supported by statutory rules and regulations that cannot be arbitrarily reversed or even modified whimsically by the Establishment. For those working for participatory management of the public irrigation system the challenge then is first to see that where it is already introduced by law, as in Andhra Pradesh and Madhya Pradesh, it works satisfactorily.

The Ministry of Water Resources (MoWR) has been managing the central scheme of the Command Area Development (CAD) for more than 30 years. The PIM was a small and not very significant part of the CAD which itself was ill-conceived, badly designed and implemented with doubtful efficacy. The members of the Working Group tried to make the Command Area Development Authority subserve the goal of the PIM by converting it into CADAM, "M" standing for management incorporating the desirable design principles of participation. The attempt was frustrated by the Establishment. CAD continues in the Tenth Plan, with the PIM constituting its small and insignificant part.

Those individuals and institutions who champion the cause of the PIM now work for obtaining financial and administrative support of the MoWR for software requirements. These requirements—training, monitoring and evaluation, and setting up consultative forums that would contribute to quality improvement in the PIM—are usually neglected even by the states which have enacted the PIM law. Inevitably, there are weaknesses and flaws in the PIM Acts and their implementation. It is extremely important that these are identified urgently and measures taken to rectify them in a manner that would strengthen the capacity, resources, effectiveness and accountability of the Farmers' Organisations and thus improve water management. There is no significant movement in this direction.

Knowing that resisting PIM initiatives of the powerful leaders—the Chief Ministers of Andhra Pradesh and Madhya Pradesh—would not work and may invite trouble, the Establishment adopted a strategy to go along with it. Then, by not providing the essential support to the initiative in the early stages, the Establishment ensured that the programme performs poorly. The Establishment then would gently but continuously harp on its thesis that replacing departmental management by participatory instruments is not a good idea. It would then suggest that there should be devolution of powers and resources, but the local institutions should function under its directions. The Establishment would continue to hold, regulate and control tightly government resources and manage them, as if the participatory phase was an aberration!

It is therefore important that the gains of the PIM in Andhra Pradesh and Madhya Pradesh are consolidated first by stabilising efficiency, equity and sustainability. Then the programme may be carried forward to obtain value addition through diversification and outreach to profitable markets. The PIM scheme, which is being introduced by law in other states like Rajasthan, Tamil Nadu, Orissa and Uttar Pradesh (and as it spreads in Maharashtra, Karnataka and Gujarat), should start on the right foot from the outset.

The Challenge

Those NGO leaders, academics and policy makers, who are are interested in and working for the primacy of the stakeholders and prefer the bottoms-up option to top-down bureaucratic alternative, have to be vigilant about the actual and potential threats. They need to work, preferably in concert, to frustrate such moves, both overt and covert.

Index